DANIEL BOONE. Painting by Chester Harding

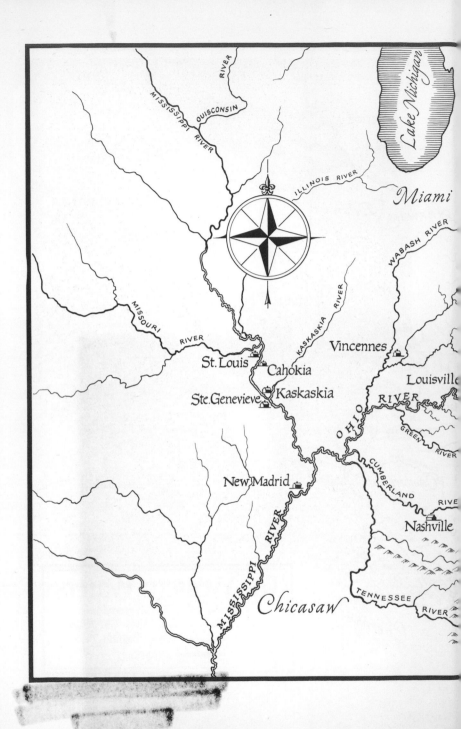

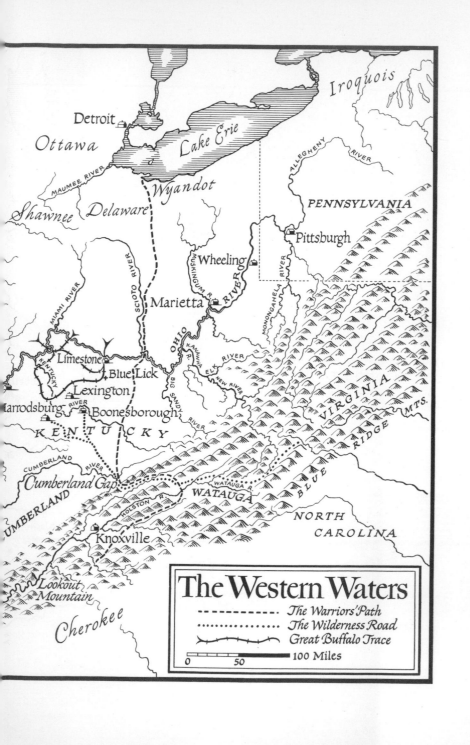

The Western Waters

The Warriors' Path
The Wilderness Road
Great Buffalo Trace

0   50   100 Miles

DAVID ZEISBURGER, THE MORAVIAN MISSIONARY (1721–1808), PREACHING TO THE INDIANS. Drawing by Christian Schussele

Men *of the*
Western Waters

A second look at the first Americans

*A second look
at the first Americans—*

BOOKS BY
DALE VAN EVERY

THE A.E.F. IN BATTLE

WESTWARD THE RIVER

THE SHINING MOUNTAINS

BRIDAL JOURNEY

THE CAPTIVE WITCH

THE TREMBLING EARTH

MEN OF THE WESTERN WATERS

Men *of the* Western Waters

by Dale Van Every

Illustrated

HOUGHTON MIFFLIN COMPANY BOSTON

1956 · The Riverside Press Cambridge

The Riverside Press

CAMBRIDGE • MASSACHUSETTS

PRINTED IN THE U.S.A.

Foreword

THIS IS not a history written for historians. I do not pretend to have turned up new facts nor will I harass my reader with innumerable citations of authority. I have relied largely for support upon the immense array of secondary studies covering the period. It is a field that has been intensively cultivated by very many eminent scholars and the harvest is there for all to enjoy. Nevertheless, I have endeavored to proceed with care. I do not think there can be much dispute of my principal statements of fact, though there may be some of the order in which I have presented them and of the conclusions I have drawn from them.

Mostly, I have written because of my real and deep affection for this First American. He is rewarding to write about and reassuring to think about. He may have been a character but he also had character. His era has been so taken for granted that we have all but forgotten it. But there can be no episode in our experience as a nation that we have more need now, as Americans, to remember. It is not inconceivable that our own world can become a wilderness more strange and confusing than his dark forest.

D.V.E.

Contents

Illustrations

A Note on the Illustrations

THE PORTRAIT of Joseph Brant was used as a frontispiece to Volume II of *The Life of Joseph Brant — Thayendanegea,* by William L. Stone, New York, 1838. The more familiar portrait by Romney is used in Volume I of that work.

The Victor Collot drawings were made by the French General Collot on his voyage in 1796 through the western lands of the United States. Collot's book was not published until 1826, when it appeared in Paris under the title *Voyage dans L'Amérique Septentrionale,* and also in an edition with the English title, *A Journey in North America.* The drawings are included, together with maps, in a separate "Atlas."

The Gilman drawing of Fort Harmar, made in 1790, was reproduced in *The American Pioneer,* in 1842.

The Bodmer painting of Cut-Off River, though made somewhat later than the period of this book, gives a good impression of the wilderness country encountered by the Men of the Western Waters. It is found in Volume XXV of *Early Western Travels,* edited by Reuben Gold Thwaites and published by the Arthur H. Clark Company, Cleveland, Ohio, 1906.

Victor Tixier's voyage was made in 1839–40, but he drew his sketch of the Charcoal Dance from life, and it is not only decorative but typical of the Indian dances of an earlier period. The drawing is reproduced in *Tixier's Travels on the Osage Prairies,* edited by John Francis McDermott, University of Oklahoma Press, 1940.

Christian Schussele was an Alsatian who came to America as a result of the revolutions of 1848 and settled in Philadelphia. His painting of Zeisburger is, of course, *ex post facto,* but a charming representation of the great friend of the Indians who lived among them for over sixty years. During the post-Revolutionary period, Zeisburger lived with Indians in Michigan, Ohio and Canada.

The three Indian portraits are found, magnificently colored, in *History of the Indian Tribes of North America* by Thomas L. McKenney and James Hall, of which a great folio edition was published in Philadelphia in 1836 by Edward C. Biddle.

Men *of the*
Western Waters

A second look at the first Americans

*They called themselves
"men of the Western Waters,"
meaning that they were as free
as those waters to seek
their own destiny.*

I. The Instinct for Survival

THE SURRENDER of Cornwallis at Yorktown, October 19, 1781, has ordinarily been considered the concluding military engagement of the Revolution. Thereafter the English ministry became resigned to the inevitable, the English army began its evacuations of Savannah, Charleston and New York, a formal peace was in sight, and Tories by the tens of thousands were in flight from the country. But west of the mountains there was no peace for another thirteen years.

This conflict in the west was no trifling war. More Americans were killed in action than in all of the major battles of the Revolution combined. Upon the outcome depended eventual sovereignty over the whole region between the Appalachians and the Mississippi, the Great Lakes and the Gulf. At issue was the possibility that the new United States might not be able to take even the first step in its later prodigious march to the Pacific.

It was a distressing war. Women and children in their homes were in as much danger as the soldier in the field. The immediate physical enemy, the Indian, was but the cat's paw of distant, aggressive world powers whose maneuvers took place out of reach beyond the ocean. Year after year and battle after battle appeared to bring neither victory nor defeat appreciably nearer. It was an inglorious war, unmarked for the participants by apparent design, policy, reason or purpose.

This ordeal was the first test of the first Americans. The men who had fought the Revolution along the eastern seaboard were Englishmen or Scotch-Irish or Germans or Dutchmen who had inhabited colonies professing loyalty to the crown and upon renouncing this allegiance had clung the more strongly to their allegiance to their respective states. But these men of 1782 beyond the mountains were unable to continue to consider themselves primarily Virginians or Pennsylvanians or New Jerseyites. They were scattered and mingled in a far wild land. Their former ties had been cut by distance, environment and peril. They were forced to fight their own battles both within and without the stockades. They could look behind them neither to the states that were nor to the nation that was to be. Schooled though many of them were in the social and political demands of the former frontier east of the mountains, they had been then but a day's walk at most from county courthouses and sheriff's offices while now they were separated by months from every manifestation of parent authority. They were obliged to contrive their own makeshift governmental machinery which, however much it might resemble in form the town meetings of their more sedate tidewater past, must in practice respond to new and infinitely more challenging conditions. Their reaction to their situation was the first intrinsically American attack upon the problem of becoming Americans.

There were other pressures than the brutalities of a peculiarly brutal war to make this test a harrowing one. While their homes and bodies burned, their minds and spirits were equally assailed. They were impelled toward some new allegiance. But an allegiance to what — or to whom? The United States was merely a new word, a concept as yet without meaning. They could have been endowed when they came west with no innate sense of loyalty to the political concept of a federal union which might one day encompass them, for that union did not begin even falteringly to exist under the Constitution until the critical period of choice was more than half over. The thirteen states, exhausted by the struggle for independence from England, had long continued to cling jealously to the principle of independence likewise from each other. There was little in this spectacle to inspire the western settlers with loyalty to the shadow central government on the faraway seacoast behind them. The feeling was widespread in both the east and the west that the natural, God-given boundary of the United States ran along the crest of the Appalachians. In such an atmosphere it is not remarkable that these intransigent westerners were so repeatedly tempted to strike out for themselves or to turn to the protection of Spain, France or England which was so ceaselessly thrust upon them. Washington himself said of their state of mind: "The touch of a feather would turn them away."

The consequences, had they turned away, give loose range to the imagination. Perhaps in later wars, on the order of the War of 1812 and the Mexican War, they might have been brought back into the Union, though we have had grim experience with the task of bringing back states that have once seceded. Possibly the area from the Appalachians to the Pacific might have been occupied by an assortment of small and competing independent nations, as occurred in Latin America when independence was won from Spain. In whatever event, the development of the United States as a continental power would have been retarded by generations.

Of course, those first Americans did not turn away. It is easy now to assume that manifest destiny so ruled. But it is not so easy to determine why they did not. Every circumstance conspired to drive them to it. The Indian War continued to inflict upon them its endless torment. Their dismal poverty was accentuated by the national government's acquiescence in the closing by Spain of the principal outlet to their commerce, the Mississippi River. Their hard-won homesteads were taken from them by land companies or eastern lawyers. The forceful and willful popular leaders who rose among them strove to deliver them to the grasp of foreign powers. Their competence to make rational decisions was distorted by divided counsels, primitive communications, sectional jealousies, race prejudices, class hatreds, and their own innate perversities. They were perpetually beset by the threats of destruction from without and subversion from within. And yet, somehow, they maintained their identity as Americans. Somehow they survived.

Courage, sacrifice, determination to resist, were not in themselves sufficient to account for this survival. Many a nation has perished while its valiant citizens battled to the last. Something beyond patriotism, beyond valor, was required of them. They must have been armed with an intuitive awareness of pre-

sibly too good for man and certainly much too good for white men.

In its outward appearance the Ohio Valley we know today resembles the land the Indians knew only in its dimensions and the location of its hills and rivers. Most striking among the physical changes have been the destruction of the primeval forest, the silting and contamination of the rivers, the extermination of the more notable types of wild life, and the disappearance of the giant cane and the giant wild grape. Perhaps not least among the changes has been the lost significance of the salt lick sites. Herds of wild animals trampled wide, beaten, concentrating paths from scores of miles away in their periodic pilgrimages to lick the salt-encrusted earth about the occasional saline springs. Man frequented the same paths and the same spots in his quest for both salt and game. The licks became centers of wilderness activity and wilderness communication comparable, in a fashion, to the cities of the region today.

The forest, then, was the paramount physical feature, conditioning the way of life of animal and man alike. It covered the entire valley except in those areas where it had been forced to give way before its one rival — fire. In good soil the trees grew to tremendous size. The naturalist F. A. Michaux measured a sycamore forty-seven feet in circumference. Another sycamore, mentioned in the *Pittsburgh Navigator,* possessed a hollow so large that thirteen men on horseback were able, with room to spare, to ride into it together. Colonel Richard Henderson described the great elm whose shade became the assembly hall for the Boonesborough Convention as "this divine tree" and "the most beautiful tree the imagination can suggest."

This boundless original forest was all things to all men. It supplied the settler with unlimited material always at his elbow with which to build his fire, his house, his fences and his tools while at the same time it extorted from him the stupendous labor of clearing, provided constant cover for the approach of his enemies, and shadowed his mind with its accentuation of his isolation. On hillsides and in stream bottoms the undergrowth was often impenetrably dense but in most other situations the treetops with their added canopy of grapevines shut off so much light that the ground below remained open and horsemen could ride at will among the gigantic pillars that supported the forest's roof. Destruction of this original forest began, at a piecemeal rate, long before the white man came. It was an Indian custom annually to set forest fires to initiate game drives. Such fires swept on unchecked until extinguished by the next rain. The barrens of Kentucky and the prairies of Ohio, Indiana and Illinois were not naturally treeless but areas from which the forest had been driven by fire and to which it had not yet returned.

The great rivers embracing the valley meandered in the same majestic curves as today but then their flowing waters were fresh and clear. The undenuded watersheds and undiminished marshlands, aided by innumerable beaver dams, produced a more even flow of water through the seasons, though in times of exceptional rainfall uprooted trees clogged lesser streams and in larger ones lodged in the shallows to form monumental obstructions so that occasionally floods were then more extensive than at any time since.

These broad western waters teemed with fish — hundred pound sturgeon, gar and catfish, forty pound perch, twenty pound pickerel, ten pound trout. Interminable processions of migrating wild fowl passed through in spring and fall. The passenger pigeon came and went in flocks so vast as to darken the sun and, when they roosted at night, to break down the forest. Flocks of red, green and gold parakeets brightened the landscape everywhere and at all seasons. Many of the birds with which we are more familiar today, such as crows and the more common songbirds, came, like the honey bee, after the establishment of settlements.

Buffalo roamed in such numbers that their trampled "traces," * several feet deep and up to hundreds of yards wide, crisscrossed the valley from favored river crossings to salt licks to seasonal feeding grounds. They were also killed in such numbers by settlers who often sought only their tongues and humps and by professional hunters who shipped hides and jerky to New

---

* Indian trails and settlers' roads tended to follow these ready made avenues and many of the buffalo routes are still followed by the paved highways of today.

Orleans that they rapidly disappeared. Buffalo were still hunted on the Kanawha as late as 1815 but long before that the great animal had become a rarity everywhere east of the Mississippi.

The original herds of elk were reduced at an equal rate. Bear were at first so numerous that hunters sighted them as often as deer. Wolves ranged the whole region in ferocious packs, attacking man almost as unhesitatingly as other prey, but shortly after the advent of white settlement they disappeared so suddenly that it was presumed that the species had been swept away by an epidemic of hydrophobia.

The single feature of the new country most discussed by the early comers was the cane. This green, jointed grass, which ordinarily grew from six to twelve feet high and sometimes to thirty feet with stalks the thickness of a man's arm, flourished in most unforested spaces from the Ohio almost to the Gulf. In some areas the canebrakes stretched for miles. But, discouraged by the freezing winter of 1780 and eradicated by the settlers' pigs, cattle and clearings, it soon disappeared as rapidly and as completely as had the buffalo or the wolf.

All early observers also dilated upon the profusion of wild flowers — azaleas, magnolias, delphinium, rhododendron — and upon the rival profusion of edible wild products: blackberries, raspberries, serviceberries, gooseberries, whortleberries, wild plums, pawpaws, haws, wild cherries, crab apples, hickory nuts, walnuts, hazelnuts, chestnuts. William Bartram wrote of his horse's legs reddened by riding through fields of wild strawberries and of the azalea making hillsides blaze as though on fire. Gilbert Imlay asserted "everything here assumes a dignity and splendor I have never seen in any part of the world." Dr. Joseph Doddridge referred sadly to the rapid diminution of the formerly abundant wild fruits that accompanied the increase of small birds following the settlers' clearings. Particularly astonishing to all who attempted to describe the early western scene was the prevalence of the wild grape with a stem a foot thick which climbed to hang its great clusters of fruit from the tops of the tallest trees. The common way to harvest the grape was to cut down the tree.

The first Anglo-Saxon white men to see the bluegrass and the towering cane were as well pleased with what they saw as had been the Indian. They were hunters and landseekers but they, too, saw more than good hunting and good soil. They, too, were carried away by the almost spiritual quality of the land's natural perfection. Few of these earliest comers could write and thus leave to us any detailed account of their reactions but they came back to Virginia and North Carolina and Pennsylvania filled with eager word of mouth accounts of what they had seen. Daniel Boone listened to one of these stories and was not able to forget it for ten years. When at last the chance came to go see for himself he came back with stories no one else could forget.

However, these long hunters who were the first white men to become familiar with the hills and meadows of Kentucky were strangely late in appearing on the scene. Jamestown was founded in 1607 but Boonesborough, less than four hundred miles to the westward, not until one hundred and sixty-eight years later. The first Englishman of record to stand on the bank of a stream which ran westward, instead of eastward into the Atlantic, was Captain Thomas Batts in 1671 when he came upon the headwaters of New River in the Virginia mountains. So little was known or even guessed of the country to the west by the Virginians of the time that the stream was measured for evidences of tidal ebb and flow and members of the party reported that they could see the glint of the Western Ocean further down the New River valley.

That same year the French, who pushed westward so much earlier and more energetically than the English, were at Sault Sainte Marie, raising the cross, deafening the astonished Indians with salutes of musketry, and proclaiming all shores washed by the Great Lakes to be the property of Louis XIV. By 1682, when the first white settlement in Pennsylvania was one year old, the French were busily buying furs, converting the heathen, and proclaiming the dominion of their king, from Labrador to Duluth and from Hudson's Bay to the Gulf of Mexico. But the French way west painfully circled the Ohio Valley. They went by the Ottawa to Mackinac, and then across Lake Superior and Lake Winnipeg to within sight of the Rocky Mountains. They went by way of Lake Michigan, Green Bay and the Wisconsin, or Lake Michigan and the Illinois, to the Mississippi, used the great river from end to end, and knew the Missouri from its mouth to the Dakotas. Finally they ventured the shorter route to the Mississippi by way of Ontario, Erie, Detroit and the Wabash. But the first Frenchman of official record to embark upon the upper Ohio was Celoron when he came in 1749 to bury lead plates upon its banks to warn off English traders and land companies.

The Spaniards had likewise kept away. They had been the first Europeans to investigate the continent's great central valley but they had soon lost interest after discovering the apparent lack of gold or natives suitable for enslavement. For a century and a half after Coronado and De Soto they had not only ignored the region but had even left the entire Mississippi off their maps lest its inclusion excite the interest of rivals.

In the white man's long continued ignorance of the Ohio Valley there had been one minor break. There were a few Englishmen circulating beyond the mountains a half century before the long hunters of Daniel Boone's time. These were traders from Pennsylvania and South Carolina who annually drove their pack horses or poled their boats hundreds of miles into the wilderness. But, being traders, they were seeking Indians with whom to trade and therefore their acquaintance with the country was confined to the areas north of the Ohio and south of the Tennessee, for there were no Indians residing in the Middle Ground between those two rivers.

This singular Indian renunciation of so favored a region was a consequence of the military and economic policies of the Iroquois. That formidable federated republic, the Rome of the Indian world, occupied a location in western New York which furnished them a trade outlet at Albany on the Hudson River and permitted them to attack competing trade routes from the interior. Early in the 17th century they determined upon gaining a monopoly of the fur trade and, revealing a remarkable talent for making war, they pressed their purpose with extraordinary vigor. For more than a hundred years they were able to deny the French access to the Ohio. Their dreaded war columns obliterated or enslaved rival Indian nations as far north as the Straits of Mackinac, as far west as the Illinois, and as far south as the Carolinas. One of the results of this prolonged bid for continental power was a permanent state of war between the Southern Indians and the Northern Indians which lasted until the Revolution. Under these circumstances communities of neither Indian group could survive in the intervening region between the Ohio and the Tennessee and it became a sort of Indian no-man's land, known to them as the Middle Ground, or the Neutral Ground, and sometimes as the Dark and Bloody Ground. Indians came to hunt, or passed through along the famous north-south Warriors' Path on their way to war, but none lived here.

Thus the beautiful heartland of the great valley remained invitingly untenanted when at long last the first white settlers crossed the mountains. But these were very late in coming. The first permanent white man's home in Kentucky was built the year of Concord and Lexington.

III. Our People

T HE HARD-BITTEN American frontiersman whose cabin in the wilderness was the steppingstone upon which the nation began its western march was something less than a hero to many of his contemporaries.

Bishop Francis Asbury, the great Methodist missionary to the West, who crossed the mountains eighteen times in the course of his labors, observed in his journal, with reference to one of his passages over the Indian-haunted Wilderness Road:

We rode down to the Crab Orchard, where we found company enough; some of them very wild. Some of them gave us very abusive language; and one man went upon a hill above us and fired a pistol towards our company. We resolved to travel in our order, and bound ourselves in honor and conscience to support and defend each other; and to see every man through the wilderness. But we could not depend upon wicked and unprincipled men, who would leave us and neglect us, and even curse us to our faces. Nor were we at liberty to mix with swearers, liars, drunkards.

Father Pierre Gibault, reporting to his Catholic superior in Quebec, was somewhat more explicit concerning the Americans in the Illinois:

There is no distinction from the greatest to the least except that by force; of the tongue, pernicious, calumniating and slanderous; of crying out very loud, and giving forth all sorts of insults and oaths. Everybody is in poverty, which engenders theft and rapine. Wantoness and drunkeness pass here as elegance and amusements quite in style. Breaking of limbs, murder by means of a dagger, sabre or sword (for he who wills carries one) are common, and pistols and guns are but toys in these regions.

James Seagrove, United States Agent to the Creek Nation, reported on the difficulty of negotiating a peace with the Indians:

It is to be regretted that the insatiable rage of our frontier brethren for extending their limits cannot be checked and kept within the bounds set for them by the general government. The United States, like most countries, is unfortunate in having the worst of people on her frontiers.

Secretary of War Knox advised President Washington:

The disgraceful violation of the Treaty of Hopewell with the Cherokee Indians requires the serious consideration of Congress. If so direct and manifest a contempt for the authority of the United States be suffered with impunity, it will be vain to attempt to extend the arm of the government to the frontiers. Indian tribes can have no faith in such imbecile promises, and lawless whites will ridicule a government which shall make Indian treaties and regulate boundaries, on paper only.

However, it was a foreign observer, Baron de Carondelet, Spanish Governor of Louisiana, who in a report to his government, got right down to the essentials of character estimation:

This prestigious and restless population, continually forcing the Indian nations backward and upon us, is attempting to get possession of all the vast continent which those nations are occupying between the Ohio and Mississippi Rivers and the Gulf of Mexico and the Appalachian Mountains. . . . Their method of spreading themselves and their policy are so much to be feared by Spain as are their arms. . . . The wandering spirit and the ease with which those people procure their sustenance and shelter quickly form new settlements. A carbine and a little maize in a sack are enough for an American to wander about in the forests alone for a whole month. With his carbine he kills the wild cattle and deer for food and defends himself from the savages. The maize dampened serves him in lieu of bread. With some tree trunks crossed one above another, in the shape of a square, he raises a house, and even a fort that is impregnable to the savages by crossing a story above the ground floor. The cold does not affright him. When a family tires of one location, it moves to another, and there settles with the same ease . . . . If such men succeed in occupying the shores of the Mississippi . . . nothing can prevent them from crossing . . . and penetrating into our provinces on the other side.

By 1782 these "prestigious and restless" people west of the mountains had found a lodgment in four widely separated centers: Watauga, in what is now northeastern Tennessee; Cumberland, on the bend of the Cumberland River in the vicinity of the present Nashville; Kentucky, in the north central part of the present state; and southwestern Pennsylvania. Estimates of their populations vary. People who moved so frequently could not well be counted. A reasonable approximation of numbers might be 45,000 in the frontier section of Pennsylvania (an area claimed by Virginia, at times by threats of force, until 1780), 10,000 in Watauga, 15,000 in Kentucky, and 3000 in Cumberland. It is some indication of how distant these people were from the majority of their fellow citizens that the census of 1790 established the center of the population of the United States to be some miles east of Baltimore.

The physical characteristics of the typical pioneer settlement were dictated by undeviating necessity. Poverty, isolation and danger compelled the settler to conform. Though he may have cleared and planted but two or three acres his cabin was separated by a mile or more from his nearest neighbor, since each claimed possession of some hundreds of acres of the intervening undeveloped land. In this clearing he lived with his family — almost invariably a large family with a new baby every year — in a one room, earthen-floored log hut. The range of his tools, utensils, furniture and equipment was limited by the weight he could pack over the mountains on the back of a horse or, more often, his own back. His perpetual concern was hunger. Corn was his staple food but he was seldom able to accumulate a supply to last until the next crop. Prowling Indians made hunting dangerous and his extreme poverty left him little gunpowder to spare. Always the first green shoots of spring were awaited with ravenous impatience though even the youngest children knew the spring also brought with it a hundredfold increase in the Indian risk.

Several more miles away, generally at the most favored location in the district, was the community center. Here each outlying landholder ordinarily possessed a lot and another hut — his town house, as it were. This collection of cabins, the settlement proper, was encircled by a communally built stockade. To this refuge the surrounding settlers resorted when the Indian danger was judged to be abnormally acute. As the recurrent Indian menace waxed and waned, each settler, with his family, shuttled desperately back and forth from stockade to farmstead, anxious to remain alive but determined to preserve his stock and crop.

These earliest Anglo-Saxon western settlements had come into existence according to a fairly uniform and discernible pattern. First in the west had been the traders. They were essentially pedlers who traveled back and forth across the mountains to sell their stocks of goods to the Indians. They were not even prospective settlers and were jealous of every advance in settlement since it threatened their livelihood but they did bring back some geographical information about the northern and southern portions of the great valley.

Next came the long hunter, so called on account of the duration of his hunts, striking out from his home on the frontier east of the mountains. Alone, or in groups of up to a dozen or so, he often spent two or three years at a time in the new and until then largely unknown country to the west. His ostensible motive was to hunt for hides and furs. But he was more activated by his innate love of freedom and adventure and the novelty of moving far and wide. The ever present risk of losing his scalp provided but an added zest. At intervals he came back to spend his slight gains, to tell tall tales of what he had seen, and to bask in the admiration of stay-at-homes.

Then came the moment when the long hunter suddenly turned settler. The Iroquois, whose military prowess had gradually weakened, ceded most of their claims to lands east and south of the Ohio River in the first treaty of Fort Stanwix in 1768, a negotiation engineered by land speculators. The hunter, who had already spied out the land, sensed his opportunity, bundled up his family, and moved into it. Before the land companies could even begin to survey or to try to sell the hundreds of thousands of acres upon which they had designs, the settlers had built cabins on the choicer sites, girdled enough trees to start their corn patches, and were no longer obliged to cross the mountains to gain their favorite hunting ground. Almost at once they were followed by swarms of their only slightly less adventuresome neighbors from the former frontiers of North Carolina, Virginia and Pennsylvania, who like them were born and bred backwoodsmen.

Among these pioneer landseekers there was an occasional individual who had previously achieved a degree of material success on the former frontier east of the mountains. He was driven not by the necessity of seeking a new opportunity but by an ambition to enlarge the scope of his enterprises. When he crossed into the new country he was able to carry with him several horse-loads of equipment, a small herd of livestock, and a number of slaves to expedite the labor of developing his new property. He had the means promptly to build a stockade at the location of his choice and his station became at once a center about which other settlers collected. Such more prosperous figures in the westward movement were outnumbered a thousand to one by their poorer neighbors, but they were no less hardy and adventuresome and as much by force of character as by superior substance they usually became militia commanders, county lieutenants, convention delegates, and the natural economic and political leaders of the new communities.

These firstcomers, the backwoods majority together with the occasional station proprietor, were the people who held the stockades of Kentucky during the Revolution, who waded neck-deep in swamps to take Vincennes, who fought the Indians from the Forks of the Ohio to the borders of Florida, and who still had left the reserve of energy to ride back over the mountains to vanquish British regulars at King's Mountain.

With the formal close of the Revolution there was a rush of

later comers. Some were veterans of the Continental Army, seeking land promised them under various obscure and conflicting grants made by the several states or by the central government.* Others were ordinary eastern farmers in quest of more land, or better land, or at any rate, different land. Many were as aimless and helpless and as little acquainted with the circumstances awaiting them as were the itinerant farm labor families who drifted about the country in search of employment during the 1930's.

But whether he came early or late the newly arrived settler was plunged into a strange and infinitely demanding environment in which, if he were to survive, he must make sure that he knew, among countless other novel arts, how to identify forest noises, how to track wild animals, how to pack a horse, how to manage a boat in a rapids, how to build a fire in the rain, how to butcher a buffalo, how to cure a deerskin, how to keep bears out of the pigpen, how to treat the ills of his animals and his children, and, above all else, how always to know when an Indian was near before the Indian himself knew it. It was one in which he must be able to make his own shoes, clothes, house, furniture, tools, dishes, soap, sugar, salt, whisky, ham, bacon, salt pork, corned beef, and still find time for the gargantuan over-all task of clearing a hole in the primeval forest to make room for his corn patch. And he must meanwhile learn to co-operate in the devising of a political framework for the government of his community upon the immediate successful functioning of which the life and death of all depended.

As the population increased and the more centrally located new communities made the transition from frontier station to provincial town, there appeared doctors, lawyers, merchants, craftsmen — and politicians. Life in the larger towns took on some of the more normal aspects of life in an eastern community. (None was very large; Louisville numbered less than 300 in 1782 and Pittsburgh 376 in 1790.) Last to come, or never to come, were the professional land speculators, who meddled so

---

* There were even some hundreds of escaped prisoners of war, mostly Hessians, from the Charlottesville, Virginia, prison camp of Burgoyne's surrendered army.

persistently in the affairs of the West, but most of whom continued to conduct their devious maneuvers in eastern counting houses and legislative lobbies.

But the original frontiersman remained the dominant type in the new society. Upon him still rested the fate of the community. The later comers tended to locate near the safer centers of the settled areas, while the backwoodsman tended to move out to the exposed perimeter where there was more room and better hunting, even though he here also bore the brunt of the Indian danger. Thus he not only remained the frontiersman but also the chief guardian of the border.

This average frontiersman of 1782 came of a family that had inhabited the wilderness edge of the settlements east of the mountains for generations. His forefathers, too, had lived chiefly by hunting, and they had known the Indian inroads of King George's War, of the French and Indian War, and of Pontiac's Conspiracy, as he now knew those of the Revolution and its aftermath. By both environment and heredity he had been stamped with characteristics as unique and distinctive as those of the Indian who had so long been his enemy.

He was lawless. He scorned every imposition of authority, including even that of his own militia officers whom he had himself elected. He was restless. Always searching for better land, he was never satisfied with what he found and kept perpetually moving on. He was lazy. Capable of the most extraordinary exertions under the stress of emergency, he was a poor workman and a bad farmer. He was poor. Keeping his family in a windowless, often but three-walled, log hut, his personal property was limited to two or three cooking utensils, his axe and his rifle. He was gregarious. Though accustomed to spending so much of his time alone in the wilds he sought companionship when he could find it and transposed unavoidable tasks such as the building of his house, the shucking of his corn, or the butchering of his pigs into community frolics by inviting the participation of all his neighbors. He was fiercely competitive. Most of his diversions were contests — horse races, turkey shoots, wrestling matches. He was superstitious. Having grown to manhood without ever having seen a church, he tended to put his faith in

and in addition most of them were Tories. In the north traders like the ex-Americans Alexander McKee, Matthew Elliott and Simon Girty lived among the Indians, took part in their councils, were given official status by the English government, and were able to keep the Indian hostility to the settlements at a perpetual boil. In the south, the great English trading firm of Panton, Leslie and Company, literally a principality in itself, was able to collaborate with Spanish policy while at the same time furthering English policy by using the law of supply and demand to animate Indian resistance to American policy.

But to the harassed settler the one great enemy was the one in the foreground — the Indian. This Indian with whom for the next thirteen years he was locked in a life and death struggle was far from the ignorant child of nature of common tradition. He might still burn his enemies but he no longer ate them. He had taken many such steps away from his original savagery. He knew the ways of the white man much better than his ways were known to the white man. He had learned certain facts of life and of world affairs in a hard school. His leaders were great orators and natural diplomats who had had far more experience in statecraft than most of the frontier militia captains who were their opposite numbers. It was a poor chief, indeed, who had not attended conferences at Montreal, New York, Philadelphia, or New Orleans, and who did not possess an acquaintance with the highest officials of white colonial, state and national governments. The various Indian nations had been recognized, consulted, cajoled and placated through innumerable sieges of treatymaking, as their favor had been sought by Spain, France, England and by every one of the thirteen states.

To this experience in diplomacy there had been added a similar experience in the art of war. For more than a hundred years Indians had served as participants or allies in every war that had been fought by the great powers over the partition of North America. Ingrained in tribal tradition was the part they had played in every battle, the mistakes that had been made by white commanders, the tactics which had proved superior. The Indian warrior was at home in his wilderness environment and schooled from childhood to take advantage of its every circumstance; he required no ponderous supply train, and was able to appear suddenly out of the forest and as suddenly disappear into it again. The Indian war chief was a skilled field leader, with an instinctive understanding of strategy and a particular aptitude for managing his forces in the thick woods in which most engagements were fought.

In material as well as moral and mental equipment the settler was possessed of no great advantage. Long before the appearance of the white man the Indian had been a confirmed trader, exchanging articles from hand to hand and from tribe to tribe until copper from Michigan appeared in Florida, sea shells from the Pacific in New England, and the famous red pipestone from Minnesota in every corner of the continent. When the white man turned up along the sea coast to display such fascinating objects as guns, brass kettles, steel axes, red blankets and the like, the Indians' eagerness to trade for them knew no bounds. In the south they fought intertribal wars to win captives to be sold to the traders for transport as slaves to the West Indies. In the north they overcame their normal repugnance to labor by devoting their winters to the trapping of the furs most sought by the traders. The westward spread of these earliest trade goods, sold from ships along the coasts of Newfoundland, Maine and the Carolinas, was incredibly rapid. When in 1609 Henry Hudson sailed up the river that bears his name he found the Indians around Albany already supplied with articles of European manufacture. And when, in 1673, Marquette became the first Frenchman to see the lower Mississippi, he also saw Indians armed with guns, knives and hatchets, wearing cloth garments, and carrying their gunpowder in glass flasks. By the time settler and Indian clashed west of the mountains the Indian had for generations been familiar with the use of the gun and the horse — the two most essential elements in frontier warfare. Owing to the diligence of his trader backers he was often better supplied with war-making necessities. Thus the settler lacked that advantage of superiority in weapons and equipment that has usually accompanied white conquests of less civilized natives.

The Indian nations confronting the settler of 1782 were grouped on his flanks to the north and south. In the south, between the Tennessee River and the Gulf, the Georgia-Carolina frontier and the Mississippi, were the Cherokee, Creek, Choctaw and Chickasaw. They had had an opportunity to adopt more of the white man's manners and morals than had most Indians. There had been a relatively long period during which they had been able to receive trade goods from the nearby coasts of the Atlantic and the Gulf before the advance of white settlement had begun to press upon them. They numbered some 50,000, relied upon farming almost as much as hunting for their food supply, lived in semi-permanent towns, and had well developed tribal organizations on the order of primitive republics. Some of the more prosperous had accumulated fortunes in horses, cattle, pigs and slaves and were as well housed, educated and clothed as white planters of the time. Traders had been among them so long that the effects of intermarriage were noticeable. Many of the most famous chiefs had Scotch or English names. However, the long period of trade rivalry and comparative peace had reduced the war effectiveness of the Southern Indians by promoting a lack of unity. Never did the four nations attack the frontier in combination. Frequently, at the most critical times, they instead attacked each other, as traditional tribal feuds overcame their common hatred of the whites. But by weight of numbers they long interposed an obstinate resistance to the advance of white settlement, year after year their raiding parties of young warriors terrorized the border from the Savannah to the Ohio, they were always ready to lend themselves to English and Spanish intrigues, and their power was not finally broken until Andrew Jackson's time.

The strongholds of the Northern Indians — Shawnee, Wyandot, Delaware, Mingo, Ottawa, Potawatami, Chippewa and Miami — were ranged across the north central portions of the present states of Ohio, Indiana and Illinois, along the southern shores of Lake Erie, and about Detroit. These Northern Indians, numbering perhaps 30,000,* no longer dwelt upon their

---

* Adjacent allied nations, such as the Iroquois, the Seven Nations of Canada, and several more primitive tribes to the west and northwest, which offered intermittent support, materially increased the military strength occasionally available to the Northern Confederacy.

ancestral lands as did their southern allies. They had for generations been relative nomads, their livelihood dependent principally
upon hunting and the rewards of war. But their towns were now
surrounded by cornfields and guarded by log blockhouses and
their more substantial citizens, owning numbers of slaves and
horses, were more comfortably endowed with material possessions
than the average settler. Every community had had at least the
opportunity to waste the never ending succession of gifts and
bribes pressed upon them by first the French and then the English. The Northern Indians had unwillingly watched and
sporadically resisted the slow hundred year-long westward movement of white settlement from the banks of the Delaware until,
now that it had at last crossed the mountains and was pouring
into the great valley, they had proclaimed the Ohio River to be
their last boundary and had sworn to each other that they would
die before retreating farther. This northern confederacy, while
not an actual political union, was more closely knit than the one
in the south and its members more accustomed to war. In a sense
they were professional soldiers. They and their fathers and
grandfathers had for more than a century lived like salamanders
in the continual fires of war; they had participated in innumerable campaigns as the three great powers, France, England and
the Iroquois, struggled for dominion over the St. Lawrence, the
Great Lakes and the Ohio; they had fought under or against
Frontenac, Vaudreuil, Montcalm, Abercrombie, Forbes, Amherst,
Pontiac, Bradstreet, Bouquet. Much of the former martial ardor
of the Iroquois had been handed on to them. They felt little awe
of white prowess. They remembered such victories over the
whites as the destruction of Braddock's army. They were to
know more such triumphs.

This Indian of 1782 was in every respect a formidable antagonist. He was a veteran of many wars who was strategically better
located and better supplied from friendly bases on the Great
Lakes and the Gulf than he had ever been before or was ever to
be again in all of his centuries of conflict with the white frontier.
The one great disadvantage under which he labored, eventually
the fatal disadvantage, was his lack of discipline. The individual
warrior took the field only when he personally felt like it and left

it when he felt like it. His impulse to quit a march, a battle, or the war might spring from a chance dream, the sound of an ill-omened bird call, a preliminary success, an unexpected difficulty, or from any whim that happened to seize him. However, this was only a comparative disadvantage. For the settler knew scarcely more discipline. The average frontier militiaman was at any given moment as likely to go back as go on and this he did whenever any feature of the campaign dissatisfied him.

The war ground on. To the settler at the time there was no apparent sign that this was a war he was predestined to win. In fact the Indians won every major battle — until the last one.

V. Peace at the Council Table

Not long after receiving the news of Yorktown, Parliament, representing the wishes of most Englishmen, resolved "that the house will consider as enemies to the King and country all who shall advise, or by any means attempt, the further prosecution of offensive war, for the purpose of reducing the revolting colonies by force."

But, though the organized war with England was now over, the desire for peace, so strong on both sides, had still to find a way through a labyrinth of diplomatic complexities. Since England was reluctant to deal directly with an unrecognized and therefore nonexistent government of a revolting segment of her own possessions, all preliminary peace feelers had to be extended by way of the good offices of the rebels' allies, the established governments of France and Spain. These two powers, thus become the brokers in charge of American interests, were infinitely more interested in their own. It was distinctly not one of these to assist in building the infant United States into a threat to their own North American designs. On the other hand, the official American reaction was that the need to preserve the favor of these powerful friends was paramount. Under these continuing stresses the West became the baby perpetually dangling from the sleigh within reach of the wolves.

The negotiations, which led to an end to the Revolution except in the west, were very nearly as devious, enigmatic and protracted as any with which we are now familiar in the divided world of our day. England was at war with France, Spain and Holland, as well as with the United States, and, now that the loss of the colonies was recognized as inevitable, much more anxious about her control of the seas and those two bastions of empire, Gibraltar and India, than about territorial dispositions in North America. Throughout the diplomatic scrambling for position that led to peace the American representatives were required to be on guard not so much against enemy England as against friends France and Spain.

We are here concerned solely with the attempted disposition of the West by the peace negotiators. All parties had claims to the West. England's rested upon the assumption that under the Royal Proclamation of 1763, forbidding settlement west of the mountains, all title to any section of the West had reverted to the crown, upon the 1763 cession by France of all of her territory east of the Mississippi, upon present occupation by Indian nations which were under the King's protection, and upon the hard fact that she was in military occupation of forts along the southern shores of the Great Lakes. The English negotiators could argue, with some reason, that recognition of the independence of the thirteen colonies no more recognized their right to the Ohio Valley than it did their right to Canada.

Spain's claim rested on a shadowy priority of discovery and exploration by De Soto in 1540 and, with immensely greater force, upon her capture of Pensacola, Mobile and Natchez from England during the Revolution. She had also captured a minor English post at St. Joseph's in southern Michigan, to give further point to her claim upon the entire west. The hard fact in Spain's case was that her armed galleys on the river, her many garrisons on both banks, and her possession of New Orleans, placed her in undeniable physical control of the Mississippi from St. Louis to the Gulf.

The Indian nations claimed their native land, which they had clearly been the first to discover and explore, which they had always occupied, and which they still occupied. Their right to this occupancy had been recognized by innumerable past treaties with France and England and had been specifically bolstered by the royal proclamation which had reserved the territory west of the mountains to the Indians for all time. Both England and Spain sponsored the Indian claim, as opposed to the American, since neither envisaged a future encroachment upon Indian lands by settlements of her own people.

France advanced no firsthand claims but urgently supported

Spain's and, to the extent that it protected Indian rights, even England's, by emphasizing the legitimacy of her 1763 cessions to Spain and England of territory that had been hers by reason of first European discovery, exploration and occupation. For France was obsessed with the presumption that whatever Spain held would eventually return to her, as, in fact, it did a few years later by Napoleon's dictate, and wished therefore to keep the Indians' power intact pending this day when she would resume her ancient sway over them.

The claim of the United States to the West rested upon the presence, lawful or no, of American settlers in Watauga, Cumberland, Kentucky and southwestern Pennsylvania, and upon Clark's seizure of Kaskaskia and Vincennes in the name of Virginia during the Revolution. The existence of the settlements was the hardest of all the facts in the entire situation. The people in them were of a sort not to be readily dislodged by the fiat of any government, including their own.

Long before the first peace overtures from England, Spain and France had pressed upon Congress Spain's claim to the West as one of the prices of their military assistance, their loans of money and supplies, and their recognition of the independence of the new nation. The French foreign office persistently proposed the crest of the Appalachians as the natural western boundary of the United States. The most favorable line ever mentioned by a French spokesman was a final proposal that England be assigned all territory north of the Ohio and Spain that south of the Tennessee.

The American plenipotentiaries, Benjamin Franklin, John Adams and John Jay, were handicapped by repeated changes in instructions from their government at home, frequent authorizations to make additional compromises, and no support at all on the western boundary question. The conduct of foreign affairs was in the hands of congress which primarily represented sectional interests. New England was far more concerned with the Newfoundland fisheries, the northern boundary of Maine, and the right to trade with the West Indies, than with the distant western wilderness. The southern states, more sympathetic to the settlements which were upon their own frontiers, were still occupied by English troops and feared a partition based upon the status quo, a suggestion slyly advanced by France as a possible alternative to acceptance of Spanish claims. The boldest members of congress regarded the occasionally voiced American claim to Canada as a less extravagant proposal than any dream of the far off Mississippi as a border.

During the late years of the Revolution it was all but taken for granted that the line of the Appalachians was to be the western boundary and many Americans accepted this as an excellent solution on the theory that such a limit was needed to promote unity and stability in the infant republic. In mid-1781 nine states supported a resolution which left the determination of boundaries to the discretion of France as the protector of American interests. The wise and good Franklin was guided by this view almost to the end of negotiations. Even Jay, most obstinate defender of American aspirations, as late as mid-1782 was proposing a western boundary running south from the mouth of the Kanawha that would have preserved Watauga and southwestern Pennsylvania but sacrificed Kentucky and Cumberland.

The final decision was not a consequence of American demands but of a sudden switch in English policy. The North ministry had fallen and though the King remained obdurate he was unable to resist the judgment of his new ministers backed by the English public's demand for peace. A ray of clarity for the moment fell upon Whitehall. It became apparent that, inasmuch as the loss of the colonies was inevitable, it might prove wiser to make some attempt to mollify the Americans than to drive them permanently into the arms of England's principal enemies, France and Spain. The offer to deal directly with the United States was eagerly accepted by the American commissioners who thereby escaped the French and Spanish pressures under which they had been laboring. More favorable terms were conceded than had formerly been so much as discussed and among them was a transfer of English title to the West with a Great Lakes boundary much as it is today. Thus the West was handed over as an English gift almost forced upon the astonished American commissioners. It is probably fair to consider this English generosity not so much as an act of justice as an impulse to mortify England's European rivals.

However, it was a gift on paper only. The treaty was signed

but not observed. England did not withdraw from her forts on the Great Lakes or from her alliance with the Northern Indian nations. France and Spain made separate treaties with England. Spain not only refused to recognize American title to the West but for the next fourteen years refused even to recognize the independence of the United States. The fate of the West was not decided at the council table. The destiny of the westerners remained to be decided by the westerners themselves.

VI. Peace Comes to the West

T H E N E W S of Yorktown, reaching Pittsburgh in November, brought to the West none of the relaxation of wartime tension it had to the East.

During 1779 and 1780 much had gone well along the western frontier. Clark had retaken Vincennes and along with it the person of Henry Hamilton, the English lieutenant-governor of the northwest. Sullivan and Brodhead had wrecked the power of the Iroquois on the Genesee and the Allegheny. Clark had successfully parried the main effort made in the west by the English during the Revolution, simultaneous drives across the Ohio into Kentucky and down the Mississippi at St. Louis. Spain had taken Natchez and Mobile. The men of Watauga had returned to the Carolinas to score their stunning triumph at King's Mountain.

But during the year that was closing most of these advantages had been lost. Two of Clark's achievements, Kaskaskia and Fort Jefferson, had been abandoned. His grand design to attack Detroit, backed by Jefferson, had deteriorated for want of supplies and men into a desperate race to save Louisville, during which the rearguard of his little army, a Pennsylvania battalion under the command of Colonel Archibald Lochry, had been annihilated. The only organized protection of the line of the lower Ohio was the remnant of Clark's forces, stationed at Louisville and on an armed galley patrolling the river. The single detachment of regular troops in the west, numbering less than 300, under Brigadier-General Irvine at Fort Pitt, was thus described by its commander: "I never saw troops cut so deplorable, and at the same time despicable a figure. No man would believe from their appearance that they were soldiers; nay it would be difficult to determine whether they were white men."

Everywhere the actual defense of the frontier against Indian inroads depended upon bodies of local militia who assembled hastily to cope with local emergencies and as hastily dispersed again. Therefore, despite Yorktown, people looked into the future with foreboding. They had reason. The coming year, 1782, was to be remembered as the Year of Sorrows.

February was exceptionally mild. The snow melted and the melting brought on a storm of Indian raids earlier in the season than had ever been known before. A feature of the favorite Indian hit and run tactic was the need to wait for the snow to disappear so that their swift advances and retreats could not be so readily tracked. The depredations this spring were not only earlier and more numerous than common but also more vicious. The smoke of burning cabins streaked the sky all the way around the long perimeter of the frontier from the banks of the Allegheny to the borders of Georgia. People were required to abandon their farms at seed time in order to place their families in the safety of blockhouses and stockades. Many lost hope and prepared to move back to their former homes east of the mountains.

A special pall of gloom hung over southwestern Pennsylvania. Scarcely a community here but had lost many of its bravest and finest in Lochry's disaster. The preternaturally early raids added new rage to the old grief. The distracted settlers became frantic to strike back. The blow they struck, the first formal campaign of 1782, cast a revealing glare upon the nature of this war they had been fighting for seven years and were to fight for thirteen more.

The nearest Indians, and therefore the easiest to get at, were in the three little villages of Christian Delaware on the Tuscarawas River, some forty miles west of the northern bend of the Ohio. These mission Indians, converted by the Moravian ministers John Heckewelder and David Zeisberger, had migrated from eastern Pennsylvania in 1769 to the solitude of the forest in search of a peace they could not enjoy near white communities. The outbreak of the Revolution, however, had found their new homes situated in what became no-man's land, with the American settlers in front of them and the war-making Indians behind them. They determined to remain neutral. But this was not a war with room for neutrals. Their pacific intentions were distrusted by both sides. The English accused them of giving information to the frontiers; the Americans of giving aid and guidance to passing Indian raiders. The year before the English had transported them bodily to Sandusky where they could be kept under surveillance but this spring had permitted some of them to return to their homes to pick up stores of corn to save the congregation from starving.

Hearing of this return, the settlers decided to do away once and for all with this reputed way station for raiders. Eighty or ninety Pennsylvania militiamen under the command of Colonel David Williamson hurriedly set out. En route their tempers were further fired by the discovery of the nude body of Mrs. Robert Wallace, victim of a recent raid, fearfully mutilated and left impaled on a stake along the trail.

The Christian Indians, as was their custom, made no attempt to defend their towns. The Americans' rage was intensified by the discovery of Mrs. Wallace's bloody clothing hidden in a Moravian hut where, according to the attempted Moravian explanation, it had been left by her Shawnee murderers. The submissive mission Indians sang and prayed while they waited upon the American decision. A verdict was reached after prolonged discussion. The unresisting captives, two or three at a time, were taken into one or the other of two selected cabins, dubbed by the executioners "slaughter-houses". Some were stabbed or axed but the most were knocked in the head with a cooper's mallet. Of the 90 who were killed, 29 were men, 27 were women, and 34 were children. The news of this exploit stirred condemnation in the east but along the frontier was received with general approbation.

The same early spring storm had been beating upon Kentucky. The northern fringe of more exposed settlements bore the brunt of this but one Wyandot war party proved how loose was the system of frontier defense by penetrating into the center of the most populated section to make an attack on Estill's Station, well south of the Kentucky River. When they failed to break into the station with their first whooping rush the Indians devoted themselves to butchering such inhabitants as they had surprised outside the walls, burned the outlying cabins, shot the cattle, rounded up the better horses, and faded from sight into the woods. Captain James Estill summoned help from the neighboring stations and went in pursuit.

So far all had gone as usual but instead of accelerating their retreat, as was the Indian custom after a raid, the Wyandot deliberately turned to give battle. It was not a big battle for there were no more than twenty-five men on either side but it was one that made a profound impression upon Kentucky. The fight was continued for more than an hour with neither side flinching though each had lost half their number. Eventually Estill tried a flank movement. The Indians countered with a charge against his center and the white line broke. Representative Indians and Kentuckians had met, as in an arena, pressed a test of comparative racial prowess to a conclusion, and the result was that the Indians, in a fair, stand-up fight on even ground between equal numbers, had proved, man for man, their military superiority.

The spring raids continued, without surcease, on into the early summer. Southwestern Pennsylvania, the most populous of the frontier districts, was again carried away by the impulse to strike back. This time the objective was the Wyandot stronghold at Sandusky, the breeding ground of so many raiding parties. Upwards of five hundred militiamen gathered and elected as their commander Colonel William Crawford, friend and land agent of Washington and a distinguished soldier whose record included campaigns in the French war and the Revolution. As evidence of how little stigma attached to Colonel Williamson, who had commanded the perpetrators of the Moravian massacre, he received 230 votes to Crawford's 235.

The column set out for the shores of Lake Erie. Every man was mounted. Despite the thickness of the woods the horse played very nearly as essential a part in the campaigns on this frontier as it did later on the plains of the Far West. Colonel Crawford soon realized that in leading a body of western militia he was not leading a military command. Each man continually decided what he would and would not do next. Swift movement leading to a surprise of the Indian towns had been contemplated but the Indians observed the march from the first day. They did nothing, however, to deter the advance, preferring to wait while Crawford's turbulent horsemen pushed ever deeper into the wilderness.

The march reached the Upper Sandusky plains. Here there was one short brisk engagement in which the losses were equal. Both sides broke off, Crawford hoping the Indians would attempt an attack in the open against his line of expert riflemen, the Wyandot waiting for reinforcements which they knew were at hand. The third day Crawford realized that the enemy had been strengthened by the arrival of a band of Shawnee allies and a detachment of Tory rangers from Detroit. Distrusting the ability of his men to cope with this augmented force, he ordered a retreat. A withdrawal in the face of the enemy is a task for disciplined troops. This retreat became a rout, with each man seeking his own road to safety. The exultant Indians were able to pick off the scattering stragglers and groups of fugitives at no cost to themselves. By the time the residue of Crawford's command reached the Ohio it had suffered catastrophic losses, estimates of which range from 70 to over 200. Crawford, himself, was captured and spared for that species of public torment which was a normal feature of an Indian victory celebration.

The burning of Crawford became one of the most often told chapters of frontier history, attracting more lasting attention than the defeat itself. It was noteworthy because of the rank of the victim and because it was the only instance in which such a ceremony has been described in detail by a responsible eyewitness — in this case Dr. John Knight, assistant army surgeon at Fort Pitt, a fellow prisoner who was forced to look on while expecting himself presently to suffer a like fate.* Dr. Knight's account throws another luridly revealing glare over the nature of this frontier war:

When we went to the fire the Colonel was stripped naked,

* Knight later escaped while being taken to another Indian town for burning.

ordered to sit down by the fire, and then they beat him with sticks and their fists. Presently after I was treated in the same manner. They then tied a rope to the foot of a post about fifteen feet high, bound the Colonel's hands behind his back and fastened the rope to the ligature between his wrists. The rope was long enough for him to sit down or walk round the post once or twice, and return the same way. The Colonel then called to Simon Girty, and asked if they intended to burn him? Girty answered, yes. The Colonel said he would take it all patiently. Upon this, Captain Pipe, a Delaware chief, made a speech to the Indians, viz: about thirty or forty men, sixty or seventy squaws and boys.

When the speech was finished they all yelled a hideous and hearty assent to what had been said. The Indian men then took up their guns, and shot powder into the Colonel's body, from his feet as far up as his neck. I think that not less than seventy loads were discharged upon his naked body. They then crowded about him, and to the best of my observation, cut off his ears; when the crowd had dispersed a little, I saw the blood running from both sides of his head in consequence thereof.

The fire was about six or seven yards from the post to which the Colonel was tied; it was made of small hickory poles, burnt quite through in the middle, each end of the poles remaining about six feet in length. Three or four Indians by turns would take up, individually, one of these burning pieces of wood and apply it to his naked body, already burnt black with the powder. These tormentors presented themselves on every side of him with the burning faggots and poles. Some of the squaws took broad boards, upon which they would carry a quantity of burning coals and hot embers and throw on him, so that in a short time he had nothing but coals of fire and hot ashes to walk upon. . . .

Colonel Crawford, at this period of his suffering, besought the Almighty to have mercy on his soul, spoke very low, and bore his torments with the most manly fortitude. He continued in all the extremities for an hour and three quarters or two hours longer, as near as I can judge, when, at last, being almost exhausted, he lay down on his belly; they then scalped him, and repeatedly threw the scalp in my face, telling me, 'that was my great captain.' An old squaw got a board, took a parcel of coals and ashes and laid them on his back and head; he then raised himself upon his feet and began to walk around the post; they next put a burning stick to him as usual, but he seemed more insensible of pain than before.

The Indian fellow who had me in charge, now took me away to Captain Pipe's house, about three quarters of a mile from the place of the Colonel's execution. I was bound all night, and thus prevented from seeing the last of the horrid spectacle.

The English had concealed the news of Yorktown from the Indians as long as they were able. But eventually the Indian leaders and their trader and Tory advisors began to realize that if England made peace they might be left in the lurch. At a midsummer council at Wapatomica it was decided to make one more great effort to break down the frontier before their English support was withdrawn. A diversionary attack under the Mohawk hero, Joseph Brant, was made upon Pennsylvania, spreading destruction across the Ohio and, among many other depredations, burning Hannastown, a considerable settlement which considered itself comparatively safe because it was situated thirty miles east of Fort Pitt. The main thrust was at Kentucky. This invading force, composed of three hundred selected warriors with a stiffening of rangers, was commanded by Ranger Captain William Caldwell, who had as his lieutenants the noted border partisans, Alexander McKee, Matthew Elliot and the three Girtys, Simon, James and George.

Caldwell's first move, a descent upon Bryan's Station, was broken off after a desultory two day siege. In border fighting stockades were seldom taken unless surprised with the gates open, unless the attackers had cannon, or unless a faint-hearted garrison surrendered. This relative invulnerability of the stockade was the physical factor upon which the survival of the frontier most depended. The Indian as a soldier was capable of the most extraordinary feats of fortitude when he could see a chance to come to grips with his opponent but to advance in the open against the accurate rifle fire that came from the loopholes of a palisade was far from his conception of a sensible way to make war. The Bryan's Station people managed to get off an express calling for aid. Stirred by this appearance of so large an enemy force in their midst, the veteran Kentucky militia swiftly gathered. Caldwell withdrew slowly, watching for an opportunity. One soon came.

The men of Lincoln and Fayette counties, under such famous and seasoned colonels as John Todd, Daniel Boone, Stephen Trigg and Robert Patterson, came up first. Anxious to get in a blow before the retreating Indians got safely away, they decided not to wait for the arrival of Colonel Benjamin Logan, known to be on his way with another contingent of militia. The Kentuckians' overconfident attack at Blue Licks produced instead of the anticipated Indian flight an equally confident Indian counterattack. The consequences were comparable to Estill's lesser engagement though far more devastating. After the exchange of the first volley, the Indians, in violation of all precedent, instead of pausing to reload charged with knife and tomahawk. In this hand to hand collision, the climactic test of battle, it was again the Kentucky line which broke. The defeat became a rout. Seventy white dead were left on the field and another twenty were captured.

The news of Blue Licks sent a shudder of despair through Kentucky. Among the fallen had been scores of their boldest and most experienced leaders and defenders, men who had been inured since childhood to Indian warfare. There were no better men than those who had been driven headlong from that field. Such a mood of depression settled over the frontier as had not been known since the dismal winter of 1776 when people had starved in Kentucky's three remaining stockades, unable to hunt in the surrounding Indian-infested woods for the food upon which their lives depended. Talk of abandoning the settlements became more general than it had been since that time. Petitions were sent off to the assemblies of eastern states and to the Congress, enlarging upon their difficulties and pleading for aid.

So stouthearted a Kentuckian as Daniel Boone was writing, September 11, 1782:

The Number of the Enemy that lately penetrated into our Country, their Behaviour, adding to this our late unhappy Defeat at the Blue Licks, fill us with the deepest concern & Anxiety, the Loss of our worthy Officers & Soulders who fell there the 19th

of Augst we Sensibly feel & deem our Situation truly Alarming,
We can scarcely Behold a spot of Earth but what reminds us of
the fall of some fellow adventurer, Massacred by Savage hands,
Our Number of Militia decreases, Our Widows & Orphants are
numerous Our Officers & worthiest Men fall a Sacrifise. In short
Sir, our settlements hitherto form'd at the Expence of Treasure
& much Blood seems to decline & and if something is not speedily done we doubt will wholly be depopulated.

Colonel William Christian, a distinguished border commander
since 1774 and himself destined to fall in an Indian attack four
years later, wrote, September 28, 1782:

Kentuckey it is supposed does not contain above 1000 men
at present, the general Part of the young men having come off
this summer, as is commonly the case when Danger appears here.
The Settlements are so much scattered, that it is difficult, and
takes some Days to collect a Force together, particularly to go
to any Distance from their own Families, when no other man
knows what number of the Enemy have entered the Country, nor
where the first Stroke will be made. . . . If no succour is sent to
Kentuckey, and the war with the British continues another Year,
it is more than Probable the whole of the Inhabitants will be
killed, taken to Detroit or driven away.

The ability of the East to send aid in response to such appeals
was probably most succinctly outlined by the remark of Governor Benjamin Harrison of Virginia in a 1782 letter to Clark:
"I am sorry to inform you that we have but 4. S. in the Treasury,
and no means of getting any more."

Spirits were revived somewhat in the fall when the two greatest western field commanders, George Rogers Clark and John
Sevier, assembled men who were still willing to follow such
leaders and struck back. In the north, Clark invaded the Indian
country and burned six Shawnee towns, while in the south
Sevier in another of his inimitable whirlwind campaigns destroyed nine Cherokee towns. These indications that the
smouldering frontier still possessed the energy to generate offensive actions were disconcerting to the Indians' English and
Tory patrons and did much to improve the state of mind in

the settlements. But little was accomplished to reduce the
actual Indian military potential. The Indians had watched the
invaders' marches and had chosen to give up their towns without risking a general engagement. Their simple dwellings could
be readily rebuilt on the same or other sites and the loss of
their stocks of corn was not fatal to people who lived largely by
hunting. The chief impression made upon the Indian mind
was that whether or no the English made peace with the Americans there could never be peace between Indians and Americans. It was becoming clearer and clearer to them, as it was to
the settlers, that Indian hunter and white farmer could not both
continue to exist in the same world.

When the snow went off the next spring the provisional treaty
between the United States and England was in effect. Among
its terms was England's ostensible gift of the West to the United
States. Washington proclaimed the formal cessation of hostilities
to his army and most of the army went home. The English army
had evacuated Savannah and Charleston and was preparing to
evacuate New York. But in the west the Indian raids again accompanied the spring freshets. The day the news of peace reached
Pittsburgh Simon Girty and his Indian pack were taking scalps
within hearing of the guns at the fort firing their celebrating
salutes.

By midsummer it became apparent that the English had
changed their minds again about relinquishing their lake posts
or their position of influence over the Ohio Indians. In the
south Spain was taking advantage of a similar opportunity to
supply and excite the Indians on that frontier. The reaction of
Congress to these continuing dangers was to pass a law forbidding the settlers to occupy Indian land and another law disband-
ing the final remnant of the national army.

Peace had not visibly diminished Indian power in the west.
In two respects the situation had worsened. Spain, a wartime
ally, had become a principal enemy. And the settlers' own government, if they chose to consider the Congress east of the
mountains their own government, had left them completely to
shift for themselves.

VII. The Real War

Marches, sieges and battles were not the decisive factors governing the outcome of the war in the west. The issue was decided by the will of the individual settler to endure the strain.

The young men and bachelors who constituted a majority of the males on the border could come and go. They tended to swarm westward when times were good and to drift eastward again when dangers multiplied. But the genuine settler, the man of family, had to stay put. He could never fall asleep without first holding his breath to listen to the night noises without. His first need upon arising was to peer from the cabin's loopholes into his familiar dooryard and his next warily to comb the fringes of the surrounding forest. Weeks and months might pass without any alarm in his immediate neighborhood but the mutter of distant thunder was always in his ears and he could never know that his own roof might not be the target of the next bolt.

This apprehension that he must daily feel was a dreadful fear. The misfortune hanging over him and over his women and children was death by butchery, accompanied by outrage unspeakable and without parallel. Yet he could not keep his family in the shelter of the nearest stockade. To feed them he had to work his farm and for this he needed their assistance. So he kept on, cultivating his corn and clearing another acre or two around his cabin, taking care, usually, to have his rifle always within reach and his senses strained to catch the first indication of danger.

The average Indian raid so closely followed the pattern set by its forerunners and its successors that these visitations were like the same nightmare, endlessly repeated. Indians occasionally lurked among the settlements singly or in pairs, watching for the opportunity to steal a horse or snatch a scalp, but the ordinary raiding party was made up of a dozen to twenty warriors. They might spring upon the most outlying cabin along the fringe of the frontier or they might penetrate deep into the settlements where people were less likely to be on guard. If on foot they took expert care to keep out of sight and to leave few tracks that might attract the notice of a chance hunter. If mounted, they traveled fast to keep ahead of the spreading alarm. Having found a place inviting attack, they crept closer, studying the ground and the behavior of the inhabitants.

A favored time to strike was just after dawn when people first emerged to deal with early morning duties but any time when surprise could be achieved was acceptable. The first rush was accompanied by a sudden din of gunshots, whistles, rattles, and the screeching whoop of the war cry, a pandemonium calculated to paralyze the victims with terror. If surprise were as planned, the adult male defenders, their positions marked in advance, were shot down or struck down in the first few seconds.

The farmstead then lay at the mercy of Indian caprice. Their next concern was loot and the premises, however poor, were ransacked for anything that was not too heavy to carry off. The Indian male was especially entranced by white women's garments and these when discovered in the cabin or stripped from the wearers were at once wreathed about his own paint-bedaubed torso. After selecting the better horses to take with them, the livestock was butchered. The Indian had a particular aversion to cows, for their possession meant the settler had milk for his children and thus was prepared to stay. The cabin and outbuildings were set afire if they had not been fired as an adjunct to the first assault.

Then came the selection of captives whom the raiders proposed to carry away with them, the most excruciating moment of all for the survivors. The old, the very young, the sick, the wounded, any who appeared likely to lag during the long march back, were killed, scalped and mutilated with special attention paid to the sex organs. These executions might be by tomahawk, knife or gunshot but the Indian had a peculiarly perverse weakness for swinging infants by their heels to pop their skulls against a tree. Half-grown boys and robust women under thirty were considered the most desirable captives and were the most likely to be kept alive. This process of selection was made the more monstrous by the circumstance that many of the Indians spoke passable English, due to their trading contacts, and were prone to prolong the agony by entering into debates with their victims upon the question of who should live and who should die.

The captive woman, who had just witnessed the murder of her loved ones, was spared but one fear. She need not dread sexual outrage upon her own person. The Indian warrior kept himself ritualistically purified by an elaborate system of fasts, self-denial and prayers and would have considered his purity and therefore his luck as warrior or hunter threatened by admitting any shadow of sex interest in an impure white woman.

The whole whirlwind of ferocious action had passed with incredible rapidity, except, perhaps, for the victims, and within a few minutes the Indians had faded from sight again into the forest. The first relief party from neighboring settlements came upon an all too familiar scene. One incongruous note added a final gruesome touch. Indians invariably ripped apart feather beds in order to carry off the ticking. Festoons of feathers hung in the trees and upon the cornstalks and drifted to and fro across the welter of smouldering ruins and dismembered human and animal corpses. If the Indians had overlooked any of the pigs these were now feeding ghoulishly. Usually the rescuers set out upon an avenging pursuit, generally a vain one, of the raiders. If they were not strong enough for this venture they hastily buried the dead and hurried back to guard their own homesteads.

Such episodes, recurring with monotonous regularity and similarity, fill the records of every year of the first twenty years of the western settlements. It was regarded as worthy of note, and, strangely enough, more than usually sad, when a man died peaceably in his bed. The great majority of these forlorn wilderness tragedies faded from community memory or, at any rate, were never recorded. Each year, from the melting of the snow in the spring until the first snow of winter, the hovering blow could fall upon any home at any time. Estimates of the period indicate certain fluctuations, connected, probably, with the ebb and flow of English and Spanish supplies to the Indians, but suggest an average annual death rate on the order of two hundred with as many more wounded or carried into captivity.*

Those who never suffered actual attack lived nevertheless in continual apprehension of one. It is an axiom of war that victory depends upon breaking the will of the enemy population to resist. Perhaps never before the era of modern bombing has a civilian population been subjected to so painful a test and never one so persistent and long enduring. It was a strain which tore at the very vitals of social relationships and, most agonizingly, at the loyalties and devotions within the family.

An occasional personal instance, selected at random from the vast store of experiences recalled by the survivors, throws a sharper light upon the stark realities of this war than could any generalization.

Peter Hendrix, in flight with his faltering mother and his infant son, realizing he could not carry both, dropped his child and saved his mother.

A young Negro woman, belonging to a migrating family suddenly assailed on the Wilderness Road, strangled the infant at her breast lest its cries betray her hiding place in the bushes.

When Harbert's Station was surprised, the adults inside the blockhouse frantically barred and held the door, while the Indians were killing or taking the eight children still in the yard outside.

Mary Ingles, realizing she could not successfully escape burdened with the infant born to her after she had been taken captive, left her three months old baby behind with the Indians in order to make the attempt to return to her husband and other children still in the settlements.

The widow Scraggs, in one room of a double cabin with two grown sons and a daughter, sternly elected to save at least one

* In relation to the West's total population this is comparable to an annual casualty rate of 640,000 in our country today.

portion of her family by forbidding her sons to go to the assistance of three other daughters being murdered by Indians in the other half of the cabin.

This compulsion to make instant difficult emotional decisions extended even into the realm of affection for the family dog. The prudent family, making for the stockade upon receiving an Indian alarm, took care to leave the dog, howling mournfully, locked in the cabin, lest its barking betray their escape route to the savages. Jennie Wiley, fleeing from closely pursuing Indians, kept in the water of a creek to hide her tracks, but seeing that her little dog, accompanying her faithfully, persisted in running along the soft bank, she was obliged to coax it within reach and hold it under water until drowned.

These same compulsions frequently stirred noncombatants into the most violently aggressive action.

The pioneer woman was of necessity as accustomed to the use of an axe as any man. One of them, Mrs. John Bozarth, a middle-aged matron, when Indians were forcing their way into her cabin, seized an axe, killed in succession the first three to enter and then managed to close and bar the door. All of her children had been cut down in the yard outside during the initial attack. Fifteen years later her house was again attacked and this time she was carried off, together with her second brood of children, but, though now so much older, she still possessed sufficient stamina to survive the captivity.

Mrs. John Merril won an even more notable victory with the same ubiquitous weapon. Her husband had been shot in the first rush and the Indians had hacked a hole in the door. She split the heads of the first four who attempted to spring through it. Other Indians were endeavoring to crawl down the chimney. She cut open a mattress and threw the feathers on the embers in the fireplace. Two half-suffocated Indians came tumbling down, likewise to fall victims to her terrible axe. The attackers, dismayed by so belligerent a garrison, withdrew.

A lame Negro, belonging to the Woods family, was alone in their cabin with Mrs. Woods and her teen age daughter. The cripple, after a prolonged tussle and some help from the girl, managed to finish off the one Indian who had burst in before

Mrs. Woods had barred the door. Much elated, he cried: "Let the rest in — one at a time."

Not all these noncombatant victories were won by force. Mrs. Samuel Daviess, when her cabin was invaded in the absence of her husband, so delayed the Indians by offering them food and drink and by opening cupboards and trunks to display trinkets and garments that rescue arrived in time to save her and her seven children.

Often women were steadier than men in an emergency. When Jonathan Jennings' boat ran upon a rock in the Tennessee River, observant Indians opened fire from shore. The other men on board dove into the river and swam off, some directly into the hands of the Indians. But the three women, Mrs. Jennings, her daughter, Mrs. Ephraim Peyton, and a young negro woman, resolutely set about lightening ship by throwing out cargo and, getting into the water, shoved the craft free, so that the party escaped, though the women's clothing and the sides of the boat were pierced by any number of bullets. The only casualty was Mrs. Peyton's baby, born the night before, which was lost during the confusion.

There were no exigencies, however, which could deliver the frontiersman from his constitutional interest in land. Clark, with all Kentucky in peril, discovered that the one way to rally volunteers to his standard was to order the land office closed for the duration of the campaign. Sullivan's soldiers, devastating the Iroquois country, took time to mark favored sites on the Genesee which they returned to claim after the war. Daniel Boone, dispatched from Virginia to warn the first land hunters and surveyors in Kentucky of the outbreak of Lord Dunmore's War, paused to blaze a claim and build a cabin upon a spot that caught his fancy, before continuing upon his mission. Simon Kenton, guiding a punitive expedition into the Indian country, during the last tense moments of crawling into the outskirts of an Indian town, took up a handful of earth, crumbled it, sniffed it, and whispered judiciously: "This is good land."

An entire literature has grown up around the adventures and vicissitudes of the thousands of people carried into captivity by the Indians. Their experiences ranged from the warmhearted hospitality which was one Indian characteristic to the protracted torture which was another. All suffered during the rigors of the march back to the Indian country when to fail to keep pace meant the tomahawk. Their initial reception was also painful. To the Indian captor a live prisoner, even if only a child or a woman, was more convincing evidence even than a scalp of his prowess in war and every care was taken for a while to view the prisoner as an enemy. During this period of boasting and vainglory captives were insulted, humiliated, beaten, and made to feel that death by torment was imminent.

Thereafter the variations began. The less numerous adult male captives were frequently burned, particularly if they were recognized as notable Indian fighters, though this was not always true. Boone, an outstanding enemy, was well treated, made much of, and even given a horse upon which presently he made his escape. Other men were sold at the standard price of 20 pounds to the English at Detroit. Most women became drudges in the families of their captors and were required to perform the more irksome and unpleasant tasks of which the Indian standard of living offered an ample supply. Boys, if at all prepossessing, were ritualistically prepared by fasting, minor torment, and bathing for adoption into the tribe to replace some fallen warrior.

After the delivery of captives, successfully negotiated at intervals by the whites, many of these youths ran off again to the Indian country, having learned to prefer the Indian way of life. The case of the occasional woman captive who had been purified and adopted and then taken in marriage by an Indian presented another harsh test of loyalties, since she was torn between devotion to her original white family and her more recent Indian family. There were even instances in which romance cast its pleasant glow over the captive's fate. William Biggs so excited the fancy of an Indian maiden that, despite his earnest remonstrances, she combed his hair, washed his feet, slept as near him as his guards would allow, and, continually voicing her need, followed him about wherever he was taken, to the great amusement of his captors, who were as much astonished by his modesty as by her lack of it. And the beautiful Marian Hanna, taken at the destruction of Hannastown, was wooed and wed by an English officer in Montreal.

Dismal as was this war in most of its aspects, a species of

humor, a shade grim as might be expected, was not always lacking on either side.

During one of Sevier's campaigns, at a stage when the Indians were withdrawing without offering opposition, a green militiaman spied an aged squaw attempting to hide. Eagerly he shot and scalped her. The rest of the day the bellowing question echoed from one end of the column to the other: "Who killed granny?" And then the roaring answer: "Ralston."

At the storming of Nickajack the warriors were given no quarter but an effort was made to take women and children alive, since they had value as a medium of exchange for white captives. "Big Joe" Logston, famed along the frontier for his size and strength and his prowess as a never defeated rough and tumble wrestler, unluckily tackled a large and powerful squaw who for some time successfully resisted his every effort to subdue her. Half the command ceased their own activities and gathered to watch, whooping with laughter, laying bets on the outcome, and cheering on his Amazonian antagonist.

A favorite frontier story was of the lone settler who, when an overwhelming number of Indians swarmed into his yard, welcomed them with open arms and every expression of delight, assured them that he had always wanted to join them, happily rushed to butcher his stock to feed them, and climaxed his transport of thanksgiving by breaking up his furniture and firing his house to demonstrate his scorn of a white man's material possessions. Convinced of his sincerity, the Indians took him to their bosoms, their unsuspecting acceptance enabling him soon to escape without having suffered the slightest injury. Another favorite was of the boy out hunting with his first rifle who rushed home crying: "Ma — I just shot an Indian." He had.

The Indian sense of humor, bawdy and hilarious among themselves, ranged from the ironic to the macabre in their dealings with whites. The Indian term for compass was "landstealer" and for courtroom, "quarreling house." They were apt to taunt an important prisoner with the question, "So you want land?" and then to stuff his mouth with dirt. At the conclusion of a successful attack sometimes their first gesture was to insist upon shaking hands with their prisoners, including those who were expiring, or, before stripping their captives, to propose sardonically, "Swap — swap?" meaning an exchange of the victors' nakedness for the losers' garments. In the relaxation of their own towns they howled with delight when a despairing victim managed by some flare-up of energy to discomfit one of his tormentors but they were also immensely diverted when a squaw urinated or defecated upon the person of a pinioned captive. Simon Kenton won undying Indian fame when he so severely bit a squaw who had seated herself astride his face that she was compelled to shriek for mercy.

However, the principal theme of the war was stark horror, endlessly repeated and seldom relieved.

At the siege of Dunlap's Station Girty's Indians burned a prisoner, Abner Hunt, within sight and hearing of the stockade, in the hope that his gradually weakening, night-long screaming might undermine the spirit of the defenders.

Thomas Mackey's nine year old son was required to stretch his father's fresh scalp on a hoop for drying.

Timothy Dorman, an indentured servant, joined the Indians and guided their raiding parties through the countryside with which he was familiar, singling out residents against whom he harbored grievances. Reaching the house of his former master he tomahawked and scalped a daughter when she resisted him as scornfully as before.

But perhaps no single episode illustrates more vividly the tensions of hatred that marked the period than the Kirk-Brown-Old Tassel series of murders. In May, 1788, Slim Tom, a minor Cherokee chief, appeared at the cabin of John Kirk, near the present Knoxville. The Kirks, who had previously befriended him, gave him something to eat. Noticing that the men of the family were absent he returned with companions and killed the eleven women and children. John Kirk and his grown son, John Jr., came back to find their home strewn with the mutilated bodies. The same month the boat of Colonel James Brown, who was en route down the Tennessee River to claim western land granted him as a Revolutionary veteran, was boarded by several Cherokee who pretended friendliness. Whipping weapons from the folds of their blankets they killed Brown, two older sons, and five crew members and carried off the six women and children of the Brown family.

These two uncommonly aggravating atrocities occurred during a lull in the war and at a time responsible authorities on both sides were laboring strenuously to work out a basis for peace. Realizing the murders had been committed by a minority faction in the Cherokee nation, American officials enjoined continued restraint. But John Sevier, the dashing border fighter, was not a man who knew restraint. Collecting volunteers, he set off to punish such Cherokee as he might first come upon. His lieutenant, James Hubbard, whose entire family had some years earlier been killed by Indians, encountered Old Tassel, principal Cherokee chief, a lifelong advocate of peace with the whites and an Indian statesman equally respected by both races, who had come out under a flag of truce to urge continued negotiation. Disregarding the flag, Hubbard locked Old Tassel in an abandoned cabin, together with the four other chiefs in his official party, handed young John Kirk a tomahawk, and advised him to take the vengeance that was his due. Kirk axed the unresisting Cherokee leaders.

Congress condemned the act by formal resolution of both houses. The governor of North Carolina issued a warrant for Sevier's arrest. But the damage had been done. Those members of the Cherokee nation who had been ready for peace rejoined the war faction and the war blazed up more furiously than ever.

Such were a few of the distinguishing characteristics of the border war to which no end could be foreseen and which the national government had felt compelled to leave to the West to wage with its own scant resources and limited manpower.

VIII. The Land Grabbers

THE AVERAGE AMERICAN of 1782 took it as much for granted as does his counterpart today that an earnest effort to make money is a prerequisite to the pursuit of happiness. To improve himself was his primary mission in life and, by common consent, to improve himself meant achieving material success. The man who was not ridden by this ambition was considered by his community a suspect and second class citizen, no matter what his other virtues.

The great difference between then and today was in the range of opportunity to make money. Commerce and industry offered few rewards. Capital was all but nonexistent. The several states had emerged from the Revolution with empty treasuries and their inhabitants with empty pockets. Continental money was worthless. Trade had been disorganized by seven years of war. Few had goods to sell and fewer the means to buy. There was but one reservoir of wealth. Land. Land still had real value. And beyond the mountains lay hundreds of millions of acres of the best land on earth.

The ordinary settler was prepared to travel for months, to endure the extremes of hardship, to risk death, in order to gain possession of the land he sought. But this was a tedious process. Men of more substance, wider vision and greater influence saw a better way. Land companies might be organized to deal not in family farms but in tracts of two and three million acres. The journeys required were no longer than to the doors of a state assembly or of Congress. No harsher hardships were incurred than accompanied the tasks of making friends among legislators and bankers and no physical risks at all. Simple arithmetic set forth the possible profit. A grant of as little as 500,000 acres secured by the expenditure of, say, 1½ cents an acre, and sold to actual land seekers for, say, 12½ cents an acre, produced a good round increment. Meanwhile, in the course of the operation, there was the opportunity that the organizers, with their inside knowledge of the company's changing prospects, might buy or sell capital stock in the company to advantage.

The land company's original grant might have sprung from various sets of circumstances. It might have owed its birth to a direct treaty with the Indians, to a pre-Revolutionary royal grant, to an act of a state legislature, to an act of Congress, to a court decision, or to the company's own repeated declaration that it was vested with the title. Since these several jurisdictions were often in conflict the grants ordinarily led to much litigation. Fierce competition among companies with rival claims resulted in lawsuits as protracted as modern patent actions among great corporations. This legalistic confusion posed the private settler a dilemma. He could not be sure that he must pay any land company for the land which he had already occupied and improved, or which company he must pay, or whether the expenditure might in any way improve his title. But whatever the settler's attitude, the land companies rolled ponderously and noisily on and for more than half a century their activities, while dealing, or attempting to deal, in western lands, played a tempestuous role in the settlement of the west.

Business men, bankers, lawyers, adventurers and politicians were the prime organizers of land companies but there was participation in the widespread operations by Americans of every type and rank. The young Washington, traveling to the Forks of the Ohio to serve notice on the French that they were trespassers, was representing a land company. The first two English-speaking explorers of the Ohio Valley, Christopher Gist and Thomas Walker, were agents of land companies. George Rogers Clark made the first of his many historic descents of the Ohio to survey for a land company. Daniel Boone led his colony to Kentucky in the name of a land company of which he was an employee. Thomas Paine, the patriot pamphleteer, also wrote pamphlets for land companies. Benjamin Franklin, from 1755 on, was actively interested in land companies. Patrick Henry, reprising his famous liberty or death theme in opposing ratification of the constitution, was demanding, among other liberties, freedom of action for land companies.

The first great burst of land company activity came between the close of the French and Indian War and the outbreak of the Revolution. The competing, overlapping, and, sometimes, merging, designs of the Ohio Company, the Indiana Company, the Loyal Company, the Vandalia Company, and the Grand Ohio Company preempted vast areas of paper on maps and memorials to the Board of Trade and the Crown but failed to reach the stage of felling trees or planting settlements. Title was claimed or sought to nearly the entire east bank of the Ohio from the Forks to the Falls but interest centered in the area on either side of the mouth of the Kanawha, a three million acre domain known interchangeably as Indiana and Vandalia. The promoters were speculators, ex-Indian traders, Virginia planters, Pennsylvania merchants, men with enough spare capital to underwrite the legal costs, men of enough political influence in England or the colonies to make taking them in advisable, and random men of enough distinction to make their signatures look well among those of other petitioners.

These various proposals that millions of acres of unbroken western wilderness be transferred by government decree to the personal possession of groups of private citizens whose purpose was resale to eventual users were based on the demands of the "suffering traders" for compensation for losses during Pontiac's Rebellion, on services rendered the Crown during the French and Indian War, on grants procured from the Indians in one fashion or another, and on the general theory that an accelerated development of the frontier was good public policy. The English government blew hot and cold, torn between a fear of precipitating new Indian wars and a desire to please some of the individual petitioners. Again and again the stockholders seemed on the verge of becoming assured of the immense fortunes that they anticipated. And again and again the prospect faded from the foreground into the background. They fumed and sweat and quarreled among themselves while each year more settlers squatted upon portions of the land itself and each ship from England alternately raised and dashed their hopes. Finally the Revolution cut them off from their English connections. Still they did not give up. Unwilling to write off their paper profits, when peace returned they continued to press their aged claims upon state legislatures, upon the Congress and before the Supreme Court.

Meanwhile a new crop of purely American land companies had sprung into being, with greater political influence and even more grandiose designs. The Transylvania Company, the Tennessee Company, the Virginia Company, the Muscle Shoals Company, the Holland Company, and the several Yazoo companies, among others, were clutching at new millions of acres in the west. A species of legal foundation for these claims was not difficult to establish. State legislatures were impressionable and especially quick to grant title to land over which there was doubt of their jurisdiction. Many would have granted land on the moon if asked. Most of the stockholders were themselves legislators or public officials. Each new land scheme was hailed with more extravagant expectations. The possibility of getting rich quick seized men with a kind of frenzy. They spoke not in terms of possessing a farm or a plantation but of acquiring tens and hundreds of thousands of acres, making fortunes overnight by the stroke of a pen. Scant heed was paid to such circumstances as that the land involved might be already occupied by settlers, might be in the heart of the Indian country, or might be claimed by Spain, and that the end result, if the project succeeded, was almost certain to be insurrection, new Indian convulsions or even war with Spain.

It is difficult for us now to imagine with any sense of reality the sudden whoop of Indians in the dooryard at dawn, or a glimpse from the kitchen window of buffalo emerging from grass twenty feet high, or the stark loneliness of a cabin in the forest, but we can have no difficulty whatever in recognizing the pattern of land company operations. The land speculator, scheming to profit by the certain increase in the product of the community, is a figure more essentially American, perhaps, and certainly more enduringly American, than the westward migrating settler

himself. No trait can be, or, at least, has been so far in our
history, more American than the assumption that the country's
future and progress are synonyms, except the general impulse to
work confidently to make them so. The land company of the
1780's was but the forerunner of the canal company and the
turnpike company and the railroad company and their many
successors in other fields, with their far heartier appetites for
feeding upon public resources. As a people we have never
strongly condemned these stages in the country's development.
We have sensed that it was a process in which the schemer, however self-seeking, presently merged, without necessarily realizing
it, into the builder, and that this was an infinitely dynamic process, making the most fantastic dreams come true and leading to
our present standard of living and national power. Neither did
the western settler, independent, belligerent and self-assertive as
he was, object strenuously at that time to the activities of the
land companies. He saw them as quite natural ventures in which
he would not hesitate to participate were he afforded the opportunity. He himself was also trying to better himself as hard
as he could. Observers of the period are agreed in the comment
that the outstanding characteristic of the early West was a universal materialism. Everybody was grasping at private advantage in a society which all assumed had not yet developed to a
point where moral or public concerns were of consequence.

The land companies ran their course. As has so often been
the case since, the original stockholders made nothing, though
many of the more active insiders did very well personally. But
while running their inglorious course they exerted a nearly
fatal influence upon what we may call the Americanization of
the West. The men who backed the land companies set themselves against every trend or proposal that might strengthen the
ties between the new country and the national government. They
opposed every step that led to recognition of national sovereignty
and from then on to every move to erect new states and to their
inclusion in the Union. These were men who seemed certain to
get what they wanted. Unlike the ordinary settler isolated in
his woodland clearing they were men in a position to make their
influence felt. Most were themselves men of military or political

rank. They were able to demand a hearing. They frequented the seats of government. They knew what made political wheels go around and how to start and stop them.

During the peace negotiations land company influence, manifested in pressures brought on state assemblies, on Congress, on the English ministry, and on the peace commissioners, was exerted in favor of abandoning American claims to the West. The old companies saw their hopes revived were England to retain the northern Ohio Valley and the new companies saw a far freer field were the Spanish claim to the southern portion of the valley accepted. At a most critical period a nine state majority in Congress, after a debate that turned on the land issue, instructed the peace commissioners to let the West go. Benjamin Franklin's long continued acquiescence in the French advocacy of a western boundary running along the line of the Appalachians was ascribed by his enemies to his land company interests.

England's sudden and unexpected cession of the West to the United States was a blow from which the old companies never recovered. But the terms of the treaty opened fascinating prospects in the southwest to the new companies. Across the whole area between the Carolina-Georgia frontier and the Mississippi were spread the conflicting title claims of Spain, of the occupying Indian nations, of the several adjoining states, and of the national government. More fruitful ground for land company operations could not be envisaged. Deals might be made with any one of the claimant authorities or, in view of the multiplicity of claimants, a company might boldly take unilateral possession of a tract under guise of planting an independent colony.

In the furtherance of these prospects the encumbrance most feared by the land companies was the assumption by the national government of jurisdiction over the west. Therefore they vigorously and progressively denied the power of federal authority to treat directly with the Indian nations, opposed the cession by the several states of their western lands to the United States, and agitated against the ratification of the Constitution. On the other hand they supported every separatist and divisive movement in the west as well as every effort to reach some arrangement with

Spain. In pursuit of these aims they in some instances went so far as to raise independent armies and to declare their projected colonies to be independent principalities.

Meanwhile, the most successful land grabber had been the individual settler. Without benefit of grant, writ, petition or prospectus he moved in with his family, and, perhaps, a horse, a cow and a couple of pigs, upon a piece of land that suited him. Seldom was he concerned about trying to secure even the most shadowy legal title to his land. His presence upon it was always violently resented by the Indians, often by a land company or large scale land operator, sometimes by a state government which had a different program, and occasionally by the national government which had by recent treaty guaranteed the Indian right to it.

But, no matter who objected, there he stayed and a kind of frontier common law grew up around him to formalize his interest. The land was regarded as his, first, by the so-called "tomahawk right," which he had gained by blazing the trees to mark his chosen site. Next came the "corn right," the result of successfully raising and harvesting a crop. When he had built a cabin and moved his family into it he was considered by his neighbors to be in full and permanent possession. This squatter's right of discovery, occupation and use was solidified as the settler defended his property from the Indians and served his time in the local militia.

Meanwhile the ordinary settler's appetitite for land was as insatiable as that of the most avaricious land company. It drove him to subject his family and himself to all the vicissitudes of the way west and obstinately to maintain his painful lodgement in the depths of the wilderness. He was seldom moved by land hunger in the sense that he yearned to possess a piece of good land, to cultivate it, to improve it, to develop upon it a permanent home for his posterity. More often than not each year he abandoned his holding and lunged off in search of another. It was actually not land that he sought so much as the money value that it represented. His grasping at land and then more land displayed all the fierce and competitive aspects of a gold rush and since, like the gold seeker, he was seeking not security but a fortune his feverish scramble remained as often unrewarded. His greed led him to hang, in the face of continuing Indian threat, to his four acre clearing which was but the token of the encircling thousand of unimproved acres which he claimed, when by every dictate of common sense he should long since have removed his family to safety, led him to keep moving to yet wider acreages on the most exposed fringe of the frontier or even into the Indian country itself, led him violently to resist every diplomatic effort to pacify the Indians by a definition of boundaries which he would be forbidden to cross.

His position began to deteriorate, however, as the settlements developed. Later comers, such as Revolutionary veterans who had been granted specific western tracts by state or national governments, turned up with more legalistic claims. Land companies began to exert more pressure. Large proprietors questioned the squatter rights. Land offices and courts were set up. Lawyers appeared. Titles became involved in litigation that dragged on for a generation. The issue was further confused by rapid changes in jurisdiction as states ceded their lands to the national government and its courts were in turn superseded by those of the new states formed in the west. As early as 1785 it was estimated at the time that the majority of the inhabitants of Kentucky owned no land. Most early settlers were overwhelmed by this legal tumult. Few could afford lawyers or prolonged lawsuits. Many gave up to move on to new and less confusing frontiers. Daniel Boone, for one, passed his old age on the banks of the Missouri, four hundred miles west of Boonesborough.

Thus we find that land hunger — surely the primary urge in the westward spread of settlement — was not a factor that promoted unity. The complexity of the land problem was on the contrary a divisive one. The man who thought he possessed land or hoped to possess land might look to the national government for protection but for long he looked in vain. If, in the face of this disappointment, eventually he chose to cling to that government it was not because of but in spite of his yearnings for land.

IX. Their Own Leaders

I N T I M E S of crisis no form of society feels more instinctively the need for leadership than does a democracy. The process of exchanging opinions and postponing decisions serves well enough to meet ordinary demands but in an emergency even a mob swings behind a leader. The western settlers' democracy was of the town meeting and grass roots essence of democracy. They lived in a perpetual state of crisis. Their need for leadership amounted to an extremity of need.

By 1782 many of their original leaders, who had commanded the stockades and fought off the Indians during the Revolution, were fading from view. They had fallen in battle, had become disgusted with changing conditions, or had been supplanted by later comers who were more literate, or more articulate, or more politically minded. In the Third Kentucky Convention in 1785 Benjamin Logan was the sole member of the original settler, county lieutenant, veteran Indian fighter type. Lawyers, merchants, politicians and town-bred men had shouldered in to deal with the problems that beset the settler.

These were stunning problems. The Indian war involved life or death for himself and his family. The Mississippi, his one avenue of escape from grinding poverty, was closed to his commerce. Political confusion from day to day altered the status even of his local government. Accumulating uncertainties clustered about his legal title to his land and his home. But behind these and every other issue there was the fundamental issue which embraced them all and upon which all depended. He was a man without a country. What country was to become his?

The grudging cession to the central government by the several states of their conflicting and overlapping claims to the West, the Ordinances of 1785 and 1787, the creeping institution by Congress of diplomatic negotiations with the Indians, the Spanish and the English, the assembling of the Constitutional Convention — all these were like pillars, dimly glimpsed as through a mist, rising shakily to support the edifice of the nation that was to be. If the western settler waited and suffered with sufficient patience conceivably this edifice might extend, in time, to shelter even him. The great issue was: Could he afford to wait? Could he hope even to survive if he endeavored to wait? He was accustomed to shift for himself. Was it not infinitely more advisable to shake off the dead hand of the East, and to strike out for himself, marshal his powers in his own interest, and make such accommodations with Spain and England as might rid him of the Indian menace, open the Mississippi and the Great Lakes to his trade, and assure his future peace and prosperity?

This was a profound and complex question to pose the average ignorant, uninformed and harassed settler. He needed advice. He had reason to look around for leadership. Men sprang up on every side to offer it — brilliant, ambitious, eloquent and forceful men. These numerous and agressive leaders spoke as with one voice. Without exception they counselled the second course. They combined, connived and conspired to lead the West to separate, to secede, to seize freedom of action, and to grasp those Spanish, French and English opportunities which were of so much greater immediate advantage than any the United States could offer.

First and most remarkable among these western leaders, there was the unbelievable James Wilkinson. He was one of the later comers, arriving in Kentucky in 1783 with the avowed purpose of making his fortune. By propaganda devices which would have earned him the acclaim of public relations experts of our time he swiftly undermined Clark's prestige and made himself the most influential man in Kentucky through all of the most critical years. He used this influence to promote every sort of activity that might loosen any remaining ties with the United States and dump the West either into the arms of Spain or the arms of England. He established contacts with English officials in Canada which extended to furnishing them detailed espionage reports on American military plans and movements. He made personal pilgrimages to New Orleans, gained the confidence of the Spanish governor, swore allegiance to the King of Spain, and was regularly advanced large sums of Spanish money. So completely developed was his talent for duplicity that at one period he was carrying on simultaneous intrigues with Spain, England and France, seeking rewards from each for betraying the designs of the other. Despite his continual treasonable activity he managed to maintain not only his standing with his fellow westerners but with the American government. High official position gave him that much more to betray. Upon Wayne's death he was appointed Commander-in-Chief of the United States Army by Washington, he remained the highest ranking officer in the service under Adams, Jefferson and Madison, was honored with the commission to accept the transfer of Louisiana to the American flag, and became first governor of that newly acquired empire.

There was George Rogers Clark, the West's undeniably outstanding hero. Though not, strictly speaking, himself a settler, he had been among the first of the pioneers, a surveyor in Kentucky in 1774, Kentucky's first representative in the Virginia assembly, and Virginia's commander in the west. Responsibility for the survival of the frontier during the Revolution had been largely his. His military efforts had been of more enduring consequence to the future of his country than those of any other man save Washington himself. After the Revolution he was discharged, his accounts questioned, and his services minimized. His influence was impaired even in Kentucky by more adroit men. Embittered and impoverished, he lost all patience with the slow course of events. He lent himself to land company schemes. He used his military reputation to attempt to promote unauthorized expeditions against Spanish possessions. He swung to the other extreme and offered to become a Spanish subject if he were invited to establish a colony of Americans in Spanish territory. Ultimately he accepted a commission as major general in the Revolutionary Army of France and organized a force of fellow Kentuckians with the purpose of capturing New Orleans for France.

And John Sevier, the very beau ideal of the frontiersman, generous, hospitable, possessed of a personal charm that captivated men and women alike, the victor in innumerable Indian campaigns, and one of the commanders at King's Mountain. He was the principal scourge of the Indian enemy in the south. His hard riding horsemen moved so swiftly through the mountains that again and again they dropped as from the clouds on surprised Indian towns. He never knew an unsuccessful campaign and the mere threat that he might take the field was enough to fill the Indians with consternation. But the terror with which he struck the Indians and the enthusiasm with which he was regarded by his frontier neighbors were matched by the dismay which he caused the constituted authorities of his state and nation. Many of his expeditions were unauthorized, even specifically forbidden, and others undertaken to further his personal land interests. He had a finger in every land company pie. He became governor of the highly irregular State of Franklin, set up by the restless Wataugans in defiance of the laws of North Carolina, of Virginia and of the United States. When his plans were threatened by the collapse of this adventure he did not hesitate to enter into correspondence with the Spanish, with Wilkinson and his fellow conspirators, with Chief McGillivray of the Creek Nation, and to throw the weight of his tremendous personal influence into the movement to unite Franklin, Cumberland and Kentucky to Spain.

And James Robertson, the archetype of all that was sturdy, resourceful and courageous in the empire-building pioneer. He promoted, organized and participated in the founding of the Cumberland settlement by that extraordinary migration during that unprecedented winter of 1779–80 when the cold was so intense that game and cattle died of it, the trees of the forest were split, most of the primeval cane was destroyed, and broad rivers as far south as the Cumberland and the Tennessee were frozen over. By force of personal example and sheer strength of character he held the settlement intact in the face of every threat, though it was the most exposed of all to the constant inroads of the Southern Indians. But he, too, played a prominent part in the devious and illegal machinations of the land companies. And he, too, lent the support of his name and his influence to the separatist movement and the Spanish conspiracy, at one stage going so far to assure Miro, the Spanish governor, of his Spanish sympathies, as to rename Cumberland the District of Mero.

And John Brown, first representative of the Kentucky district in Congress. He associated himself with the efforts of Gardoqui, Spanish envoy to the United States, to take advantage of the crisis in the west and advised his Kentucky constituents, then engaged in a series of conventions to determine whether to seek statehood, separation from the United States, or union with Spain, to delay decision until the Spanish alternative had been fully explored.

And James White, Superintendent of Indian Affairs for the Southern Department under the Confederation and member of Congress for North Carolina. He became Gardoqui's most active American agent, traveling widely through the west, exchanging views with other leaders such as Wilkinson, Sevier and Robertson in an attempt to knit together the movement to place the West under the protection of Spain.

And William Blount, member of the Continental Congress, of the Constitutional Convention, and of the United States Senate, and appointed by Washington Governor of the Southwest Territory and Superintendent of Indian Affairs in the South. He alone among the conspiring western leaders suffered contemporary official rebuke. Charged with attempting to ally American frontiersmen with their Indian enemies in an attack upon Spanish Florida and Louisiana in behalf of England, then again at war with Spain, he was impeached by the House of Representatives and expelled by the Senate.

And any number of lesser fry, such as Wilkinson's henchmen, the federal judges Benjamin Sebastian and Harry Innes, who were open advocates of Spain and on Spain's permanent payroll.

Finally, and possibly not least, there was the *Kentucke Gazette,* the first and for years the only newspaper in Kentucky, which was a howling partisan of the separatist, Spanish and French movements.

The West did, eventually, elect to remain American. But in our search for the explanation we must keep in mind that it was an instinctive and impulsive decision reached without benefit of the counsel or advice of patriotic and farsighted leaders. Every outstanding westerner to whom the rank and file had a right to look for guidance perpetually urged them to turn the other way.

X. The East's Helping Hand

To find fault with the government's conduct of foreign affairs is a traditional public preoccupation in a democracy. No function of government is so constantly criticized. Scarcely a citizen, however uninformed or indifferent with regard to other matters, but regards himself sufficiently an expert in this field to hold the most definite opinions. The western setttler was no exception. He had, however, a considerable basis in personal experience for his criticism. Among his array of troubles those connected with foreign affairs were the most pressing and the most serious. His commerce was strangled and his very existence threatened by forces beyond his reach which could be restrained only by international negotiation or by war. No matter how self-sufficient and intransigent in other respects he could not escape looking to the national government's support in this one.

After ratification of the peace treaty almost the sole power left to Congress, under the Articles of Confederation, was responsibility for dealing with foreign governments. This involved merely the authority to negotiate, since in practice each state reserved the right to accept or reject any agreement. Congress was obliged to conduct these negotiations as a kind of committee in which each state had one vote and a majority of nine out of the thirteen was required to take any significant action. Three ominous questions, all bearing upon the survival of the West, demanded immediate answers:

1. England was declining to surrender the lake posts and maintaining her threatening grasp on the northern Ohio Valley.

2. Spain was claiming and occupying or controlling all of the territory south and west of the present states of Tennessee and

Georgia and closing the Mississippi to American trade to under-line the fact.

3. The Indian nations were continuing their attacks on the frontier and refusing to admit that the peace treaty to which they had not been parties could have any reference to their rights to their own homelands.

The congressional formula for dealing with these unhappy problems was to postpone making any serious attempt to deal with them. There was a general conviction that things were so bad that they must surely, in time, get better and that only by patience and by delay could solutions be approached. There was not, in the east, too much concern for the fate of the West. There was, instead, a disposition to regard the whole idea of western settlement with alarm and disapproval. One fear, held by smaller states and those without claims upon western lands, was that rival states claiming vast domains in the west might so expand in size, population and importance as to break down the whole principle of equality among the states. Another anxiety was that the westward migration represented a disastrous drain upon the nation's resources. Many public leaders shared this view. Rufus King considered the premature settlement of the west a total loss to the nation. Governor George Clinton of New York characterized the drift of people from the east to the west as a national calamity. Even so firm a friend to western aspirations as Jay had proved himself during the peace negotiations declared over-rapid settlement "will, unless checked, scatter our resources and in every view enfeeble the union" and in a 1786 letter to Adams suggested: "Would it not be wiser, gradually to extend our settlements, as want of room shall make it necessary, than to pitch our tents through the wilderness? . . . Shall we not fill the wilderness with white savages, and will they not become more formidable to us than the tawny ones who now inhabit it?"

The most widely held opinion of the time, voiced by informed observers in the United States, England, France and Spain, and most of all on the frontier itself, was that geography had des-tined the West to be a separate nation. Considered in the frame of these contemporary judgments there can be little wonder that Congress did not rush to succour the West.

The English government's impulse to hold the lake posts in defiance of the terms of the treaty might have been initiated by secret pressure from the fur trade, which since the earliest days of the great Hudson's Bay venture had had a powerful voice in London, but the English spokesmen had a not unreasonable public justification. By another clause of the treaty Congress had undertaken to persuade the states to compensate the Loyalists. Some 60,000 of them had fled or been driven from their homes. Most had been substantial citizens. The several states had made a special point of confiscating their property and in most cases of distributing it among deserving patriots. England felt a natural obligation to protect people who had made such painful sacrifices to demonstrate their loyalty to the empire. Congress proved unable to persuade one state to pay a single penny of compensation. England seized upon this excuse to hold the lake posts as a kind of mortgage.

Congress made several mild appeals, largely to keep the record straight, and then let the question hang fire. The bankrupt United States with its powerless central government was in no condition to threaten resort to force. Moreover, many rational observers saw some justice in the English case. Washington said at the time, "I think there is more wickedness than ignorance mixed with our councils." And it was Jay's opinion that "there has not been a single day, since the treaty took effect, in which it has not been violated by one or another of the states." As Secretary for Foreign Affairs he feared to press a peremptory demand for the posts lest refusal "involve the United States either in War or Disgrace." As a consequence of this diplomatic deadlock the English hammer in the north remained poised over the heads of the western settlers for another thirteen years.

In the south, on the other flank of the frontier, there was the Spanish anvil. Spain was at the peak of that strange brief resurgence of imperial energy that marked the last third of the eighteenth century. The mighty empire which had subsided into inaction after establishing her overseas dominion from the West Indies to the Philippines and from the southern

Rockies to Cape Horn had stirred like a sleeping giant. New Orleans and the west bank of the Mississippi had been acquired from France, new colonies founded the length of California, the Spanish posts in Texas strengthened to guard the link between Mexico and Louisiana, and the two Floridas wrested from England. It became Spain's settled policy to keep the ball of her new fortunes rolling by adding the Ohio Valley to her many other recent acquisitions. This seemed an achievement within her certain and easy reach. The chief result of the aid Spain had rendered the colonies during the Revolution had been that Spain had gained a near stranglehold upon the entire region.

Spain had been understandably confident that, with the ardent support of France, all that she sought would fall into her lap at the council table during the peace negotiations. When these expectations were disappointed by England's sudden diplomatic about face she did not by any means give up. Taking advantage of the circumstance that, in ceding the West to the United States and the Floridas to Spain, England had thoughtfully left the line of demarcation between the two cessions to be worked out by the recipients, Spain claimed the entire Southwest and maintained her garrisons there to enforce the claim. Taking further advantage of her formidable geographical position, she began to put on other pressures. She refused the loan that formerly had been contemplated and declined even to regard the young republic as an independent nation. She closed the Mississippi to the commerce of the western settlers. She supplied the Southern Indian nations with arms and encouraged their hostility to the American frontier. And she embarked upon a complicated series of intrigues with western leaders, offering them pensions, special trade advantages and bribes in return for their support. These were powerful pressures.

John Jay had been appointed minister to Spain during the Revolution and sent to Madrid to negotiate a treaty of assistance and alliance. He remained there for nearly five years, except for the period he collaborated with the other American peace commissioners in drafting the treaty with England, but was unable to work out an understanding. Spain did enter the war against England but did so entirely in pursuit of her own purposes. From the first Jay's chief difficulty at the Spanish court was the right of navigation of the Mississippi. Eventually realizing that not only was there no hope of a treaty but that Spain was embarked upon a course actively opposed to the interests of the United States, Jay returned in 1784. During the war Spain had permitted traffic on the Mississippi, waiting to see which way the wind blew, but in June of this year proclaimed formal closure of the river. This body blow to the West found Congress in recess from June to October and thus no national government in existence. When Congress did reassemble no feasible counter-pressure to exert upon Spain occurred to anyone. As Jay grimly pointed out, the alternative to yielding to Spanish inflexibility was war. Under the circumstances the country had no more stomach for war with Spain over the Mississippi than with England over the lake posts.

The next year Diego de Gardoqui came to the United States as Spanish envoy with the ostensible mission of negotiating a treaty of commerce. A necessary first step had to be some solution of the Mississippi question but this step he could scarcely be brought to discuss. He devoted most of his time and energy to organizing intrigues with Americans of influence, in the east as well as in the west, to enlist their support for Spanish maneuvers in the Mississippi Valley.

The arrival of Gardoqui attracted the East's attention for the first time to the unique difficulties facing their fellow citizens beyond the mountains. The proposal to insist upon Spain's opening the Mississippi became a heated political issue, with the northern states, primarily interested in seagoing trade, disposed to let the matter drift, and the southern states, whose borders were adjacent to the frontier settlements, leaning toward support of the West. Those arguments in this dispute which were not based altogether on sentiment and prejudice revolved about the assertion that aid to the western settlements was against the best interests of the United States. According to this theory the West was certain to become an independent nation the moment it grew strong enough to stand on its own feet and that therefore any effort to expedite this moment was a nonsensical waste of the parent country's resources. Even Washington, who felt a personal sympathy for the landseeking frontiersman and was certainly no advocate of the little America school, welcomed the closure of the Mississippi. He thought that a Mississippi open to the West's commerce was bound to draw the frontier's interest toward New Orleans and union with Spain and that the one slim hope of holding the region within the United States was to require the bedeviled settlers to trade over the mountains with the East. Jay, disturbed lest this division within the councils of the new republic take an even worse turn, sought to remove the issue from the political arena by making Gardoqui an offer to give up the navigation of the Mississippi for the next twenty-five years.

News of this move stirred a roar of rage in the West. The name of Jay, who had, after Clark and Washington, been the West's most effective friend, became anathema everywhere on the frontier. Not only the desirability but the necessity of opening the Mississippi to his trade was obvious to the simplest settler. The recent experience of one Jacob Yoder cast a glaring light upon the situation. Before the Spanish had closed the river, Yoder, a German-Kentuckian, had left Redstone on the Monongahela with a boat laden with wheat, floated his cargo down to New Orleans, there exchanged the wheat for furs, exchanged the furs for sugar at Havana, sold the sugar in Philadelphia, and crossed the mountains back to Kentucky with a fortune in his pockets. All understood the moral of this tale. The Ohio-Mississippi was the providential avenue for their commerce which offered all a release from poverty. On the other hand, their chief products, wheat, corn, and pork, were of a bulk that would not pay transportation by pack horse over the mountains to the eastern market. The feeling swelled among the settlements that they were being calculatingly betrayed by their eastern brethren. Meanwhile, the Spaniards kept a hand on their stopper in the Mississippi bottle and did what they could to aggravate the discontent.

With the third great foreign policy problem, the Indian threat to the frontier, Congress was more disposed to deal but even less able to cope. Under the Articles of Confederation Congress did not have undisputed authority to treat with Indians occupying lands claimed by any of the several states. The handling of such Indian problems was a prerogative reserved primarily to the state concerned which was prepared to do so without regard for national policy. North Carolina's first act, for example, was to open all lands between her borders and the Mississippi, no matter how deep within admitted Indian territory, to entry by settlers.

In the area north of the Ohio River the authority of Congress, however, was soon more clearly defined. Virginia, New York, and the Iroquois, respectively, ceded their claims upon the region to the central government. This simplification did not make the task less difficult. The nations of the warlike Northern Indian confederacy, with the English forts and trading posts at their backs, were the parties at interest who were actually in possession. Congress proceeded to forbid entry by settlers and to appoint commissioners to deal with them. A long period of haggling ensued in which the United States commissioners prevailed upon such Indian representatives as could be persuaded to meet with them in conferences to cede a portion of the area to be opened for settlement in return for their being guaranteed possession of the remainder in perpetuity. United States commissioners were also dispatched to the Southwest to render what assistance they could in smoothing the rough path to peace in that quarter.

Treaty after treaty was negotiated with various groups of Indians with respect to both frontiers. As more states ceded their western lands the role of the central government grew in importance. But everybody continued to get into the act. Treaties were as solemnly signed by land companies or the nearest organized settlement as by the various states or the national government. Each conflicted with the others and none was ever observed by anybody. In this spate of treaty making the pattern of negotiation became as conventionalized as was the case with the Indian raids which meanwhile continued without respite. The white delegation, whatever its credentials or lack of any, approached the Indians with an invitation to hold a conference. There were always Indians to accept with alacrity. They flocked to conferences as children to a circus. For an invariable feature of the proceedings was that the white delegates had brought gifts and bribes and a generous supply of as much as even an Indian could eat and drink. After days of gorging and whoopee the satiated Indians were usually ready to accept the presents that had been spread before them and to sign anything. Nothing ever came of it except a pseudo-legal point which could later be cited by the white participants if it chanced to suit their purpose. For when the Indian delegates returned home their authority to bind their nation was promptly denied, with or without justification, by that portion of the tribe which had not attended the festivities. The white delegates had embarked upon the transaction with even less intention of abiding by their commitments.

The consequences were much the same when the most formal treaties were negotiated by representatives and respected head chiefs and officially accredited plenipotentiaries of the national government. The essence of every treaty was the drawing of a line up to which the Indians would sanction settlement and across which the United States would forbid settlers to trespass. Invariably the next surge of settlement swept over the line and invariably the young Indian warriors continued the raids which were the treasured proofs of their claims to manhood. By and large, the whites, being the stronger party, were the more arrant treaty breakers. The United States has never made an Indian treaty up to, possibly, our generation which it has not speedily broken.

Two elements were required to make the treaties of the 1780's effective in restoring peace. First, sufficient force was required to compel Indians and settlers to abide by them. The national government possessed no such power. Second, the Indians had to be regularly supplied with those trade goods upon which they had come to depend, especially guns and powder to continue their hunting for food. Even had the United States been in a position to offer such supplies the enraged settlers would not have permitted it. Therefore, the Indians were forced to rely for their necessities upon the Spanish in the south and the English in the north and to govern their behavior accordingly.

This threefold failure of the national government to relieve them in the slightest from the chief dangers that oppressed them was naturally resented by the western settlers. Their country, and every day the doubt was more loudly voiced that it was their country, had weakly acquiesced in the English retention of the lake posts and the Spanish closure of the Mississippi. With respect to the Indian menace, truly a life and death issue, the only notable reactions in Congress had been to forbid settlers to encroach upon Indian lands and to disband the remnant of the Continental Army. The common assertions that the East was indifferent, jealous or hostile and that the one hope of the West was to break away received increasing attention.

One very great help, however, was being extended by the East. It was a form of aid totally unplanned and deeply deplored along the seaboard. At the end of the Revolution a veritable surge of new landseekers poured over the mountains. Without regard for the uncertainties of the fearful journey or the yet more fearful uncertainties awaiting them at their destination they kept on coming. This sudden disorganized growth of an already disorganized population added little to the political stability of the West but added greatly to its sense of self-sufficiency.

XI. Self Government — Plus
Separation, Secession and Sedition

THIRTY-SEVEN DAYS after the shots heard round the
world were fired at Lexington and Concord the Boonesborough
Convention met. The latter event set in train consequences
of scarcely less moment. Seventeen newly arrived settlers assembled under a gigantic elm on the banks of the Kentucky
River to set up the first American government west of the mountains. They were treading upon legal ground even less explored
than the wilderness that they had penetrated. There was neither
precedent nor justification for what they were doing.

Their claim to the land upon which they stood was based
upon a "purchase" by Richard Henderson, a young North
Carolina attorney, in the name of the newly formed Transylvania Company, of all Kentucky from the Cherokee, who themselves had no clearer title to the region than a dozen other
Indian nations might have advanced. No power to govern it
had been delegated to this handful of leather-shirted lawmakers
by the Crown, by any royal governor, by the Intercolonial Committee of Correspondence, by the First Continental Congress,
by either of the legislatures of the states of Virginia and North
Carolina from which most of them had come, or by any other
then existing political authority which might conceivably have
cast a mantle of legitimacy over their deliberations.

But they did not hesitate. There is no evidence that they
suspected the significance of what they were doing or that they
had the faintest inkling that they were setting off a chain reaction which was presently to compel the not yet born United
States to become great. They simply took it for granted that
the power to govern themselves was a right inherent in their
persons and in their situation.

Perhaps on one of the three days of this first of the series of midwestern political conventions which has continued to our day there was first voiced the endlessly repeated saw which became the foundation principle of western democracy: "Any fool can put on his pants better than the wisest man can do it for him." In sounding the keynote of the convention, Colonel Henderson, though himself a principal official of the proprietary land company, lent himself wholeheartedly to this first expression of wilderness democracy and placed his finger precisely upon the source of the power it presumed to exercise:

Our peculiar circumstances in this remote country, surrounded on all sides with difficulties, and equally subject to one common danger, which threatens our common overthrow, must, I think, in their effects, secure to us an union of interests, and consequently, that harmony in opinion, so essential to the forming of good, wise, and wholesome laws. If any doubt remain amongst you with respect to the force or efficacy of whatever laws you now, or hereafter, make, *be pleased to consider that all power is originally in the people;* therefore, make it their interest, by impartial and beneficial laws, and you may be sure of their inclination to see them enforced. For it is not to be supposed that a people, anxious and desirous to have laws made, — who approve of the method of choosing delegates, or representatives, to meet in general convention for that purpose, can want the necessary and concomitant virtue to carry them into execution.

The seventeen delegates, representing the three settlements which had sprouted in Kentucky that spring, accepted the challenge and calmly set about making laws for establishing courts, for punishing crimes, for regulating the militia, for punishing swearing and Sabbath-breaking, for providing for writs of attachment, for fixing fees, for preserving the range, for improving the breed of horses, and for preserving game.

Here we have come close to the heart of the mystery. Here in its simplest elements, the test of survival has been disclosed. These seventeen men were the prototypes, the first representatives of coming generations of conquerors. On this spot, this year, the First Americans had appeared upon the world scene.

Their like had never before been witnessed. Two thirds of a continent was to come within their grasp; they were to build upon a scale altogether beyond the conception of the most far-sighted of the founders. Before them Spaniards from Florida and Mexico, Frenchmen from the St. Lawrence, Englishmen from Hudson's Bay, had penetrated far more deeply into the western unknown, had ranged far more widely across forests and mountains, plains and deserts. These others had spied out the vast interior of the continent years, even centuries before, had founded forts, trading posts, missions, and occasional settlements, from the northern tundra to the southern gulf. But nothing enduring had so far come of any of this. The boldest of those venturers had remained the tools and delegates of the authority that had despatched them. Now, at last, had come intruders of a different breed. After so perilous a journey, still uncertain of enough to eat, still uncertain of everything except continuing Indian attack, their first thought was to claim the power to govern themselves.

These were men whose every action, word and thought, whose almost every breath, was setting precedent destined to shape the whole proportion of a nation. They were not inventing a new type of democracy. Their primitive convention was in form but a replica of the town meeting with which they and their forefathers had long been familiar. But they were taking one earth-shaking stride. Having arrived in the midst of the wilderness, they conceived that their power to govern themselves stemmed in nowise from any existing political authority behind them. It was a conception from which most of them were never to waver. Of it was to be born a then undreamed-of departure in democracy — the principle of the Union's continual augmentation by new and equal states.

The names of the first four of them to bring their families to Kentucky were Boone, McGary, Hogan and Denton. They were outriders of that strong current of earliest frontier migration, composed mainly of Scotch-Irish, which had sprung from central Pennsylvania in the middle 1700's. Denied a flow directly westward by Indian power on the upper Ohio, the migration had pressed steadily southward down the valley of Virginia to the western border of North Carolina. During this long march, continually abandoning new locations for more promising ones beyond, their children's children growing up on the frontier, these restless and land-hungry migrants had become seasoned backwoodsmen, hunters, Indian fighters, more land hungry than ever, and as tough and hardy a stock as the world has ever seen. Now, at last, they conceived that they had found a gap, not only in the mountains but in the Indian defenses. The mountain gap was a way over the ridges that a goat might surmount, with enough assistance, and the Indian gap was merely the circumstance that the nearest Indian towns were far enough away on the Ohio and the Tennessee to give settlers a chance, if they worked fast enough, to get up a stockade before they were attacked in force. But the land in Kentucky appeared so much more attractive than that on the eastern slopes of the mountains that first by tens and then by hundreds they yielded to the temptation to go for it. Accustomed to peril they embraced infinitely greater peril. Of Boone's three companions on his first Kentucky hunt, one was killed by Indians and one devoured by wolves. His first effort to lead settlers over the mountains was turned back with the loss of six killed, including his own eldest son. Yet, amid so many dangers and the prospect of greater hazards, with their pitiful fortunes at stake and the lives of their families as much at pawn as their own, the first impulse, before they had even raised a stockade, of these illiterate, lawless, reckless, and unruly first Anglo-Saxon settlers in the west was to devote three painstaking days to defining their declaration that they were their own political masters.

The Boonesborough assertion of independence soon collapsed. It was the impulse that counted. For it was a fundamental and an inherent impulse that persisted. It counted because nothing like it had ever happened before. No early Spanish or French colonist, however wayward occasionally his acts, could conceivably have dreamed that he was, in political theory, anything but the creature of his king. He remained in principle the servant of parent state or church or both. The early English colonist on the Atlantic seaboard had recognized as unquestioningly his status as subject of the mother country. Royal governors and governing proprietors remained the representatives of ultimate authority. The most rebellious colonial protestations were related to the words of charters, grants, memorials and petitions. Since Leif Ericson this was the first new colony in the New World to proclaim at birth its independence.

An almost equally significant feature of the Boonesborough convention was its conformation to the essentially American pattern of empire-building of which it was the first clear manifestation. Free enterprise had joined free men in asserting freedom from previous authority. The moving spirit at Boonesborough was Henderson, head of the land company, who required freedom of action to protect his assumption that the company actually owned the land that he had purchased from the Cherokee as much as did the individual settler need it to protect his title to the land upon which he was building his cabin. This fluctuating but recurrent alliance between unbridled settler and uncurbed investor was to endow the development of western settlement with tremendous vitality by offering rewards to self interest at every economic and political level. But it was also a chaotic process that was to keep the West in tumult for many years to come.

The tumult began at once. There were also in Kentucky that spring surveyors laying out tracts of land for the old Ohio Company, most of whose shareholders were Virginians. Virginia, become belatedly aware of how long a march Henderson had stolen, denounced him as an unprincipled land pirate and his adherents as a pack of lawless scoundrels. There was also in Kentucky another handful of independent landseekers who, unlike the Boonesborough people, had come over the mountains without benefit of encouragement from Henderson. These several currents of varying self interest promptly clashed.

To the Boonesborough example of the western settler's summary assumption of the power to govern himself there was added the next year the first example of his equal readiness to rebel against any rule, including his own. The Boonesborough settlers were beginning to squirm under their agreement to pay the Transylvania Company for their land. Other Kentuckians took less time to deny the right of the company to charge them for land which by what they considered a deeper right belonged to them already. A second convention at Harrodsburg, after a little nudging by such Virginia partisans as the young Ohio Company surveyor, George Rogers Clark, petitioned Virginia to assume jurisdiction over the Kentucky settlements. For good measure the Harrodsburg dissidents resolved, in advance of receiving any reply, to declare their complete independence in the event their petition was disregarded. The language of this petition, denouncing the Boonesborough Convention which many of the petitioners had supported a few months before, sharply emphasized the western conception that the basic authority of government rested not only upon the free choice of the governed but upon their privilege to change their minds so often as they chose: "We, therefore, *are not willing* to obey those, or the authority they have assumed, or indeed, to acknowledge any power or prerogative which is not derived from the Convention of Virginia." This early secession movement in the west, the forerunner of so many to come, led to Virginia's acknowledgment of the Kentucky settlements as a county and to the Transylvania Company's involvement in a maze of litigation which helped to becloud Kentucky land titles for the next twenty years.

These first two political steps taken by the newest and most westerly settlements established the two principles that were to guide the frontier's political thinking for a generation. The first was that it was the settler's implicit and inalienable right to govern himself as he saw fit and without regard for other considerations than his own interest. The second was that it was his privilege when pressed by necessity to turn for support either to a neighboring state or to the central government, whichever best served his purpose at the moment, without this action committing him to ties which he could not later cast off whenever this in turn suited him. This view provided a remarkably simple and serviceable pattern which enabled him always to dance to his own tune without, he assumed, ever having to pay the piper.

The Transylvania Company was only the first victim of this manifestation of headlong self-interest. The characteristic irresponsibility of pure democracy when confronted by problems above the local community level was to provide many more. State and national authorities, military commanders, and, when these high officers at length came into being, presidents of the United States, were driven to distraction by it. Spanish, English and French officials charged with advancing their respective governments' Mississippi Valley designs were perpetually confused. And nobody was more continually baffled than the West's own leaders.

The initial Kentucky experiment in self-government differed from comparable earlier and later experiments in other settlements only in a bolder assumption of the inherent right of the settler to govern himself. Three years before, the first Wataugans, uncertain whether the land they occupied belonged to Virginia or North Carolina, filled the jurisdictional gap by drawing up their Articles of Association. Cumberland, most isolated of all the settlements, later filled a similar void with the declaration in the Cumberland Compact: "We do most solemnly and sacredly declare and promise each other, that we will faithfully and punctually adhere to, perform, and abide by this our Association, and at all times, if need be, compel by our united force a due obedience to these our rules and regulations." In southwestern Pennsylvania the impulse toward self-determination was distorted by violent differences of opinion among three factions, those who favored allegiance to Virginia, those who preferred Pennsylvania, and those who advocated a separate state, with, at times during the Revolution, a not inconsiderable fourth faction which envisaged a return to English rule as the best way out.

The democracy born of necessity in the western clearings was a living, active force that impregnated the day to day existence of the community and impinged upon every action of the individual. There was no pre-existing framework of law or even of custom to keep order, apportion civil tasks, or provide for the common defense. These were compelling necessities and the newcomers had to meet them extemporaneously. Since no man acknowledged another his superior, differences of opinion could otherwise only have been settled by resort to force. But private violence could not be afforded on account of the constant danger threatening the group from without. They could, perhaps, have drawn straws or cast lots, which at times they did, but usually they chose to abide by the will of the majority. This spontaneous democratic process was not at all times so far separated from an appeal to chance since the majority was as often swayed by glib talk, gusts of passion, inter-group jealousies, and plain ignorance, as by reason. But decision was reached.

A sterner school of practical democracy could scarcely be imagined, for any new settlement's hope of survival depended upon any number of such decisions involving divisions of labor and responsibility which needed to be reached without an hour's delay. The newborn community's first cry of life was the clamor of its first town meeting. By rule of majority the meeting determined the location, size and type of the stockade, the apportionment of adjacent lots which were certain to become more valuable than ordinary land if the community did survive, and a fair assignment of duties to meet the requirements of scouting for Indian sign, hunting game for the common larder, guarding the grazing stock, and keeping watch at night, all of which extra demands must synchronize with the labor of building, clearing, plowing and cultivating a first crop. In those cases in which the station had been founded largely by the efforts of a single man or family any attempted rule by proprietor soon developed into the same rule by majority, since the acceptance of more people into the community was required for defense and these people invariably demanded a full and equal say in the conduct of their affairs. The most important elective office in the infant government was that of militia captain for all else depended upon a successful defense. In common practice every man capable of bearing arms was therefore eligible to vote, regardless of his other qualifications, and, as late as the first all-Kentucky convention in 1784, the militia captain was the community's representative at all more comprehensive political gatherings.

This primitive western democracy became possessed of the tremendous political vitality of the citizenry's almost universal participation. Men were unable to apply themselves to their private affairs without first dealing with public affairs. There is no substitute for experience, and daily experience in facing the details of self-government was forced upon the settler. He became conditioned to the circumstance that he himself was obliged to take a hand personally in shaping the manner in which he was governed.

But there were weaknesses, also, which were the reverse of vital and all but fatal. Men, paradoxically, tend to take lightly the laws that they themselves make. The westerner was primarily an individualist. He had sought freedom of action as well as freedom of opportunity when he had come west. The determination to remain his own man had become an obsession. He considered that laws which he had made could be as readily unmade so often as he chose to change his mind. If the majority disagreed he could ignore their personal application to him. If the majority insisted he contemptuously moved on to another and more complacent community. Freedom more often than not became license. The ordinary conduct of the individual verged on anarchy. His self-will persisted even on the life and death level of his attitude toward measures for the common defense. The militia commander was not so much a military commander as a spokesman for shifting public opinion. He had been elected and therefore could be as readily deposed. Men obeyed him and followed him only so long as they felt like it. Democracy permeated every aspect of the daily life of the western citizen but he was a brawling and lawless citizen nevertheless.

Possibly an even greater disadvantage under which the western democratic process labored was the state of communications. Information passed slowly through the Indian-infested wilderness, even from one station to its nearest neighbor. News of Clark's capture of Vincennes was thirty-two days reaching Louisville a hundred miles away and the fastest courier service that that most energetic of commanders could set up along his line of communications to the capital of Virginia at Williamsburg involved a round trip of four months. The first postal service between east and west over the Wilderness Road was not established until 1792 and this main land route of migration and trade was not open to wagon traffic until 1796. Throughout its most critical period the frontier was dependent for news of national and world affairs upon occasional private letters brought by chance travelers and upon tales relayed by the more recent immigrants from the east. The uninformed settler was left prey to ignorance and rumor. Garbled person to person accounts of distant events swept like winds through the forests, losing all resemblance to fact, to become the chief topics for discussion in political gatherings met to make the most important decisions. Unprincipled men were able to take advantage of the circumstance that the most extravagant lie might seldom be overtaken by the truth. In such an atmosphere there flourished that tendency to doubt and to suspect which has always been a mark of the American temperament. The westerner came to distrust the probity of all public figures, not only of the most eminent national leaders but of his own elected representatives as well, almost as much as he distrusted the designs of his overt enemies. Unashamedly materialistic in his own personal endeavors he was perpetually cynical in his estimate of the motives of others.

Nevertheless, it was this essentially anarchic course taken by western democracy that led to that unique departure in governmental structure, a political experiment without precedent in the history of nations, that opened wide the way to the American nation's resistless surge to the Pacific. This startling project was the insistence from the first by the western communities that they be accepted as free and equal states on a par with their elder sisters. A more strikingly successful political invention has never been contrived, for it provided the one workable means possible for the new republic's limitless growth. And it was entirely a western invention. This was not one of the basic principles to spring from the inspired imaginations of the founding fathers who wrote the Declaration of Independence. The eastern leaders during the early Revolution had no other dream than of a union of the thirteen original states. That there should be new states was an idea born in the west from the seed planted at Boonesborough and Harrodsburg.

However, the grandeur of the new idea and what we now

tend complacently to regard as the inevitability of its fulfillment were not then more clearly recognized on the western side of the mountains than on the other. From the beginning the westerners had proclaimed themselves free men. They called themselves "men of the Western Waters," meaning that they were as free as those waters to seek their own destiny. Again and again they stated this conception of their future. While they might accept some form of association with seaboard America, that choice, like all others, was entirely theirs, and they categorically reserved the right to seek instead a Mississippi Valley arrangement with Spain, England or France, and most of all the right to set themselves up as an independent nation. Their suggestion of future admission as equal states was not made so much in the form of an appeal or even of a demand as in the form of a tentative offer that might be withdrawn. All was on an or-else basis. Their petitions were accompanied by a clamor of threats and abuse and a continual discussion of alternative actions. It was this rebellious and belligerent uproar that gained and held the attention of the East, which might well have remained long oblivious to a more diffident approach. The principle of new statehood was at length accepted. But it was to most undutiful and prodigal sons that the fatted calf of equality was offered.

The separatist movement among the western settlements was active from the moment of their establishments. The desperate stresses of Indian warfare during the Revolution caused them to dispatch appeals for help eastward, for they were dependent upon the East for gunpowder and military supplies, but at every lull in the war the acceptance of support was forgotten and the independence agitation renewed. This was not at first an impulse toward secession from the Union, for there was then no union from which to secede, but a demand for freedom from the interference with their affairs by individual eastern states claiming western lands. There was every variety of such interference. The territory of Watauga was split between the claims of Virginia and North Carolina. Cumberland was considered within North Carolina's sphere, dependent upon a survey of the westward extension of the Virginia-North Carolina line when and if it was made. Southwestern Pennsylvania was bitterly disputed by Virginia and Pennsylvania until 1780. Virginia's claim to Kentucky was uncontested, except by the Kentuckians, and strengthened by the circumstance that Virginia alone among the states had offered significant aid to the defense of the West during the Revolution.

The independence movement was born of the westerner's fierce, almost infantile resentment of any restraint and stimulated by his special resentment of the assumption by the claimant eastern states of jurisdiction over the validation of his land titles. The trend from the outset was to appeal to Congress for protection and to urge that Congress consider admitting the western districts as separate and equal states but even in mid-Revolution the ugly alternatives of total independence or foreign protection were in men's minds. In 1778 Daniel Boone, upon his escape from Indian captivity, was court martialed by his neighbors, charged with having become an English agent during his retention in Detroit. He was acquitted but that he was tried at all is significant evidence that people at the time considered it quite likely that even such a man as Boone might go over to the English side. Such notable border figures as Alexander McKee and Matthew Elliot had done so that same year.

The prospect of respite from the Indian war as an accompaniment to restoration of English authority in the west was not an altogether unwelcome one to many people along the frontier, particularly to the large number of Tories who had fled westward to escape the attentions of earnest patriots on the seaboard. The Indian attacks, the land question, the state jurisdictional disputes, and local disagreement over defense policies produced endless confusion and made loyalties difficult to clarify.

Colonel George Morgan was writing in 1780 for the secret information of Congress:

> We have distressing news from Kentucke which is entirely owing to a set of Nabobs in Virginia taking all the lands there by office warrants, & Pre-emption Rights — Hundreds of families are ruined by it. In short it threatens a loss of that county — Should the English go there and offer them Protection from the Indians the greatest part will join.

The same year Clark was writing his brother of his refusal to accept solicitations advanced by discontented settlers that he become "Governor-General" of a "new Government" for the West. Also in 1780 Jefferson, then Governor of Virginia, was writing to Colonel William Preston, on the Virginia frontier, "I am sorry to hear that there are persons in your quarter so far discontented with the present government as to combine with its enemies to destroy it," and three months later, "It will probably be better to seek the insurgents & suppress them in their own settlements than to await their coming, as time and Space to move in will perhaps increase their numbers." The rebellious opposition of the frontier to Virginia's attempted draft of local militia to reinforce Clark's projected attack upon Detroit forced the hand of the General Assembly to such a degree that on June 21, 1781 it passed a joint resolution "desiring the Executive to take such steps, by offering a pardon or otherwise, as may effectually suppress certain Insurgents and their associates in the Western and Northwestern Frontiers" and "authorizing the Executive to put a stop to the Expedition lately ordered to Detroit, and to take steps for disposing of the Stores, etc., provided for that purpose."

In 1780 a memorial signed by 672 Kentuckians was presented to Congress demanding that Kentucky be admitted as a new and separate state. The same year the people of Southwestern Pennsylvania sent a similar memorial to Congress, renewing petitions that had been in circulation since 1776, demanding with new urgency the recognition of "Westsylvania" as a state. Both Pennsylvania and Virginia sternly objected to these proposals and Congress discreetly took little notice. When the agitation continued Pennsylvania enacted a law declaring such attempts to form new states treason and prescribing the death penalty. Virginia presently followed suit. The westerners were left no alternative to the discussion of outright secession.

However, there was some eastern support for the strange new statehood program, chiefly from old states such as Maryland which had no western land claims and were anxious to check the threatened aggrandizement of those that had. Congress, seeking a way out of the dilemma, weakly promised that if and when the western lands were ever ceded to the national government, the western communities might be considered eligible for statehood. Such cessions were eventually and grudgingly made

(North Carolina's not until 1790) but only after the West, increased in population by an ever-accelerating migration from the east, had become so strong as to make any other course preposterous.

The formal end of the Revolution found the restless West too impatient to wait longer upon eastern hairsplitting. In 1784 the people of Watauga, without asking permission or approval of anybody, set themselves up as the separate and independent State of Franklin and elected the great border hero John Sevier their governor. The same year the people of Kentucky, meeting in the first of a seven year series of increasingly importunate state conventions, were unanimously in favor of separation from Virginia and recognition as a state. Cumberland was so exposed to Indian attack that the chief thought there was help from anybody and was ready to turn to Spain, if necessary. The people of Southwestern Pennsylvania were slightly mollified by the rapid improvement of a road over the mountains from Philadelphia to Pittsburgh and somewhat subdued by reflections upon the cost of breaking away from Pennsylvania but a seething discontent remained that was to break out ten years later into open and armed rebellion against the national government.

Meanwhile Congress was beginning dimly to glimpse the facts of life in the west. It adopted in 1784 a resolution introduced by Jefferson proposing to the several states, for it was not within the power of Congress under the Confederation to dispose, a future program for the eventual formation of ten new states in the Ohio Valley. But as evidence of how far this flight of fancy extended not only into the world of the future but into the world of dreams the names of the states were to be: Sylvania, Michigania, Chersonesus, Assenisipia, Metropotamia, Illinoia, Saratoga, Polypotamia, Pelisipia and Washington.

However, this slight break in congressional apathy did indicate a dawning awareness of the central problem. The issue no longer was how the western settlements might be kept attached to their claimant parent states. The time for that had already passed. The question now was how, in whatever fashion, to keep them attached to the nation at all. Still there remained continued hesitation, with Congress pulled by eastern prejudice and hauled by western recalcitrance. The United States, as a nation, was not to seek greatness. It was to have greatness thrust upon it.

XII. And Still They Came

ALMOST NO FORM of insecurity was spared the western settler of the early 1780's. His future appeared no less uncertain. However well he planned or hard he worked the want of a market for his surplus kept him poor. Smallpox and malaria were as prevalent as doctors and medicine were scarce. Though his own home might continue to escape Indian attack he was continually being summoned to defend his less fortunate neighbors and from time to time was required to abandon his family and private affairs in order to go off with his militia company on long, always mismanaged, usually fruitless, general Indian campaigns. He could not be sure that the land he had cleared and improved was to remain his. By the middle of the 1780's he could not even be sure that he had a country. Every political gathering that he attended was devoted to increasingly strident demands for separation. The trend seemed ever stronger toward compromise with foreigners, perhaps even domination by foreigners.

There can be little wonder that many pioneers became disillusioned and toiled back over the mountains to the relative peace and quiet of their former homes. But there must be very great wonder that this eastward retreat breasted a tenfold greater wave of westward migration. The movement west in the years immediately after the Revolution amounted to a major shift in population on a national scale. The more discouraging the news of conditions in the west the more determined people seemed to be to go there. In 1784 an estimated twelve thousand reached Kentucky. In 1785 more than a thousand boats, averaging several families each, were counted on the Ohio. In 1786 a thousand were counted in the first forty days. In 1788 so many more came that this was called the year of the Great Migration. Many of these were no longer hardened backwoodsmen, born and bred on the frontier, accustomed to camp and trail, strange noises in the night, and feeding their children on game. They were townsmen, eastern farmers, often men who had never owned or fired a gun. Bringing their families along, they swarmed into the west, camped along riverbanks like a disorderly army of invasion, wandered about, half starved, looking for land or merely looking for something to eat.

A word was coined for these streams of people who crowded the routes leading westward. They were called movers. This was a faintly contemptuous term with the connotation that movers were so footloose because they had little but themselves to move. Many continued to move after they reached the west and never became true settlers. Landless, or, at best, temporary squatters on other men's lands, their restlessness persisted and they kept on moving, often before the last crop they had planted had had time to ripen. The mover continued to be a common and typical western figure for the next several generations. Abraham Lincoln's parents were movers. The family moved again and again before he came of age and took root in Springfield.

This sudden human tidal wave surprised the West as much as it outraged the East and it upset the calculations of politicians on both sides of the mountains. The more conservative easterner regarded this incredible exodus of so many of his neighbors as an imbecility on the order of the legendary march of the lemmings to destruction in the sea. The West accepted the influx more philosophically but still with mixed feelings. Many of the newcomers, such as continental veterans, were useful additions to the community, able to pull their own weight upon arrival, but many more were refugees from a habit of failure which no change of scene proved sufficient to break, some were criminals, and, most important of all, few were prepared to be much help in fighting off the Indians. But all were people and in a democracy the people rule. By 1790 the population of Kentucky had leaped to 73,000 and Congress was at its wits' end to find new excuses to withhold statehood.

Many aspects of the settlers' existence are as difficult for us now to comprehend with any sense of reality as it might have been for them then to anticipate the differing complexities of our time. We cannot place ourselves in a position where we can begin to feel the terrifying day to day and year to year uncertainties with which they wrestled because we have read the history books and know that finally it all came out very well indeed. But no feature of that distant world is more incomprehensible than this sudden mass impulse of so many tens of thousands of perfectly average Americans to step, of their own volition, into the whirlwind. The more we attempt to examine the mover's conceivable state of mind the more incomprehensible the matter becomes. He was undertaking a journey longer than any that can today be made on this earth, a journey of months, an essential part of it through a roadless wilderness where he was to be in daily danger of losing his life and the lives of his wife and children, in order to reach a far country to cast his lot with people who, according to every report, were having about as bad a time as people can have.

Bearing upon his decision, no doubt, were such influences as the postwar depression in his community, the apparent lack of opportunity in the east, a taste for adventure, a temptation to gamble, a wish to escape the demands of landlord, employer or tax collector, a hope to own land, more land or better land. But by far the greater impulse driving the average settler west appears to have been an acute desire to get rich quick. He could see about him in the east slight prospect of his ever getting rich, even by the hard work of a lifetime. But in that far mysterious land beyond the sunset he could foresee at least the possibility of mounting at a bound from the status of sharecropper to that of plantation owner, from the situation of unemployed clerk to that of merchant prince, from the station of a man who owned two slaves to that of one who owned two hundred. Such dreams may well have filled his mind. But there must have been room in it for a few other considerations. He had not been living in a box. He must have been listening to every report he could gather on conditions in the west. No news travels like bad news and he had heard some of the worst. Accounts of the outstanding disadvantages of life in the west were eagerly circulated in the east and he must have heard a good many. So he knew that except for a fortunate few everybody out there was poorer than they had ever been in the east. He knew about the closure of the Mississippi and about the painful uncertainties of title legalization. He knew that if he did find land he might not be able to hold it and that however big his crop there might be no market in which to sell it. He had heard a good deal about the more disagreeable features connected with Indians in the dooryard. He was aware that the move might cost him the privilege of continuing to be an American. He knew in some detail, because this was a topic upon which he had had to ask the most questions, about the fearful journey required to get there. And still he went.

Let us attempt, briefly, to trace a typical experience. We can only surmise what led our average mover to make the final decision to set out by what we can deduce from his actions. Perhaps he has had neighbors who went the year before and a winter of brooding over their possible fortunes has made him too restless to sit still. Perhaps he is a veteran with a grant to a piece of land which will be his if he can find it and if someone else is not already in possession. Perhaps he has naively taken at face value the glowing circulars broadcast by land companies. Perhaps he just feels he cannot stand it any longer where he is. At any rate, he has sold his farm, paid off his debts, and is starting out with his family, a few tools and utensils, and such farm animals as he thinks he can keep alive enroute.

We pick him up at Lancaster in eastern Pennsylvania where he must make his second great decision. There are but two routes he can take. Will he go northwest over the mountains to the Monongahela and there build a flatboat upon which to float down the Ohio to his destination? Or will he strike off south to the great misnamed "gap" in the mountains and turn west over the Wilderness Road? If he has much property to freight and the money to afford a flatboat he will probably take the Ohio route. Otherwise, being a landsman, he will go by land. Let us say he chooses the latter alternative.

First he has 440 miles of travel southward down the Valley of Virginia. This takes him a month or more, since what with intermittently bad weather and uniformly bad roads, he cannot hope to average more than ten or twelve miles a day.

Having reached Watauga he has reached the limit of inhabited country and has yet before him the famous Wilderness Road, stretching two hundred miles more over the mountains to the first settlements of Kentucky. He finds that like the gap the road is misnamed. It is not a road but a mere pack trail, climbing one rocky ridge after another, descending into cane-choked mountain valleys, fording wild streams, and unmarked, anywhere along its length, by a single habitation. Before braving this ordeal he must dismantle his wagon and sell or give away anything he cannot carry on his back or the backs of his animals. He must also wait until a sufficient number of fellow movers accumulate to form a company strong enough to defend one another during the passage. For the Wilderness ahead is the most dangerous Indian country anywhere along the frontier. Another historic road, as famous in its own right as the Wilderness Road, cuts across it — the Warriors' Path, the route once traveled by Northern and Southern Indians during their endless wars on each other and now a favorite avenue for their endless wars upon the whites.

(There is no need that the tales told to warn him of the Indian danger be exaggerated. The grim truth was sufficient. More than a hundred were killed along the Wilderness Road in 1784. Year after year a comparable toll was exacted. In 1792 the loss ran to 102. In 1793, Thomas Ross, one of the victims, attracted attention because he was the first mail carrier over the Road, and the next year there was an added shock in the circumstance that four ministers were butchered in a single day. The way did not become safe until the general peace of 1795.)

Our mover, if he has had the good fortune to struggle successfully over the rockbound escarpments and across the rushing rivers of the Wilderness, to keep his horses, his cow and his children from drowning at fords or falling from cliffs, and meanwhile to escape Indian ambush, has now at last reached the outskirts of Kentucky, where he must summon new energies to begin looking for whatever it was that he had come to look for.

Now let us go back and assume that he decided instead to

take the other possible route. His first task is to get 230 miles over the Pennsylvania mountains to Redstone on the Monongahela, over a road which is not nearly as passable as when General Forbes cut it in 1758 on his way to the taking of Fort Duquesne. After a while he will stop counting the times his wagon overturns or his team is mired.

At Redstone he must compete with hundreds like him for the materials to build his flatboat and do what he can to guard his remaining resources against the profiteering designs of the local inhabitants. When his boat is finally finished, a process which he must expedite with desperate energy since if he misses the spring freshet he may have to wait months for the next high water, and is loaded with his family, and his animals, and everything he owns, and he is afloat on the river, he can, he thinks, breath a great sigh of relief. But it will prove a short sigh. For he immediately discovers that of all the devices ever contrived by man a flatboat is the most maddening. Dependent upon the current of the river for motive power, its tremendous weight animated by incredibly contrary impulses is all but impossible for even the most experienced riverman to control. It runs upon every shoal, strikes every rock, catches on every snag, spins in every eddy, and seems never to make direct and rapid progress except when headed on a beeline for a mudbank.

Navigation, however, is not our mover's chief concern. Floating down the Ohio he is proceeding as slowly as in a bad dream through a region where the Indian danger is second only to the Wilderness Road. The northern bank is the "Indian side" beyond which live the most warlike of all the savage nations, and as yet no settler has ventured to establish himself near the river on the south side. For hundreds of miles he drifts through an unbroken wilderness without sighting a habitation or another white man except an occasional boatload of fellow movers as nervously uncertain of what they are about as is he.

(Again the warnings that have been dinned into his ears have not been exaggerated. A wallowing family flatboat with its cargo of farm animals, tools, prospective captives, and easily taken scalps, possessed an irresistible fascination for the Indian. Upon sighting it, war parties crossing the river to raid the settlements invariably turned their attention to this easier prey. Other parties made it a practice to lurk in hiding along the banks, waiting for a boat to run aground, or, in the event a feint proved the crew's marksmanship to be ineffective, to dart out by canoe to make a direct attack. A favorite device was to require captured women and children to appear on the bank and wail for help when the next boat passed. If the people aboard this second boat yielded to humanitarian impulse and poled ashore to pick up the weeping victims they in turn met disaster. There are few contemporary records or estimates of losses on the Ohio during these years. They must have been considerable for at the time innumerable stories of catastrophe were in circulation. Most of those who failed to get through seemed merely to have disappeared. Few clues were left to their fate. Their boats were burned, their bodies swept away by the river.)

Among the many perils threatening our mover as his boat drifts on day after day through five hundred miles of seemingly endless wilderness, one, purely psychological, begins increasingly to oppress him and his family. On land, had they become discouraged, or dismayed, or overcome by homesickness, they could have changed their minds, turned around and started back. But here there can be no turning back. The current of the mighty river runs but the one way. It sweeps them inexorably on into the unknown. Whatever their fate they are irretrievably committed to it.

If it is our mover's fortune to get through, as do most of his fellows, by sheer weight of numbers, for there are so many of them that the Indians suffer from an embarrassment of victims, he will reach Limestone (later called Maysville), the first settlement in Kentucky, where most movers disembark. Here he finds hundreds of such boats as his pulled up on the shore. His family gathered around him, he stands gratefully upon the shore of Kentucky. His problems are only beginning.

These cursory glances at the itinerary of an average mover cast little light to improve our understanding of his state of mind. The hardships and dangers were so well known and the rewards to be attained so delayed that by every rule of reason or common sense only the most reckless should ever have embarked on the venture. Yet tens of thousands of quite ordinary citizens did so without hesitation. Every attempt to examine the circumstances but deepens the mystery. Perhaps it was a sort of racial impulse, comparable, after all, to the herd instinct of the lemmings. One thing is certain. Had there been a guiding purpose at work, devoted to making our country great, all would have happened just as it did happen.

Travel journals detailing the personal reactions of participants in this amazing migration, of the kind so numerous in the later, covered-wagon days, are few. But a priceless one, kept by William Calk, a very early mover, has come down to us. It has been printed and reprinted but it is a classic which merits every addition to the number of its readers. It may be that a few excerpts from his terse story may tell us more about what moved the mover than the most labored attempt in our time to rationalize:

Mond. 13th — I set out from prince wm. to travel to caintuck on tuesday Night our company all got together at Mr. Prises on rapadan which was Abraham hanks* philip Drake Eaneck Smith Robert Whitledge & my Self, thear Abrams Dogs leg got Broke by Drake's Dog . . . . 22nd — We start early and git to foart Chissel whear we git some good loaf Bread & good whiskey . . . . 24th — Come to a turabel mountain that tired us almost to death to get over it & we lodge this night on the Lawrel fork of holston under agrait mountain & Roasft a fine fat turkey for our suppers & Eat it without aney Bread. Satrd 25th — We start early travel over Some very Bad mountains one that is caled Clinch mountain . . . . 30th — We set out again & went down to Elk gardin and there suplid our Selves With Seed Corn & irish tators then we went on a littel way I turned my hors to drive afore me & he got scard ran away threw Down the Saddel Bags and broke three of our powder goards & Abrams beast Burst open a walet of corn & lost a good Deal & made a turrabel flustration amongst the Reast of the Horses Drakes mair run against a sapling & noct it down we cacht them all agin & went on . . . . April Satrd first —

---

* Maternal grandfather of Abraham Lincoln.

this morning there is ice at our camp half inch thick we start
early & travel this Day along a verey Bad hilley way cross one
creek whear the horses almost got mired some fell in & all wet
their loads we cross Clinch River & travell till late in the Night
& camp on Cove creek having two men with us that wair pilates
· · · · · · · 5th — Breaks away fair & we go on down the valey
& camp on indian Creek we had this creek to cross maney times
& very Bad Banks Abrams saddel turned & the load all fell in
we go out this Eavening & kill two Deer · · · · · · · fryday 7th
this morning is a very hard snowey morning we still continue
at Camp Being in number about 40 men & Some neagros this
Eaven Comes a letter from Capt Boone at caintuck of the indians
doing mischief and some turns back. Satrd April 8th — We all
pact up and started crost Cumberland gap about one oclock
this Day We Met a great maney peopel turned Back for fear of
the indians but our Company goes on Still with good courage
we come to a very ugly Creek with steep Banks & have it to cross
several times · · · · · · · tuesday 11th — this is a very loury
morning & like for Rain But we all agree to start Early we cross
Cumberland River & travel Down it about 10 miles through
Some turrabel cainbrakes as we went down abrams mair ran
into the River with Her load & Swam over he followed her &
got on her & made her Swim Back again · · · · · · · we come
to Richland Creek it is high we toat our packs over on a tree
& swim our horses over & there we meet another Company going
Back they tell such News Abram & Drake is afraid to go aney
further · · · · · · · thursday 13th this morning the weather
Seems to breake & Be fair Abram & Drake turn Back we go on
& git to loral River we come to a creek Before wheare we are
able to unload & toate our packs over on a log this day we meet
about 20 more turning Back we are obliged to toat our packs
over loral river & swim our horses one hors Ran in with his
pack & lost it in the River · · · · · · · sunday 16th — cloudy &
warm we start early & go on about 2 mile down the River and
then turn up a creek that we crost about 50 times Some very
bad foards with a great Deal of very good land on it in the
Eavening we git over to the waters of Caintuck & go a little
Down the creek & there we camp · · · · · · · tuesday 18th fair
& col and we go on about 10 oclock we meet 4 men from Boons
camp that caim to conduck us on · · · · · · · we come to where
the indians fired on Boons company & kild 2 men & a dog &
wounded one man in the thigh · · · · · · · thursday 20th this

morning is clear and cool. We start early and git Down to caintuck to Boons foart about 12 oclock wheare we stop they come
out to meet us & welcom us in with a voley of guns fryday 21st
warm this Day they Begin laying off lots in the town . . . .
Sunday April 23rd this morning the peopel meets & Draws for
chois of lots this is a very warm day. monday 24th We all view
our lots & Some Dont like them . . . . Wednesday 26th
We Begin Building us a house & a plaise of Defense to Keep
the indians off . . . . Satterday 29th — We git our house
kivered with Bark & move our things into it at Night and Begin
housekeeping Eanock Smith Robert Whitledge & my Self. May,
Monday first I go out to look for my mair and saw 4 bufelos
the Being the first that I saw & I shot one of them but did not
git him . . . . tuesday 2d I went out in the morning &
kild a turkey and come in & got some on for my breakfast and
then went & Sot in to clearing for Corn."

Thus our William Calk made his way over the Wilderness
Road, reached Kentucky safely, built a cabin, shot his first
buffalo, started getting in his first crop, and left us about as
successful an account of the mover as a person as we are ever
likely to get. Evidently the all inclusive explanation is that the
mover was a positively incurable optimist. Until recently this
was a rather common American trait.

XIII. Half Sold Down the River

THE FOURTH KENTUCKY CONVENTION, scheduled to meet in September, 1786, to forward the process of separation from Virginia, was postponed for lack of a quorum. A majority of the delegates was off fighting Indians. Attacks upon the frontier had been more numerous and violent this fourth summer of the peace with England.

In the last two years the national government had laboriously negotiated the treaties of Fort Stanwix, Fort McIntosh, Hopewell and Fort Finney, seeking Indian recognition of the fact that the United States, not England or Spain, was now the sovereign authority with which they were obliged to deal and Indian agreement to a definitive line between the area open to settlement and that reserved to Indian use. But, as usual, these treaties were signed by only some representatives of some Indian nations. More as a result of the treaties than in spite of them Indian hostility became more vigorous and more calculated. The government of the United States which had sought the treaties was powerless to enforce them. The only federal troops in the west, a handful at Fort Finney, had not been paid for months and were being weakened daily by new desertions. Congress was unable even to find the $1000 required to pay for the transportation of gunpowder to arm them.

The emergency was again, also as usual, left in the frontiersman's lap. Kentucky had no authority to send militia beyond her borders. Clark easily got around this legalistic difficulty by calling for volunteers to cross the Ohio with him. He proposed to attack the raiders in their northern lairs and to inflict a punishment so severe as to put an end to the inroads. No project could have been more popular in Kentucky. Something of the sort had to be done if the border was not to be nibbled to death by little wars. However, no more than 1200 of the needed 2400 volunteers assembled. People on the frontier, except those who inhabited the more exposed outer fringe of settlements, had become increasingly preoccupied with their private affairs. Clark, himself, did not move with his old energy and the men who had joined him were not up to the old standard. Once men had followed him through neck-deep swamps. Now they first inquired how well they would be fed. When Clark pushed on without waiting for what his men considered sufficient supplies some hundreds mutinied and went home. The hungry army gave up any idea of punishing Indians and descended upon the little French-American community of Vincennes, where it lived off the country not of the enemy but of friends.

Taking advantage of the circumstance that the main Indian forces had shifted to meet the threat of Clark's initial advance, another Kentucky column under Logan had more success. Logan burned five Shawnee towns and brought back forty Indian prisoners, valuable as exchange media for white captives. This stroke, however, was not sufficient punishment to achieve any significant result. More angered than impressed, the Indians were raiding the frontier again before snow fell.

So far western discontent had centered about the Indian question and the Separatist question. Now, suddenly, the Spanish question stirred so much popular excitement that for the moment all else was forgotten. News, somewhat garbled, had come of Jay's proposal to acquiesce for the next twenty-five years in Spain's closure of the Mississippi. Instant rage flared throughout the west. It was a fury directed almost as much against the East as against Spain. All clearly recognized the issue. The East at last had flown its true colors. Rufus King of New York was accepted as a spokesman for the prevailing view in the east when he said: "Should there be an uninterrupted use of the Mississippi at this time by the citizens of the United States I should consider every emigrant to that country from the Atlantic states as forever lost to the confederacy." Westerners found their worst suspicions of the East confirmed and their last doubt of Spain's imperial purpose removed. The East proposed to stand idly by while Spain used her navigational control as a club to stunt the growth of the West.

Appreciation of the sudden threat to what unity remained between the sections was not confined to the west. There were perceptive easterners who also saw the danger. Madison said the westerners could well consider themselves absolved "from every federal tie." Monroe called the eastern attitude "an attempt to break up the settlements on the western waters."

Such expressions of concern were well enough founded. Men in the west were not of a temperament to submit gracefully to any type of pressure. Always their first impulse was to strike back, to meet force with force, to take the offensive. The Third Kentucky Convention, meeting the year before when the Mississippi controversy had not yet reached its present pitch, after listing twelve specific grievances connected with the West's geographic separation from the eastern seat of government and from eastern interests, had unanimously resolved:

That it is the indispensable duty of this convention, as they regard the prosperity and happiness of their constituents, themselves, and posterity, to make application to the general assembly, at the ensuing session, for an act to separate this district from the present government forever, on terms honorable to both and injurious to neither; in order that it may enjoy all the advantages, privileges, and immunities of a *free, sovereign, and independent republic.*

Their impulse now was to defy Congress and to compel Spain to open the Mississippi. There was immediate talk of an expedition to take Natchez and New Orleans. The temper of the moment is revealed by extracts from heated letters, exchanged by western leaders or written to friends in the east, many of which, as it was intended that they should, found their way into the hands of congressmen:

To sell us and make us Vassals to the Merciless Spaniards is a grievance not to be borne, Should we tamely submit to such measures we shou'd be unworthy the name of Americans and a scandal to the Annals of History.

Shall all this country now be cultivated entirely for the use of the Spaniards? Shall we be their bondsmen as the children of Israel were to the Egyptians? Shall one part of the United States be slaves, while the other is free?

Our situation is as bad as it possibly can be, therefore every exertion to retrieve our circumstances must be manly, eligible and just.

Preparations are now making here (if necessary) to drive the Spaniards from their settlements at the mouth of the Mississippi. In case we are not countenanced and succoured by the United States (if we need it) our allegiance will be thrown off, and some other power applied to. Great Britain stands ready with open arms to rescue and support us. They have already offered to open their resources for our supplies.

Clark, always the direct actionist, immediately started taking some action. He held his army in Vincennes, though his abortive Indian campaign had ended, enlisted additional forces, and seized a considerable quantity of Spanish property which was there in the custody of French traders. This was admittedly a hostile act of a type only to be taken against a recognized enemy. Clark did not publicly admit that he was gathering his forces for an expedition down the Mississippi but it was widely and approvingly believed in the west that this was what he was preparing to do. The Spanish, well-informed as usual, began making feverish preparations to improve their defenses at Natchez and New Orleans.

The story of the West's survival can never be made to follow the sedate path of proper history. Forever it is being carried away into what more resembles the rankest melodrama. There is little order in the succession of cause and effect, suspense is piled on suspense, our heroes escape danger only by falling into greater danger, and what transpires, more often than not, is not only the totally unexpected but the totally unrelated. At this critical moment, when the current of events was rushing toward an irregular assault upon Spain with the most unforeseeable consequences, the West was saved from the rash venture not by the reasoning reflection of responsible leaders but by the plotting of a traitor. The incredible Wilkinson, whose fortune hunting had included increasing political activity at the recent Kentucky conventions, saw his great opportunity to destroy Clark and usurp his position as the West's standard-bearer.

Above all Wilkinson was articulate. By tongue or pen he was wonderfully persuasive. He wrote a series of letters, some under his own name, some under others', to influential men in the east, dilating, with diabolic cunning, upon Clark's alleged personal weaknesses, warning that Clark was breaking up, had become a confirmed drunkard, and that if not promptly restrained he was certain to get the country into a general war. Clark's reputation was never to recover from this shrewdly timed attack, and most historians since have complacently assumed, basing the conclusion almost entirely on reports broadcast at this time by Wilkinson and his political supporters, that the West's most energetic and successful champion had at the age of thirty-four suddenly degenerated into a kind of senile inebriate. An immediate consequence was that a disturbed Virginia assembly and a no less alarmed Congress denounced and reprimanded him. Wilkinson, in control of the interim committee sitting during the adjournment of the Convention, was able to add even Kentucky's official condemnation as a final blow to Clark's prestige. For he had gained the ear of fellow Kentucky leaders with the adroit reminder that there was more than one way to skin a cat. Before making war on Spain a try should be made at taking advantage of Spain. The war fever died down. Clark was left stranded and alone. From now on and for years to come Wilkinson was to be the dominating figure on the Kentucky scene.

But there were certain confidences he did not yet whisper into the ear of his most sympathetic associate. Upsetting Clark was but one facet of the opportunity he had seized. At the very time he was writing American statesmen in the east he was dispatching other missives to Spanish authorities on the Mississippi. He warned them of Clark's designs and presently was able to assure them that it was due to his efforts and his alone that an American attack upon Spain had been prevented. These contacts encouraged him to undertake a private trading enterprise down river. Other Americans had occasionally made such ventures in order to discover if the Spaniards might not, after all, be in a mood to do some business, only to have their cargoes confiscated by beaming Spanish officials. But Wilkinson's goods were not confiscated and he was personally welcomed at New Orleans by the Spanish governor.

His unprecedented commercial success was made known at once and word of it sent back to Kentucky where it created a sensation. What was not made known at the time was that in his efforts sufficiently to impress his new Spanish friends he had taken an oath of allegiance to the King of Spain and had written an elaborate memorial advising the Spanish government how most certainly the West might be brought under the Spanish flag. Wilkinson's principal proposal was that Spain encourage the development of a Spanish party in Kentucky by granting its leaders, meaning himself and his chosen associates, exclusive trading privileges. Meanwhile the river was to be closed more rigorously than ever to all others in order to deepen the ordinary Kentuckian's resentment of the inability of the United States to come to his aid. Thus by carrot and stick the West could be hastened toward separation from the United States and union with Spain. A secondary feature of the Wilkinson program was Spanish encouragement of the establishment of American colonies in Spanish territory. By this device, he pointed out, large groups of Americans would find their interests coinciding with Spanish interests and Spanish power in the Mississippi Valley be increased at the expense of American power.

Wilkinson devoted the whole year of 1787 to the launching of his Spanish intrigue. He had reason to feel that success was in sight. He had made a great impression upon Miro, the Spanish governor. He knew that he could count upon the support of practically every important American in the west. Men who were grasping at landholdings the size of medieval dukedoms could not fail to appreciate what he now had to offer. All he needed was a little time. But he had less time than he knew.

That same year the march of events was also accelerating in the east. Congress had so far awakened from its lethargy as to draft and pass one of the noblest and most farsighted governmental charters of all time, the Ordinance of 1787. And delegates had met at Philadelphia to draft a sturdy new constitution to take the place of the ramshackle Articles of Confederation. Neither event attracted much attention that year in the west. The territory dreamily contemplated as one day to be governed by the Ordinance was still in the possession of violently hostile Indians. And the constitutional convention was considered mainly a forum for disputes among rival eastern commercial interests. Instead, all of the West's attention was fixed upon the outcome of Wilkinson's New Orleans venture.

He returned by sea to Philadelphia and when he appeared in Kentucky it was in a coach and four and with a retinue of newly purchased slaves. Over night he became the West's hero and darling. His disclosure that he had found a way to trade profitably through the Spanish blockade stirred overwhelming excitement. Prices doubled and then doubled again. Men who had been convinced that they were destined forever to remain poor began to realize that after all they might be upon the verge of becoming rich. Tobacco sold for $2 a hundredweight one day and $9.50 the next. All elbowed to get aboard this miracle-working bandwagon.

The reversal of feeling was as sudden and as complete as if a curtain had been drawn to disclose a new stage, a new set of characters, and a new play. Before, Spain had been the chief enemy and had been regarded with such hostility that preparations for an unauthorized war had been under way. Now, Spain had become the West's best friend and Spain's control of the Mississippi not the barrier but the door to prosperity for all. There was a concerted rush to take advantage of this stunning opportunity.

Through all the early months of 1788 every indication supported the conclusion that the West was stampeding pell-mell into the arms of Spain. As Wilkinson had foreseen, literally every commercially important and politically influential figure in the west was scrambling for Spanish privileges. Trading fleets were organized and colonies projected. No one wished to be left out of the distribution of glittering advantages that seemed in prospect. The formerly heroic Clark, now completely disillusioned and embittered, was among the first to change sides.

He wrote Gardoqui of his conviction that "no property or person is safe under a government so weak and infirm as that of the United States" and offered to become a Spanish subject in return for approval of his proposal to found an American colony in Spanish territory. Others were at his heels. Sevier, Robertson, Blount, Morgan, Hutchins, White and Brown appeared as ready to commit themselves and their futures as was Wilkinson himself, or his immediate associates, Sebastian and Innes. All embarked upon eager consultations with each other and upon negotiations with Gardoqui and Miro, seeking Spanish approval of their various land company, trading company, or colonizing company projects. These were not ignorant dupes or men operating with their eyes closed. None had any doubt about the implications. All knew they were taking a road that led directly to separation of the West from the United States and to some kind of union with Spain. All realized this as fully as did Clark when he offered to become a Spanish subject or Wilkinson when he actually did take his oath of allegiance to Spain.

Wilkinson's first great trading fleet, freighted with hopes for Kentucky's prosperity and schemes for Kentucky's secession, was on its way to the Spanish market in New Orleans. But other events did not wait. In this year 1788 almost everything else was happening too. All over the west there was more tumult and shouting, more Indian trouble, more sudden change, than ever before. The "free" State of Franklin was torn by a minor civil war between partisans loyal to North Carolina and the adherents of Sevier who favored his turn to Spain. Following the Kirk-Brown-Old Tassel series of murders the Indian war along the Southern frontier reached a new pitch of violence and this was accompanied, as usual, by bolder raids by the Northern Indians. Houston's and Bledsoe's stations were besieged, Harman's abandoned, and Gillespie's taken. A formidable attempted counterattack under General Joseph Martin resulted in a notable Indian victory at Lookout Mountain. As winter approached, the Creek and Cherokee nations, for once resolving their differences, took the field together and in force. In the north the survey of Cincinnati and the founding of Marietta, demonstrating an American intention to push settlement as inexorably north of the Ohio as south of the river, stirred Indian hostility there to new intensity.

The western settler was deluged with reports, accounts and rumors of near and distant developments, all with a significant relation to his personal fortunes that he was required to make an effort to estimate — Wilkinson's trading venture, the Spanish-American colonial projects at Muscle Shoals, Chickasaw Bluffs, Walnut Hills, and New Madrid, the defection of the western leaders, the accidental destruction of New Orleans by fire, the campaign to elect delegates to the convention which was to implement Kentucky's separation, the insurrection in Franklin, the new settlements north of the Ohio, the extraordinary number of new immigrants, and the mounting flames of Indian war.

East of the mountains, also, portents and prodigies marked this momentous year. There, too, there was the kind of suspense that only melodrama ordinarily provides. The nation had no government. The old congress of the Confederation had all but ceased to exist, in effect bequeathing the western problem and all other problems to the new congress provided by the Constitution, if such a body ever materialized. The Constitution, to everybody's enormous surprise, had been drafted and signed. The thunderous roll call of the states was in progress to decide the question of ratification. There were the most agonizing doubts that ratification would prevail. Failure meant a state of chaos in the place of the state of being a nation and yet opposition was violent and prolonged. States were voting ratification by margins which were excruciatingly narrow. But, after bitter debates, state after state was ratifying. Slowly the number approached the magic number of nine which would mean that the new Constitution had become the law of the land. January 2, Georgia. January 9, Connecticut. February 7, Massachusetts. April 28, Maryland. May 23, South Carolina.

The West, which had so long complained of a central government too weak to protect the frontier, nevertheless watched dubiously this attempt actually to create a stronger central government. There was no enthusiasm for the Constitution along the border. Of the nine delegates from southwestern Pennsylvania to the Pennsylvania state constitutional convention seven voted against ratification. The Kentucky delegates toiled over the mountains to Richmond to vote ten to four against ratification. This surprising western opposition to a stronger national government may be ascribed in part to the influence of politically powerful land companies and land speculators. These were interests which quite naturally feared federal restraint. But it is evidence, too, of how general was the rapidly growing separatist sentiment and how basic was the determination of the West to choose its own course. There was also a deeper prejudice, imbedded in public opinion and felt as much by the landless as by the proprietor class. This was an objection to the creation of a national government with full treaty-making power to deal with the Indian problem. Even in the glare of his own burning home the settler remained a rugged individualist. He did not want federal interference with his own Indian program. He wanted to reserve the right to decide for himself when the Indians should be told to back up and turn over more land for settlement. In actual practice this was to be a right the border settler continued to exercise for the next century.

The news that the new Constitution had been ratified was brought to the West, appropriately, by a new young prosecuting attorney sent to Tennessee from the East, Andrew Jackson.* He was to become the greatest westerner of his time and to live to see the West, in his own person, seize political dominance in the nation. There was news for him, too, scarcely less significant than that he brought.

The Sixth Kentucky Convention had met to decide upon the future of Kentucky. Wilkinson and his Separatist Party followers were in the saddle. Prices were still up as a result of his personally conducted Spanish trade program and enthusiasm for everything Spanish was high. His party had no hesitation in proposing on the floor of the convention that Kentucky give up fooling around with requests for statehood and turn to the obviously far more prosperous association with Spain that was indicated. But to his immense astonishment, and to the surprise of almost everybody else, there was hesitation about taking

---

* The party immediately following Jackson's through the Wilderness was destroyed by Indian attack.

this so manifestly sensible a course. The ordinary people of Kentucky had taken a sharper interest than formerly in the election of delegates to this convention. There were many members who were here not merely because they were prominent citizens or colonels of militia or big landholders but because they had been singled out by the votes of their constituents. There was a new disposition to ask questions and to question the answers. Delegates on the back benches were taciturn but inclined to be skeptical of some of Wilkinson's glib enthusiasms. They professed no special loyalty to Virginia or to the United States but a most practical disposition to wait and see. They felt like waiting to see how this Spanish trade boom held up. And they also saw no harm in waiting to see how the new American national government worked out. The vote was close. But this unexpected wait and see attitude prevailed. The decision reached by the Sixth Convention was simply to postpone any decision to the next convention.

The immediate storm had been weathered. But the crisis had not been ended. It had merely been prolonged. The various schemes of ambitious western leaders were still in full course. Trading fleets were still descending the Mississippi in quest of Spanish profits. George Morgan was winning Spanish authorization for his New Madrid colony. Gardoqui and Miro were still pulling their many strings. Wilkinson had been disappointed but not confounded. The Spanish threat was to become more dangerous before it finally faded.

Meanwhile another entrant had appeared in the race to win the west. Lord Dorchester, English Governor General of Canada, had not failed to observe the opportunities offered in the Mississippi Valley by the unrest of the American settlers. Dr. John Connolly, the perennial English intriguer who had played so active a part in troubled Pittsburgh during the first year of the Revolution, reappeared in Louisville in this eventful year of 1788. The West, he said, could readily possess itself of the Mississippi, which it needed so desperately, if it accepted English assistance against the Spaniards. He offered the aid of "four thousand British troops in Canada, besides two regiments at Detroit," together with "arms, ammunition, clothing and money" for the purpose of capturing New Orleans. This English overture offered advantages possessed by no other course the West could have taken and it was the one development most feared by Spain. The frontiersmen could conceivably have taken New Orleans whenever they made a determined effort but they could not have held the city or made use of the port without control of the sea. An alliance with England supplied this missing element. Nevertheless, though his case might appear so much more promising than Wilkinson's, Dr. Connolly found few in Kentucky, other than former Tories, ready to listen to him. The Revolution was too recent and it was too difficult to believe his protestations that England had had nothing to do with the continuing Indian war. Even the argument that an English alliance would bring relief from that war did not overcome the average settler's ingrained anti-English prejudice.

However, all was grist to Wilkinson's mill. First he improved his credit with the Spaniards by informing them of the English move, making it seem more dangerous than it was in order to make his continuing friendship seem more useful to Spain. Next he sent an emissary to Canada to inform the English of the Spanish design and to explore the possibilities for him if the English accepted his offer to join them. Then, as final insurance, in case the worst came to the worst, he took care to warn his own government of both Spanish and English plots. And all the while he fought tooth and nail, by vilification, misrepresentation, and tale-bearing, against any trading or colonizing venture, whatever its origin, in which he had not been offered a major interest.

His most favored project, however, remained his Spanish intrigue, which offered the more immediate profit. He had no reason yet to lose hope. In 1789 Kentucky was no nearer statehood than it had been, the largest trading fleet yet swept down river, land values in Kentucky were rising as an accompaniment to the Spanish trade boom, he himself was more popular than ever, the colonizing projects were going forward with Morgan's at New Madrid actually established, Spanish emissaries were circulating their promises through the west more busily than ever, and such a figure as Robertson was writing Miro, "Unprotected, we are to be obedient to the new Congress of the United States but we cannot but wish for a more interesting connection. . . . For my own part, I conceive highly of the advantages of your immediate government."

Wilkinson returned to New Orleans that summer to draft a second memorial and to reassure the Spaniards of their continued need for his indispensable services. This time he received an outright grant of money that was not under the guise of a trading profit. Wilkinson accepted, he protested, not for himself but for the sake of winning new adherents to his Separatist Party. "Two or three of the right men" in each Kentucky district, he said, if brought over to the Spanish interest, would bring with them the whole West. He returned to Kentucky on Christmas Day of that year with two mule loads of silver in his pack train. His return was also marked by the suicide of Isaac Dunn, his auditor, whose spirit may well have been broken by the task of keeping what must have been as complicated a set of accounts as ever existed.

The West survived the crisis of 1788–89. There was much trembling on the brink but, as always in melodrama, never the fatal fall. This was in part due to the peculiar ineptitude of the Spanish governmental system. All that was required to tip the quivering scale was, as Washington said, "the touch of a feather." But, for all their devious scheming and plotting and spying and bribing, the Spanish officials charged with the conduct of Spanish affairs in the Mississippi Valley were not even featherweights. Whenever the situation took a turn that demanded some outright action, even the slightest action, so long as it was overt and definite, they sidled away from their commitments, resorted to double talk, and left their more aggressive American associates baffled and stranded. Miro and Gardoqui were jealous of each other, worked independently or at cross purposes, and neither was bold enough to take any action without waiting upon a time-wasting reference of the decision to his home government. And their home government was ridden by fears. The Spanish ministry feared to give the Southern Indians the quantity of supplies required to join the Northern Indians in a full-scale Indian war lest the enraged settlers turn upon the Spanish settlements. They feared to excite an open rebellion of the American settlers lest an independent and belligerent West prove a more uncomfortable neighbor than the relatively complacent United States. They feared most of all an alliance of the American West with English Canada, a conjunction of interests which they considered inevitable since it would so obviously advance the interests of both parties to the combination, because this would mean the immediate and certain loss of every Spanish holding northeast of Mexico. So the faraway Spanish government continually cautioned and restrained their already uncertain representatives in North America and their long delayed final instructions were, in effect, to wait until the Americans of their own volition separated themselves from their country and of their own volition sought union with Spain.

But the survival was also due to that innate stability in the democratic process which now and then crops up when least expected. The citizens of a democracy may rant and rave, denounce and criticize, they may loudly declare that their current government is surely the worst of all possible governments. But when these same citizens are drawn into positions of governmental responsibility, and the moment is also marked by crisis, they tend to become themselves responsible. It was so with the members of the Kentucky conventions. They were bitter men who had little faith in Virginia or in the United States. But, confronted by the demand that they make an irretrievable decision, they dealt with the crisis as responsible men. They were not appalled by the idea of secession. Men of the same stamp were to prove that in 1861. They merely felt it their duty to pause to consider, to rely upon sober reflection and common sense. They chose to wait, a while longer, and see.

They were to wait some years before there was any diminution in the number of their grievances, any lessening of the stresses that were tearing them away.

XIV. Yazoo and Nootka

Yazoo and Nootka were the somewhat outlandish names, previously as unheard of as recently were Panmunjom and Dienbienphu, of two wild and widely separated spots on the earth's surface, but during 1790 they were names which had become household words in New York and Charleston, in Louisville and New Orleans, in Madrid, London and Quebec. Yazoo was the name of a small river flowing into the Mississippi near the site of the present city of Vicksburg. Nootka was the name of a sound denting the shore line of Vancouver Island in the northeastern Pacific. The connection between these two remote places, which had so little in common other than that each was still unbroken wilderness inhabited only by savages and visited only by traders, was established by an act of the Georgia legislature of December 21, 1789.

Georgia had unanimously ratified the Constitution. She was the youngest and in many ways the weakest of the thirteen states. She had been founded as a colony to provide a buffer between South Carolina and the Spanish and Indians in Florida. She was still a buffer state, confronted by an Indian power strong enough to hold her frontier to the seaboard lowlands. She needed the support of a stronger federal arm. But before this new federal arm became strong enough to take over Georgia's as yet unceded western land claims the need was felt to take such hurried advantage of them as seemed most practical. By the act of December 21 Georgia sold some 25,000,000 acres along the eastern bank of the Mississippi and the southernmost bend of the Tennessee for five-sixths of a cent per acre to three land companies, the Tennessee Company, the Virginia Company, and the South Carolina Yazoo Company.

This land was from four to five hundred miles west of the Georgian frontier. (The sites of the future cities of Macon and Atlanta were then 80 miles west of Georgia's westernmost settlements.) Such American claim as existed to it resided entirely in the new government of the United States. All of it was claimed and the most of it controlled by Spain and all of it was within the recognized borders of the Indian nations that occupied the region. Georgia did not pretend by the act to deny the jurisdiction of the United States over the area included in the transaction and expressly disclaimed any intention of attempting to exercise any political authority over such colonies as might be founded. All that she did was to go through the motions of selling the land. All else was left to the devices of the land companies that had gone through the motions of buying it. They were to have complete freedom of action.

A more nearly ideal field for land company maneuvers could not be imagined. The superimposed and overlapping claims of Georgia, of the Indian nations, and of the United States and Spain, opened doors to their agents to attempt the negotiation of every variety of deal. The land had cost the companies almost nothing and at the worst the issue could be kept in litigation indefinitely. At the best the reward within reach was a domain the size of a European principality or an American state. The regular crew of land speculators swarmed, almost without exception, to join the companies, merging their former independent schemes in the new more comprehensive pattern. And to the roll of such practiced western entrepreneurs as Wilkinson, Blount, Clark, Sevier, Morgan, White, Cox and Ross were added such eminent easterners as Alexander Moultrie, Wade Hampton, Patrick Henry, Isaac Huger and even such foreigners as Baron von Steuben and Dr. James O'Fallon.

The latter soon led all the rest. O'Fallon was a middle-aged Irishman who claimed to be descended from Irish kings and who was said formerly to have been at one time a doctor and at another a Catholic priest. He had come to America just before the Revolution, as Wilkinson had to Kentucky just after the war, to make his fortune. Apparently at first unable to decide which side to take he was denounced by both but eventually was recognized as a patriot and, in the course of his Revolutionary adventures became the friend of such widely dissimilar figures as Anthony Wayne and Tom Paine. The fortune, however, continued to elude him. Now opportunity knocked. He was appointed general agent of the Yazoo Company, which, because of its larger holdings, more substantial backing and more aggressive policy, took the lead in the new land company program. Those personal qualifications which did most to gain him his appointment were that he was Irish, Catholic and not an American. It was felt that these attributes would prove helpful in making the necessary approaches to the Spaniards, upon whose initial complacence the whole design depended.

O'Fallon speedily established contacts with Gardoqui and Miro, expatiating upon the age-old sympathy between Irishmen and Spaniards and upon the Company's desire to adapt itself to every Spanish interest, and hurried to Kentucky to enlist colonists. The recruit he was most eager to enlist was Wilkinson. Though no one then realized how deeply Wilkinson had committed himself to the Spaniards the favor that they had shown him had made him a marked man and one whose support was essential to such a campaign as O'Fallon's. Wilkinson was miffed that he had not been named to the post of general manager of the Company but the project had already gathered such momentum and he needed money so badly that he went along for a while.

O'Fallon's proposal to Miro, so far as his soaring Irish imagination permitted him to make a coherent proposal, envisaged a colony of ex-Americans on the Mississippi just north of the existing predominantly English and Tory settlement at Natchez, to be devoted not only to land development but to the establishment of a center for the slave trade, the Indian trade, and general Mississippi Valley trade. The phase of the proposal supposed most to appeal to the Spanish authorities was the suggestion that the new colony become a kind of buffer state between the American and Spanish frontiers, a state politically half independent, half Spanish, but not at all American. At the same time O'Fallon was writing Washington, begging official American support and insisting that he was only endeavoring to make fools of the

Spanish. When Miro and Gardoqui, interested but suspicious, showed an inclination to withhold judgment until the project had assumed a clearer shape, O'Fallon began at once to hint darkly that however well disposed he and his company were to Spain their Kentucky backers were in a position to take by force whatever was not freely offered.

Washington had become first President of the United States and was busy picking up the pieces of national policy left him by the late government of the Confederation. He saw the perils of treason and secession toward which the Yazoo project was plunging but he possessed no physical means to oppose it. Trading on the prestige of his great name he promptly issued a proclamation denouncing the scheme. About all else he could do was to quicken negotiations with the Southern Indian nations, striving to halt their aggressions against the frontier and to encourage them to resist the encroachment of the land companies. Then, like a distant thunder clap, there came the news of Nootka, making the situation a thousand fold more dangerous.

Spain, claiming territorial rights in the waters bordering the Pacific Northwest, had seized at Nootka Sound several cargoes belonging to English traders. The fur trade still enjoyed its traditional influence with the English government. Stimulated also by the centuries-old enmity between the two countries, England issued an insulting ultimatum and openly prepared for war. A prominent feature of England's war plans was to authorize Dorchester in Canada to push ahead with his own earlier proposal to enlist the restless Kentuckians in a campaign to sweep Spain from the Mississippi Valley in combination with English military and naval assistance. Thus the cloak and dagger talk of Dr. Connolly in 1788 became an immediate political reality in 1790.

O'Fallon, impatient with Spanish tardiness in welcoming his overtures, enthusiastically hailed this sudden vast shadow cast over the international scene. He burned the bridges of his negotiations with the Spaniards and blatantly threatened Miro with the announcement that he would soon be on his way to take what he wanted by force. O'Fallon turned to Clark, the Kentuckian above all others who was always ready for action and who, his own colony proposal having been ignored by the Spaniards, was as anti-Spanish as formerly. The alliance between the two, as between royal families, was cemented by the marriage of the middle-aged O'Fallon and Clark's fifteen-year-old youngest sister, Frances. Clark, whose imagination had since his youth been fired by the great designs to take Detroit or New Orleans, or both, set energetically about the assembly of an expeditionary force with the approval of most Kentuckians.

Washington's emergency cabinet meetings were wrapped in indecision. All agreed that the O'Fallon-Clark expedition must be prevented but no one knew how. The government had neither money nor military and naval forces. The imminence of war between England and Spain enormously complicated the situation. To tear the grip of Spain from the Mississippi was one thing but to have it replaced by the infinitely stronger grasp of England was quite another. It was realized that the West would be even more likely to turn to a union with English masters of the Mississippi than it had ever been with Spanish custodians. Hamilton was inclined to make the best of a bad job by siding with the English and hoping possibly to come out with Florida as a consolation for the loss of the West. Jefferson clung to the pious hope we might remain neutral and retrieve what we could at the council table but if the Yazoo expedition made neutrality impossible he advised an alliance with Spain in return for the cession of New Orleans and the Floridas. He was deeply conscious of the threat to the country of a constricting ring of English possessions extending from the mouth of the St. Lawrence down the Mississippi Valley and around to St. Augustine in Florida.

Other far distant events as suddenly changed the picture again. Spanish seamen clambering over the sides of English trading barks in the shadow of Vancouver Island's towering pines were now joined as American scene changers by mobs swarming through the streets of Paris. The accelerating pace of the French Revolution left Spain facing her traditional enemy, England, without the support of her traditional ally, France. Cornered by unhappy circumstance, Spain made her surrender to the English ultimatum so abject that England was left without excuse to proceed with her threatened declaration of war.

The passing of the war clouds, which came as suddenly as

had their gathering, revealed how far out on a limb O'Fallon had contrived to place himself. He had precipitately cut himself off from every hope of a reconciliation with the Spaniards and had as recklessly flouted the authority of Washington's new government. He was now confronted with the united opposition of Spain, the United States, and the Indian nations. Clark, accustomed to adversities, stubbornly persisted for a time with his expeditionary preparations but for most Kentuckians the zest had gone out of the venture and it gradually withered.

Wilkinson, with his rat's talent for sensing a ship's sinking in good time, had earlier abandoned the Yazoo Company to hasten back to the service of his Spanish employers. Now he completed O'Fallon's downfall by the exercise of another of his talents, an unerring perception of a rival's weakest point. He arranged that a report upon certain O'Fallon financial transactions come to the attention of major stockholders in Charleston. O'Fallon was discharged and the Yazoo Company withdrew its forces from the field to await a new and wider opportunity.

Another crisis had passed after having for a few weeks taken the proportions of the most deadly threat yet to national unity. This time the escape had been due almost entirely to fortune and the turn of distant events. Certainly it had not been due to good management or sober foresight, either in the west or along the seaboard.

XV. The Indians Close Ranks

So far we have considered events primarily in the light of the settlers' attitude. But there was another attitude, as distracted, as bitter, and as violent — that of the Indians. England's sudden and unforeseen surrender of the Ohio Valley had filled them with dismay. Before the Revolution all their commercial relations had been with traders who drew their goods from English sources. During the Revolution they had been England's fully committed allies. They had been led by English commanders, furnished with English war materials, and their ranks stiffened by detachments of Tory rangers. They had pinned their hopes on English victory. Now they were thrown back upon their own resources and yet faced by the same implacable enemy, the inexorably advancing American settler.

The simultaneous cession of the Floridas to Spain rounded out the picture of Indian disaster. The great chance to drive the Americans back over the mountains had passed with the Revolution. That hope had now to be abandoned. The Americans had gained too firm a lodgment in that Middle Ground between the Ohio and the Tennessee into which originally they had trickled before either Northern or Southern Indians had realized the dimensions of the threat. There remained the absolute necessity of preventing a breakout from this deep salient. Every Indian nation was fully conscious now that the one escape from certain doom was to halt every further advance of American settlement. The next loss would represent in our time not another Korea or Indo-China but an India or a Germany. This line which must be held at whatever cost was the river line beginning along the mountain headwaters of the Allegheny and running down the Ohio and up the Tennessee to its mountain headwaters.

The array of Indian nations guarding this fateful line of Indian defense, which once breached could never again be reestablished elsewhere, presented situations of alternating strength and weakness. In western New York where Indian power had formerly been strongest it was now weak. The Iroquois had been so mauled during the Revolution that most of them wanted peace at any price. Brant had taken his Mohawks to Canada to lick their wounds under the British flag but the other nations of the League had chosen to remain in their old homes to make such deals as they could with the victorious Americans. A few Iroquois migrated to their western hunting grounds beyond the Ohio, where these minor bands were commonly called Mingo.

To the west of the Iroquois, in what is now northern Ohio, and Indiana, stood the principal Indian stronghold, north or south. Scattered across the forested hills and creek bottom meadows of the watershed dividing the streams running into the Great Lakes from those into the Ohio were some scores of the small, semi-fortified towns of a group of Indian nations, dominated by the warlike Shawnee, Wyandot, Miami and Delaware, who were both determined and able to fight. At their backs, but close at hand, were the lakes which were the avenue of approach for the supply-laden barges of their fur trader friends. Across their front extended a belt of wilderness between them and their American enemies, wide enough to give cover to their own assaults on the frontier and to make counter-attack difficult. They could strike at will and without warning yet need never be surprised by retaliation.

Beyond, in the Illinois, was more weakness. Here were the degenerate remnants of nations destroyed by the Iroquois in their heydey a century before. To the north were the Sacs, Foxes and Sioux who were too far away to count, as were the Iowa, Missouri, and Osage across the Mississippi.

Continuing along the Indian defense line to the south face of the salient, the Chickasaw, in what is now northern Mississippi and western Tennessee, represented the weakest link in the Indian chain. Numerically a small nation, their military capacities nevertheless had been second only to the Iroquois. They were famous for the speed of their horses, the beauty of their women and the prowess of their warriors. They had a record of extraordinary success in their many wars with the French and the Spanish. But, most unfortunately for the general Indian cause, they decided now upon an isolationist policy and made a separate peace with the Americans which they never broke. It was to prove a policy which brought down upon them destruction as complete as the contrary one did upon their neighbors.

Closing the salient, between the Chickasaw and the Carolina mountains was the Cherokee nation. The Cherokee were a vital and talented people but their strategic influence was lessened by their division between a peace party which fought only when driven to desperation and a war party under the grim chief, Dragging Canoe, who waged unrelenting war upon the Americans, year in, year out, to the day of his death. Due to Dragging Canoe's tenacity the southern frontier was never quiet, least of all when attempts at peace negotiation were in progress.

Below the Chickasaw were the Choctaw, numerous but militarily unimportant, and below the Cherokee the Creek, most populous and politically the most organized of all the Indian nations. The Creek republic was situated along the Gulf Coast from which its supply lines were safe so that it could exert a continuous pressure against the Georgia frontier and, so often as it chose, send war parties through the Cherokee country to attack the Watauga, Tennessee and Kentucky frontiers. The Creek nation represented the second strongest bastion in the Indian line but its effectiveness was reduced by its intermittent quarrels with the Cherokee and the Chickasaw and a recurring tendency to consider first its own immediate interests.

From a strategic point of view the Indian position was immensely strong. Their chief strength was massed against the flanks of the salient and specifically concentrated against the settlers' long and exposed lines of communication, the upper Ohio and the Wilderness Road, while their principal centers of military power, the Shawnee-Wyandot-Miami-Delaware coalition in the north and the Creek republic in the south, were sufficiently distant from the white frontier to add enormously to the hazards of counterattack. Had the Indians contrived to place so many as half their available warriors in the field at any one time they could have confronted the settlers with overwhelming force but this proved a feat they never found possible.

The effectiveness of the force the Indians were able to bring to bear to maintain their river life line, upon which their future hinged, was governed by four major factors: First, a continuing supply, which could only come from white sources, of those material necessities upon which their way of life had come to depend, primarily guns and gunpowder. Second, adequate leadership on the part of their own leaders. Third, substantial diplomatic and military support from England and Spain. Fourth and more essential than all else, the development of a political and military confederation of the several Indian nations to enable them to make a united effort to achieve their common purpose.

The first requirement was met almost at once. England decided to hold the lake posts and in order to maintain the Indian friendship which made this possible was obliged to continue to supply the Northern Indians. The official English policy was to encourage them only to defend themselves but the implementation of this policy, so far as most personal contacts with the Indians were concerned, was in the hands of traders, ex-traders and ex-Tories who were as hostile to the settlements as were the Indians themselves. The Northern Indians soon discovered that about the only limitation placed upon the range of their military activities by the Anglo-American treaty of peace was that their war parties were no longer accompanied by companies of Tory rangers. This was an advantage, in the judgment of most Indians, in that they were no longer expected to seek arduous and dangerous strategic objectives but were free to scatter their forces among smaller and more profitable hit and run raids.

In the south, Spain, the new master of the Floridas, almost as soon realized that the simplest way to keep the threatening advance of the American frontier at a distance was to arm the intervening Indians. Spanish logistical talent was not even up to an adequate supply of their own garrisons but Spain found a practical way out by turning over the Indian trade to the baronial English firm of Panton, Leslie & Company. Soon the same supply routes from the Gulf that had activated Southern

Indian hostility during the Revolution were again in operation.

The supply system was rounded out when upwards of a hundred French traders, furnished with English trade goods from Detroit, established themselves at Muscle Shoals on the Tennessee, midway between the northern and southern supply bases, where their enterprise was guarded by escorting bands of Shawnee and Delaware warriors. From now on, no Indian, wherever located, who felt moved to take his personal crack at the frontier, but found the means to do so always at hand.

As a result the border was kept year after year in the same state of insecurity, ranging from alarm to despair which it had known during the Revolution. Only occasionally were there Indian attacks on a scale large enough to permit organized resistance. Most of the damage was done by small parties perpetually coming and going under cover of the wilderness. Seldom was there sufficient warning to gather even the local militia. The usual victories sought were over families, hunters, herdsmen and surveyors or parties of travelers, salt makers, churchgoers or school children. The depredations were so numerous and so common that few single disasters were considered worthy of record unless featured by some unusually atrocious circumstance. Most excited the concern only of immediate neighbors who feared a like fate. So many people were in movement in search of land and were so far separated from their friends and relatives in the east that their disappearance often escaped notice. But in the aggregate these lonely tragedies mounted to an annual death list running into the hundreds. Seldom except when the victim was a figure whom we now would term newsworthy did one of these continually recurring minor calamities find a place in the records of the time. In 1786, for example, more comment was excited when the Indians killed Colonel William Christian, a most respected and long experienced border commander, near Louisville, John Donelson, co-founder of the Cumberland settlement, in the Kentucky barrens, and 21 members of a traveling party of well known Virginia families, the Fords, the McNitts and the Barnes, on the Wilderness Road, than by the over all total of losses in that year of greatly accelerated Indian raiding. The calculated cumulative effect of Indian tactics was a painful and unrelenting pressure against each separate segment of the frontier. The exact phrase may not yet have been coined but the Indian slogan was "Americans go home" — meaning back over the mountains.

The second requirement, for adequate native leadership, was met by the rise of Indian standard bearers who were more vigorous and picturesque than ultimately successful. In the south the most noted Indian field commander was the Cherokee war chief, Dragging Canoe, but his full time followers were too few to permit him to seek decisions. The outstanding Southern Indian was the Creek, Alexander McGillivray. McGillivray was a figure to stand out colorfully even against his colorful background. He was as much at home in the salons of Charleston or Savannah as beside a wilderness campfire. His father was a Scotch trader and his mother the daughter of a French officer and an Indian "princess." Born to wealth he was as well educated as any white youth of his time and his early career was devoted to the conduct of a mercantile business in Savannah and Pensacola. When the Revolution broke out he returned to the Creek nation and the English recognized his stature as a prominent Tory as well as a distinguished Creek by appointing him assistant commissary and commissioning him a colonel. He took an active part in the confused and peculiarly vicious campaigns of the Revolution along the southern frontier. In May 1783 the Creek National Council elected him Chief and Head Warrior and thereafter he was commonly known as King of the Creeks. His policies during the troubled years that followed were marked by a care to maintain his English connections, through a silent partnership in Panton, Leslie & Company, by efforts to frighten Spain into a less cautious support of the Indian cause, through alternatingly conspiring with and against them, and by an unwavering hatred of the Georgians whom he never forgave for confiscating his father's estates, which he fed by waging a continuous and intermittantly aggressive war upon their frontier. His education and his familiarity with the white world were of great assistance in his conduct of Indian affairs. His chief weaknesses were a love of extravagance and barbaric display, a savage streak of cruelty and treachery, and a tendency to think first of his private interest which extended to occasional conniving with American land companies in the hope of sharing in their prospective profits. But there can be no question that his was a personality that dominated the Southern frontier in his time or that his leadership greatly prolonged the period of successful Indian resistance.

In the north another Indian towered above his fellows. Joseph Brant — his more musical and appropriate Mohawk name was Thayendanegea — was perhaps the most multi-talented figure his race ever produced. He was by turns soldier, statesman, teacher and preacher. In him were combined much of the political sagacity of a Pontiac, the scholarship of a Sequoia, the martial vigor of a Crazy Horse, and the loyalty to his people of a Chief Joseph. Unlike McGillivray, he was a full blooded Indian but like him he was familiar with the white man's world. He was educated at the Lebanon, Connecticut, Indian School which was the forerunner of Dartmouth. In 1775 he visited England where he was lionized by society and became the intimate of such literary figures as James Boswell. Returning to America at the outbreak of the Revolution he saw how clearly every Indian interest was dependent upon an English victory and he took a leading part in the general Indian rebuff of American efforts to enlist them in the patriot cause. Throughout the Revolution he was the most active and the most successful Indian war commander, campaigning as impetuously in Pennsylvania and Kentucky as along his own New York frontier.

When England made a peace with the United States that left Indian interests unprotected Brant again saw clearly that there could be no end to the Indian war against the Americans and he became more committed than ever to opposition to everything American. The first necessity was an Indian united front and he threw all of his energies into the organization of a confederation of Indian nations in which he envisaged himself as a second Pontiac. Having got this movement under way at Indian congresses at Niagara and Detroit, he rushed off to England to seek that stronger support of England's former forest allies which was the necessary second step. His arrival at Salisbury was thus described in the London press:

Monday last, Colonel Joseph Brant, the celebrated King of the Mohawks, arrived in this city from America, and after dining with Colonel De Peister, at the headquarters here, proceeded immediately on his journey to London. This extraordinary personage is said to have presided at the late grand Congress of confederate chiefs of the Indian nations in America, and to be by them appointed to the conduct and chief command in the war which they now meditate against the United States of America. He took his departure for England immediately as that assembly broke up; and it is conjectured that his embassy to the British Court is of great importance.

In London Brant became the hero of the season. Among celebrities who made much of their enjoyment of his company were Sir Guy Carleton, Lord Rawdon, General Sir Charles Stuart, the Duke of Northumberland, the Earl of Warwick, the Bishop of London, Charles Fox, the Prince of Wales, and George III himself. Nothing delighted Brant more than his personal popularity in the highest English society but he had come to the English seat of government on a more serious mission. In a formal address to Lord Sidney, Minister for the Colonies, he bluntly stated the Indian case: "We desire to know whether we are to be considered as his Majesty's faithful allies, and have that support and countenance such as old and true friends expect."

His English admirers found it very difficult indeed to frame an adequate reply. The fur trade influence which had triggered the initial and rather impromptu decision to hold Indian friendship by retention of the lake posts was no longer a compelling factor. Such Indian agents and local government advisors as Alexander McKee and Matthew Elliot, whose private trading interests centered about Detroit, remained as pro-Indian and anti-American as ever. But the vast preponderance of fur trade activity was now deployed west and northwest of Lake Michigan and Lake Superior. The Ohio fraction was not of itself worth risking a border war. On the other hand there was a feeling among many Englishmen that their honor was involved. It was not deemed strictly cricket to abandon these Indian allies who had served them so faithfully during the Revolution. Moreover, government circles were beginning to sense that, with the general international situation so precariously uncertain, it might be just as well to maintain the Indian barrier to American settlement, under one subterfuge or another, as long as possible.

The English official reply was filled with expressions of warm friendship and deep sympathy and accompanied by veiled allusions to a prospective firmer association. Disappointed in gaining an immediate public alliance but consoled by the hope of a future one, Brant rushed back to the New World to a new series of wilderness conferences. No fellow Indian leader could fail to recognize the need to unite and his efforts produced the formal demand of the Northern Indians, in 1786, that the United States treat them as equals, not as subjects, and negotiate treaties with the entire confederacy, not with separate Indian nations. To this Brant, the next year, added, in a letter of his own addressed to Congress, the announcement that the Indians northwest of the Ohio had formed a "defensive and offensive alliance" and the demand that American surveying for settlement beyond the Ohio forthwith cease. (That same year of 1787 Brant found time between conferences to translate the Prayer Book and St. Mark's gospel into Mohawk.) Brant had not yet succeeded in achieving so solid a confederacy as he had hoped but he had united the Northern tribes and succeeded in establishing himself as the recognized spokesman for the Indian cause.

The third requirement, for genuine diplomatic support from England or Spain, or both, carrying with it the assurance of military assistance in the event of a decisive crisis, was met by more promise than performance. The Indian was left in the position of the countryman at the carnival. What he wanted was there in front of his eyes but he was never able to turn over the right shell.

In the south Spanish officials were profuse with their protestations of friendship, lavish with advice, but calculatingly thrifty with supplies. Of the most essential item, gunpowder, they underwrote enough to hunt and enough to kill a certain number of settlers but not enough to kill too many. Spain yearned to discourage the advance of the American frontier but desperately feared to provoke the aggressive frontiersmen into full scale retaliation. She wanted also to keep the door open to the West's separation from the United States and consequent union with her.

In the north English policy was almost identical. The Indians were privately encouraged to strike the frontier often but not too hard. Sufficient punishment to prevent the spread of settlement without bringing on a general war in which England must participate was the perfect balance sought. For England, too, wanted to keep the door open for a possible alliance with the West when the opportunity came to sweep the Spaniards from the Mississippi Valley and achieve the encirclement of the United States.

The English policy was, in one respect, more anomalous than the Spanish. Spain, after all, was attempting to hold territory she considered rightfully hers. England, in holding the lake posts, was clinging to territory admittedly American under the terms of the peace treaty. She therefore strove to burden the Indians with the onus of keeping the Americans at a distance from the posts and baited her persuasion with glowing but prudently vague promises. This attitude was evident at every level of England's governmental hierarchy. Sir John Johnson, Superintendent General of Indian Affairs for British North America, was writing Brant:

You have no reason to fear any breach of promise on the part of the King. Is he not every year giving fresh proofs of his friendship? . . . Do not suffer bad men or evil advisers to lead you astray; everything that is reasonable and consistent with the friendship that ought to be preserved between us, will be done for you all. Do not suffer an idea to hold a place in your mind, that it will be for your interests to sit still and see the Americans attempt the posts. It is for your sakes chiefly, if not entirely, that we hold them.

Major Matthews, speaking for Lord Dorchester, Governor General of Canada, was writing Brant:

His Lordship cannot begin a war with the Americans, because some of their people encroach and made depredations upon parts of the Indian country; but they must see it is his Lordship's intention to defend the posts; and that while these are preserved, the Indians must find great security therefrom, and consequently the Americans greater difficulty in taking possession of their lands. . . . In your letter to me, you seem apprehensive that the English are not very anxious about the defence of the posts. You will soon be satisfied that they have nothing more at heart, provided that it continues to be the wish of the Indians, and that they remain firm in doing *their* part of the business, by preventing the Americans from coming into their country, and consequently from marching to the posts. . . . Lord Dorchester has been pleased to permit me to take the command of Detroit, which is garrisoned by the regiment I am in, and has ordered that another regiment be sent up for the protection of the posts in general . . so that I think we shall have but little to apprehend from anything in the power of the Americans to attempt.

While the original reply to Brant of Lord Sidney, English Minister for the Colonies, stated:

His Majesty, in consideration of the zealous and hearty exertions of his Indian allies in the support of his cause, and as a proof of his most friendly disposition toward them, has been graciously pleased to consent that the losses already certified by his Superintendent General shall be made good; that a favorable attention shall be shown to the claims of others, who have pursued the same system of conduct; and that Sir Guy Carleton, his Governor General of his American dominions, shall take measures for carrying his royal commands into execution immediately after his arrival at Quebec. This liberal conduct on the part of His Majesty, he trusts, will not leave any doubt upon the minds of his Indian allies that he shall at all times be ready to attend to their future welfare; and that he shall be anxious, upon every occasion wherein their happiness may be concerned, to give them such further testimony of his royal favor and countenance, as can, consistently with a due regard to the national faith, and the honor and dignity of his crown, be afforded to them.

The nature of the support, then, which was provided the Indians by both England and Spain was designed to excite them to commit continual excesses against the frontier and at the same time to dissuade them from attempting decisive campaigns. The precise aim was to discourage and limit the spread of American settlement. This resulted in a test of endurance which lasted thirteen years. It was an excruciating process for both Indians and settlers.

The fourth requirement, the Indian organization of the political means to take united action, was the factor upon which all else depended. No Indian was so simple-minded as to fail to grasp not only the virtue but the absolute necessity of a united front. Every chief and subchief was a voluble advocate of a general confederation. Brant in the north and McGillivray in the south worked incessantly to bring one about. Every nation conferred eagerly with its neighbors. Every year delegations of Northern dignitaries visited Southern council fires and delegations of Southern ambassadors attended the great conferences in the north. Wampum by the yard was unrolled and oratory by the hour delivered. Everybody was for the salvation of confederation. Nobody was against it. Always achievement of the ideal seemed at Indian fingertips. Yet a practical and strategic union of Northern and Southern Indians never emerged from the realm of words to become a consistent guide for action. The constitutional inability of the Indian to remember future commitments and to submit to personal discipline lost him each year much of the progress he had seemed to make the year before. The great opportunity to construct a workable confederation in the 1780's before the United States had itself contrived a workable confederation was lost.

The diplomatic attitudes of Spain and England toward Indian union were not helpful. Spain was definitely opposed to a general Indian confederation, lest the Southern Indians come under the influence of their more belligerent Northern fellows and the whole Indian world come under the sway of England. England assiduously encouraged Indian confederation but until 1794, when it had become too late, made her support contingent upon the confederation's waging a defensive war.

The cause of confederation received other blows. Brant's influence waned, in part due to other chiefs' jealousy of his preeminence and in part to a growing disgust with English vacillation, leading to the suspicion that Brant was too deeply committed to English interests properly to guard Indian interests. McGillivray, too, lost stature as an all-Indian leader as a result of his continuing feuds with the Cherokee and the Chickasaw and of his dabbling in American land company schemes.

An approximate Indian united front was finally brought about, not by Indian political sagacity but by American aggression. The continual advance of the settlers' frontier, the insistence of the United States upon procuring ostensible land cessions by the negotiation of separate treaties with individual Indian nations, and the decision of Congress to authorize settlement northwest of the Ohio, left the Indian no other recourse than to close ranks. This in turn made it apparent that no longer could the settlers be expected to deal on a local basis with an Indian hostility that was universal. The Indians had ceased being a collection of tribes separately subject, theoretically, to state or federal sovereignty and had taken on most of the aspects of a foreign power in conflict with the United States. Upon the struggling new national government therefore was imposed as one of its first and unhappiest tasks the need to back its national diplomacy with the alternative of national war.

XVI. The Regulars to the Rescue

The next most consequential attitude — that of the United States — had for long far less influence on the course of events than that of either settlers or Indians. The fierce stresses of the thirteen years following Yorktown presented another historic test than that of the ability of the settlers west of the mountains to survive. They provided as well a trial of the ability of the federal government to become a government.

Under pressure from the several states, each intent upon guarding its independence and enlarging its importance, Congress began by divesting itself of almost every government function. The feeblest attempt to exercise federal authority was denounced by patriots as big government and a threat to the liberty that had so recently been won. To the men who had fought against England's military power the new government's possession of any military force whatever was a definite ideological error. The smallest federal military establishment was considered a "standing army" and bound to become an "agent of tyranny." Congress speedily disbanded the remnant of Washington's Continental Army.

The war continued in the west but it continued without the enemy being confronted by a single soldier in the uniform or under the flag of the United States. Many Americans were fighting for their lives while the American national government was able to lift not a finger to aid in their defense. The resentment stirred by this failure of their own to support them began to rival any resentment provoked by the enemy. The West was alternately discussing separation and drifting toward Spain but the average westerner did not feel that he was abandoning his country. His country, if he had one, had already abandoned him.

At this unhappy juncture a fortunate turn of circumstances thrust upon the national government a bristling and many-horned problem which no congressional casuistry could find excuse to pigeonhole. England's sudden cession of the West to the United States had included not only the region south and east of the Ohio in which were located the western settlements but the territory northwest of the river which was still occupied by the belligerent coalition of Northern Indians. Congress had been able to let the existing western settlements shift for themselves on the theory that all were within the jurisdiction of one or another of the various states with western land claims. But this cloak of immunity could not be stretched to cover the barbarous country in the northwest.

Every state had clung stubbornly and jealously to its claims below the Ohio but no state wanted any part of the bear's den beyond the river. New York's claim to the Northwest rested on her assertion of jurisdiction over the Iroquois whose claim to the Ohio country rested on conquests of the preceding century. For whatever it was worth New York hastily ceded this claim to the national government even before the end of the Revolution. Virginia's claim rested principally upon Clark's conquest of Kaskaskia and Vincennes which he had made as an officer not of the United States but of Virginia. Virginia followed New York by ceding her claim to everything north of the Ohio, with the thrifty reservation of certain tracts of land earmarked for bounty to her veterans when and if settlement became possible. Congress thus was confronted by the inexorable fact that the one area within the bounds of the United States which was not within the jurisdiction of any of the several states was this grim Indian stronghold. Here was one buck that could not be passed in any direction.

The first congressional reaction was to sidestep. To placate the Indians a resolution was passed forbidding settlement north of the Ohio. But the central problem still remained. It was unthinkable that even so designedly weak a government as that of the United States under the Confederation should permit a vast region, formally pronounced American by the peace treaty, to fail to become American territory through sheer neglect to take possession. And to take possession, even in the most narrowly technical sense, it was necessary to occupy the lake posts. This in turn required the creation of at least a minimum federal military force to garrison the posts, lest they at once revert to the Indians or to fur traders equally unfriendly to the United States. To this, on second thought, another requirement was added. The treaty with England must be supplemented by Indian treaties in which the resident Indians also recognized American sovereignty in the area. Here, too, some federal force was necessary to protect the peace commissioners in their approach to the still hostile Indians. It became self-evident that the so recently disbanded national army had to be in some measure resurrected.

Congress grasped this nettle with the utmost circumspection. To disarm critics of a standing army the states of Connecticut, New York, New Jersey and Pennsylvania were asked to place detachments of their militia, totaling seven hundred men, at the disposal of the federal government. To make certain the force did not become an agent of federal tyranny all officers were to be appointed by the states that furnished the men. The national government's chief role, at first, was the issuing of broad policy directives and there was immediate confusion regarding what proportions of the expenditures involved should be paid by the states and by the nation, providing either found funds available. Pennsylvania, furnishing the largest contingent, had the privilege of appointing the lieutenant colonel to command the regiment and selected Josiah Harmar, an honest, portly, hard-drinking and none too distinguished Revolutionary veteran. Lieutenant Colonel Harmar was ordinarily referred to as General Harmar, since he was the senior officer in active service, and his command became known, though not officially, as the First American Regiment. This first experiment with the National Guard system, in which state militia was called into the federal service, was attempted because soldiers were, in the language of the act, "immediately and indispensably necessary for taking possession of the western posts, as soon as evacuated by the troops of his Britannic Majesty, for the protection of the northwestern frontiers, and for guarding the public stores."

The several companies of militiamen marched laboriously overland from their respective states to Pittsburgh. Provision for their care and supply en route fell between the stools of state and national parsimony. Some light is thrown on the state of federal military organization by a letter of September 30, 1784, from John McDowell, regiment surgeon, to Governor Dickinson of Pennsylvania, informing the governor that:

When the troops marched this morning, three men were left on the ground too sick to go on with the detachment. I am of the opinion that they will be able to follow the regiment in the course of two or three weeks, if they are properly attended to. It is a pity to leave them lying on the ground friendless and money-less. I therefore ordered them, with the advice of Col. Harmar, to be removed to Carpenter's Hall, where they must stay until I have the pleasure of your commands concerning them.

The first company reached Pittsburgh December 5, 1784. Harmar proceeded to reoccupy Fort McIntosh, a Revolutionary frontier defense post on the northernmost bend of the Ohio, and to build Fort Harmar at the mouth of the Muskingum and, somewhat later, Fort Finney, a temporary post near the mouth of the Little Miami. But fulfillment of the principal purpose for raising his force, the occupation of the lake posts, was beyond his reach.

The year before Baron von Steuben, sent with instructions from Washington and Congress to discuss arrangements for the delivery of the posts, had been met at the Canadian border by Governor General Haldimand's bland reply that he had as yet no instructions to give them up. Haldimand's parallel response to the demands of New York for possession of those posts within her borders was that the state had scarcely been a party to the treaty between England and the United States. By the time Harmar reached Pittsburgh the English refusal to relinquish the posts had become revealed as a settled policy. The fur trade had brought its influence to bear in London but there were other factors involved. General Allan Maclean, in charge of supplying the Indians at Niagara, thus voiced the current English concep-tion of England's relationship with the Indians:

The Indians get this day from the King's Stores the bread they are to eat tomorrow, and from his magazines the clothing that covers their nakedness; in short they are not only our allies, but they are a part of our Family; and the Americans might as well (while we are in possession of these Posts) attempt to seduce our children and servants from their duty and allegiance.

Haldimand, in reporting to his government, also placed the matter on security grounds:

To prevent such a disastrous event as an Indian war is a consideration worthy of the attention of both nations, and cannot be prevented so effectually as by allowing the Posts in the Upper Country to remain as they are for some time.

This view was presently endorsed by his government. English policy makers belatedly had realized how precipitate had been the impulse to cede the Northwest during the treaty negotiations. The decision, taken on second thought, to hold the posts, was based upon a determination to maintain the Indian barrier in order to guard the security of Canada by preventing the expansion of American settlement.

With the small force at his command Harmar could not, even had he been so instructed by Congress, make so much as a gesture toward the posts on the lakes, since any move in that direction would have meant he must first fight his way through the Indian country. Instead he set about carrying out his other instructions. Detachments were dispatched to search out and dispossess the American settlers north of the Ohio. Some hundreds of truly hard-bitten frontiersmen had already crossed to commence the cutting of clearings and the building of cabins on the Indian side. Harmar's reports refer frequently to the Indians killing numbers of these "adventurers," as he called them, but it appears that on the whole these most exposed of all settlers were not in much greater jeopardy than their former neighbors on the presumably safer side of the river. It is possible that most Indian raiding parties, free to choose their victims, passed them by in order to attack the richer and less watchful settlements beyond where greater profits were to be had at less risk. It is also possible that the Indians, as became clearly evident a little later, were waiting to see what the American government had in mind and did not at the moment wish to attract unnecessary attention to this most critical of all frontiers. In any event there had not been any concerted Indian attempt to root out the adventurers and some hundreds were left for Harmar to deal with. The soldiers evicted them and in some cases burned their cabins to discourage their return. Thus the first frontier campaign of the new army of the United States was devoted to protecting the interests not of the settlers but of the Indians.

Meanwhile, the peace commissioners appointed to treat with the Northern Indians were at work. The same Congress which had felt unequal to the task of raising an army, which had accepted without serious argument the English decision to hold the posts, and whose dread of Indian hostility had led to the settlers' eviction, paradoxically had instructed the commissioners to require the Indians to open the territory northwest of the Ohio to settlement. The guiding principle seemed to be the hope that the cake could be had and eaten, too — that at one and the same time the United States could have peace with the Indians and possession of Indian lands.

The pressure upon Congress to manage somehow to get the land was politically strong and from several quarters. Northern speculators had begun to see north of the Ohio an opportunity to rival that enjoyed by their southern counterparts south of the Tennessee. There was also a school of economists who argued that federal sale of western lands could be relied upon to pay the national debt and there could be no argument to which any Congress could be more receptive. Congress was perhaps the most susceptible of all to the demands of Revolutionary veterans for their promised bounties which could conceivably be satisfied by doling out western lands to them. This latter agitation had been gathering force and was spotlighted when Washington in 1784 made a tour of his western holdings on the Kanawha which he had accumulated by buying up the bounties of his fellow veterans of the French and Indian War.

With eyes closed, in effect, Congress therefore made the try. The first treaty was a windfall. At Fort Stanwix the Iroquois gladly accepted their presents and handed over title to their former lands northwest of the Ohio which they no longer occupied or controlled. Next, at Fort McIntosh, representatives of the Wyandot, Delaware, Chippewa and Ottawa faced the commissioners. There was more argument here but the Indians were as yet none too certain of their own next moves and quite willing that the Americans should first unveil the nature of their designs. Knowing that there would be no ratification by their national councils the delegates went through the form of signing a treaty opening most of southeast Ohio to settlement. A few months later the recalcitrant Shawnee came to Fort Finney where Clark, as belligerent in the role of peace commissioner as he had ever been as field commander, threatened them until they, too, signed.

These treaties provided sufficient legal excuse for opening the edges of the northwest Indian country to settlement but they were not treaties that produced a cessation of hostilities. The war was to grow fiercer for another ten years before a peace was to be obtained. Evidence of how far the treaties fell short of the Indian surrenders which they presumed to define was that the transactions were conducted in American army posts on the American side of the frontier and not in the wilderness council halls of peoples who had been forced into submission. Moreover, in seeking the treaties at all, Congress had placed the cart before the horse. The primary necessity was to gain possession of the lake posts in the Indians' rear which were their bases of supplies. So long as these were left in English hands the Indians were certain to remain unmanageable. The arrogant English refusal to give up the posts presented a problem from which Congress had flinched but it could not have been one marked by more pains and perils than the accelerating Indian war which was to be the alternative.

The principal immediate result of the treaties was to acquaint the Indians with the enormity of the danger which threatened them. No longer was the frontier to advance by one forest clearing at a time. Now it was to go forward by leaps and bounds, propelled by the authority of the American national government. Indian determination to resist was inflamed. Indian congresses were held at Ouiatanon, Niagara and Detroit to organize their resistance. Brant rushed off to London to enlist English aid.

Meanwhile, government surveyors crossed the Ohio under military guard. This was to be no hit and miss settlement as in Kentucky and Tennessee. All was to be done in a planned and orderly manner. There were to be no more title suits handed down from father to son, no more property boundaries running from the forks of the creek to the oak stub on the hill to the big sycamore by the spring. All was ruled off in neat square townships and sections. When a man bought his land he was to get the exact acreage he had bargained for and a title that would stand.

There remained a more complex difficulty than those presented by soldiers and Indians, English commanders and fur traders, surveyors and speculators, premature settlers and claimant veterans. The country northwest of the Ohio had as yet no government whatever. Every other square mile of American territory could look, willingly or unwillingly, to some state legislature, but this vast section of a continent could look only to Congress. Congress had postponed facing this incongruous and perplexing poser but pressures were accumulating to make further postponement more and more embarrassing.

The little French towns in the Illinois had passed dizzily from the rule of France, to that of England, to that of Virginia, to their present state of no government at all. Unlike American settlements they had no genius for self-government. They kept begging that they be furnished a resident governor of some sort to take charge of their affairs. Their situation had been complicated by the arrival of a number of disorderly and aggressive Americans who disturbed their civil peace and excited their Indian neighbors.

The recently evicted adventurers kept returning to their lands, presenting a growing threat to congressional plans for an orderly settlement. They wanted no government except their own. One of their spokesmen, John Amberson, issued a call to his fellow squatters to hold a convention, in which he set forth:

I do certify that all mankind, agreeable to every constitution formed in America, have an undoubted right to pass into every vacant country, and there to form their constitution, and that from the confederation of the whole United States, Congress is not empowered to forbid them, neither is Congress empowered from that confederation to make any sale of the uninhabited lands to pay the public debts, which is to be by a tax levied and lifted by the authority of each state.

In ceding her claims to the Northwest, Virginia had reserved certain bounty lands for her veterans and before making the cession had granted 150,000 acres across the river from Louisville to Clark and his men. She now proclaimed her principal reserve between the Scioto and the Miami open for settlement. A growing population without a government was in early prospect in both districts.

Kentucky, harassed by Indian raids, was continually sending unauthorized expeditions across the river Ohio in pursuit or retaliation, making infinitely more difficult the national government's relations with the Indians. The Kentuckians could hardly be charged with trespass when the region they entered had no government of its own.

And finally Connecticut, the last of the states to cede its claims in the Northwest, had made its cession, withholding only the famous Western Reserve upon which the city of Cleveland was to rise. The national government no longer had even the nominal excuse of a cloud upon its jurisdiction further to postpone action.

Still Congress hesitated, inhibited by that restriction upon every federal assumption of authority or responsibility which was the basic tenet of the Articles of Confederation. Members of Congress had been disregarding, though with increasing uneasiness, the ticking of these several time bombs when another bomb went off right under their chairs. This was the kind of explosion to produce immediate action. New England, long the foe of western expansion and western emigration, had formed a land company of her own, the new Ohio Company, under the distinguished sponsorship of such men as General Rufus Putnam, General Samuel H. Parsons, and Reverend Manasseh Cutler, and was proposing that the territory across the Ohio be opened to the settlement of thousands of New England veterans. So galvanic was the reaction of Congress that Cutler laid his final proposal before a committee of Congress on July 5 and the Ordinance of 1787 was enacted on July 13.

The famous Ordinance must be regarded as second only to the Constitution among the foundation stones upon which the republic was to rest. The emergency presented a magnificent opportunity to the inspired and creative imaginations of the founding fathers. They were masters of political theory and exponents of political idealism and they had a clean slate upon which to write. A vast expanse of utter wilderness, perhaps eventually to become populous and prosperous, lay before them. It had no existing government to reform or revise, none of the handicaps or obstructions that might persist from former political mistakes or injustices. They rose to the challenge and gave it a government more nearly perfect than any then existing, including the one under which they served. Though they were pressed for time the charter that they drafted was neither sketchy nor theoretical. It covered everything, from such details as the manner in which the next of kin might inherit an estate to such exalted principles as freedom of religion, equality under law, and the prohibition of slavery.

But the overwhelming significance of their achievement lay in the establishment in the Ordinance of the formula for the admission of new states. This had been a right demanded from the beginning by the western settlers but the principle was first fixed in the American system by the Ordinance of 1787. There it was specified that when a newly settled district reached a population of 5000 voting males it was to elect its own General Assembly and send a delegate to Congress and that when the number reached 60,000 it was to be admitted into the union as an equal state. This unique political invention was to provide the opportunity for a natural and healthy growth such as no nation in history has enjoyed.

Further to demonstrate how serious, suddenly, had become its intentions, Congress appointed its own president, Arthur St. Clair, Governor of the Northwest Territory. New England meant business too. On April 7 of the following spring Marietta, the first permanent American settlement across the Ohio, was founded. The new Ohio Company was a new kind of land company. It sold land to actual settlers, selected the kind most likely to succeed under frontier conditions, planned its operations, and followed through with its projects. The arrival of the New Englanders marked a more substantial trend in the field of western settlement. More orderly, more businesslike, more thrifty and less volatile than their forerunners south of the Ohio, they tended to pick a location and stay to develop it. Among them were more builders and fewer movers.

Congress, however, still attempted to evade the Indian issue. Defense of the new frontier was a federal responsibility but adequate military preparations to undertake this responsibility had not been so much as contemplated. Harmar was instructed to beg his militiamen to reenlist in order to keep his already inadequate force in being and St. Clair was authorized to spend $14,000 to "conciliate" the Indians. Without waiting to see what effect this attempt to conciliate might have, the expansion of settlement north of the Ohio meanwhile was encouraged. Other land companies were endorsed. Columbia and Losantiville (presently to be rechristened Cincinnati) were founded.

Indian repudiation of the recent treaties and their formally announced defiance, expressed by their several congresses, brought no response from Congress. The drafting and ratification of the new constitution were under way and Congress could grasp at this new excuse to postpone dealing with problems. For once there appeared a certain virtue in congressional inaction. The Indians, finding their defiance unchallenged, also hesitated, their councils divided between the relative advantages of assuming an offensive or defensive posture. One party advised waiting until England was forced by the developing threat to her own interests to come to their assistance, the other urged a general attack before the new settlements became too strong. The dispute produced indecision. The more belligerent Indians intensified their raids against Kentucky and along the banks of the Ohio. But under the influence of the defensive school few committed depredations upon the weak new border north of the river.

But there was one circumstance which waited upon neither American nor Indian congress. The year 1788 was the year of the Great Migration. Many more settlers were swarming westward than in any former year. Most were headed for Kentucky but a fair number turned northward into the newly opened Ohio country where their arrival edged that frontier nearer the Indian towns and made more imminent as well as more inevitable the crucial clash between the will of the United States and that of the Northern Indian confederacy.

St. Clair devoted his early energies as Governor to the establishment of the local governments authorized by the Ordinance. On July 26 he proclaimed at Marietta the organization of the County of Washington. A witness thus describes the opening of the first Anglo-Saxon court of justice in the Ohio country:

The procession was formed at the Point (where most of the settlers resided) in the following order: 1st, the high Sheriff, with his drawn sword; 2nd, the citizens; 3rd, the officers of the garrison at Fort Harmar; 4th, the members of the bar; 5th, the Supreme Judges; 6th, the Governor and Clergymen; 7th, the newly appointed Judges of the Court of Common Pleas, Generals Rufus Putnam and Benjamin Tupper. They marched up a path that had been cut and cleared through the forest to Campus Martius Hall (stockade) where the whole countermarched, and the Judges took their seats. The Clergyman, Rev. Dr. Cutler, then invoked the divine blessing.

The account goes on to say:

Our first ball was opened about the middle of December, at which were fifteen ladies, as well accomplished in the manners of polite circles as any I have ever seen in the old States. I mention this to show the progress of society in this new world; where I believe we shall vie with, if not excel, the old States, in every accomplishment necessary to render life agreeable and happy.

St. Clair, pressed to get on with his "conciliation" of the Indians, summoned them to a new peace conference at Fort Harmar. Again the Indian representatives who attended, by far the least pretentious batch of delegates that had so far been rounded up for such a purpose, were prevailed upon to sign, but as a gesture of conciliation it was none too successful, for St. Clair had also been pressed by Congress to demand yet more land, though the validity of the cessions that had already been made had been denounced by every Indian nation concerned. The delegates signed, picked up their presents, and went home to sit comfortably among their fellow citizens at Indian conferences which, listening to the speeches of Alexander McKee and his assistant English agents, formally reiterated the Indian declaration that any American settlement northwest of the Ohio was an invasion of Indian territory and a continuing cause for war.

The new national government, taking office under the constitution in the spring of 1789, was beset by so many desperate problems that there was little opportunity to concentrate upon the one in the Northwest. President Washington had a grasp of frontier affairs denied to most easterners but this only made him the more aware that the perils of the new northwestern border were overshadowed by greater perils elsewhere in the west. Not one of the older settlements but was on the verge of revolt nor was there one important western leader, many of them his own personal friends and former trusted lieutenants, who was not actively trading with the Spaniards, seeking to establish Spanish colonies, or participating in intrigues directly aimed at deflecting the West into the Spanish orbit. Considered against such a background, intervention of federal forces in the Indian war remained what Secretary of War Knox had termed in 1787 "an unlimited evil." The basic fear was that the approach of a federal column to the English posts required by any attempt seriously to threaten the Indian centers of resistance might bring on a renewal of the war with England. In assuming the presidency of a new and untried form of government, which was being assailed by every sort of foreign and domestic danger while shackled by a bankrupt treasury and supported by a scant majority of its people, Washington had taken on a heavier burden than he had known at Valley Forge.

However, Kentucky's continual counter raids across the river against the Indians, so often and so ineffectually forbidden by federal authority, presently made it clear that continued federal inaction could but make the situation worse. The national government reluctantly prepared to act. Harmar's rag-tag little army was transferred in name as well as fact to the federal establishment, though this meant no increase in numbers or improvement in supply, and Harmar was authorized to build and garrison the more advanced post at Cincinnati which became Fort Washington. Next, St. Clair was told that if the worst came to the worst he might call out the western militia to serve under federal command but that first he must make another endeavor to persuade the Indians to consider peace.

This faint stir of federal activity included a glance at the southern frontier where for the past two years Indian attacks had been even more persistent than along the Ohio. Major John Doughty, the most able junior officer in Harmar's command, was detached with a small force and sent up the Tennessee to visit the Chickasaw, reassure them that they had chosen wisely in electing to ally themselves with the United States, and make arrangements for furnishing them with trade goods to replace those withheld from them by English and Spanish disapproval of their diplomatic heresy. Though Doughty was his friend, Wilkinson betrayed him by giving Miro and McGillivray advance notice of the expedition. As a special object lesson to the Chickasaw, a body of Creek and Cherokee overwhelmed Doughty and drove him not only from the Tennessee but across the Mississippi, where he was given hypocritically sympathetic asylum by the Spanish authorities at New Madrid. Such was the result of the first appearance of federal troops on the southern frontier.

St. Clair set about conscientiously making a final effort to win a peace with the Northern Indians. It was incumbent upon him to learn the "true sentiments" of the Indians, to ascertain to what extent their repeated expressions of defiance represented a genuine determination to resist. He was at his wits' end to determine what stone next to turn. It had been proved impossible to persuade any of their major chiefs to attend the "peace conferences" held in army posts along the Ohio and it was considered unsafe to send American commissioners to their towns. As a last resort St. Clair employed the services of a neutral emissary, a respectable French trader of Vincennes, Anthony Gamelin.

Gamelin made his way into the Indian country where he was given a ready hearing by the principal chiefs, though he was forced to make his representations in the presence of anti-American French and English traders. The Indian reply, in keeping with the traditional evasiveness of Indian diplomacy, was that they could give him no reply. If he was in a hurry for an answer, they said, he should go to Detroit to get it for they could not treat with the Americans except with the consent and advice of their English allies. When he attempted to press them, they challenged him to name one chief who had signed the recent Fort Harmar treaty. Not representative delegates but only unimportant and mischievous young men had agreed to that pact, they said, and it was without effect.

Gamelin returned to report his failure and upon his heels came news that scarcely had he left their council fire than the Indians had added emphasis to their challenge by formally burning an American captive in it. St. Clair realized that time had run out. There was no longer any possible alternative to the recognition that a state of war existed not only between the Indians and the settlers but between the Indians and the United States. The national government must proceed by military force to require the Indians to abide by the recent treaties and to cease their attacks upon either new or old settlements, he advised.

Washington's anxious gaze was fixed on a wider picture which included the then imminent Yazoo-Nootka threat of an English advance down the Mississippi Valley against the Spanish possessions. Hamilton was of the opinion that this was no time further to excite the English by launching a federal military expedition in their direction but Jefferson felt the assembling of such an expedition might have a salutory effect in giving the English the idea that we were prepared to resist their contemplated descent of the Mississippi. Washington took a middle ground, approving a campaign against the Indians but instructing St. Clair to take the greatest care to notify Detroit that no hostility against England was intended and that particularly he had no intention of attacking the lake posts.

That spring of 1790, Congress had established a War Department, retaining Knox as Secretary of War and Harmar as senior field officer. An army was created with the until then novel proviso that every commissioned and enlisted member must take an oath of allegiance to the United States. The strength of the army was raised to 1,216 enlisted men, to receive $2 per month in pay and "one pound of beef or three quarters of a pound of pork, one pound of bread or flour and half a gill of rum, brandy or whisky, daily, and two quarts of vinegar, two pounds of soap and one pound of candles every hundred days." St. Clair issued his authorized call for Pennsylvania and Kentucky militia to reinforce his federal troops and instructed Harmar to begin organizing the first offensive Indian campaign initiated by the United States since Sullivan's memorable punishment of the Iroquois in 1779. It was taken for granted that this one would prove as successful.

Harmar gathered his forces at Fort Washington, the militia, as usual, coming in more slowly than expected, and his supplies accumulating even more slowly, owing to the circumstance that most of Kentucky's surplus provisions were en route down the Mississippi to Wilkinson's Spanish market at New Orleans. On the last day of September Harmar marched out of Fort Washington with 1100 militia and 320 regulars, his column in continuing disorder on account of the lack of discipline among the militia and bitter jealousy between militia and regular officers.

The Indians, adopting their customary tactic, fell back, waiting for what might seem to them an opportune moment to strike. Advancing without opposition, Harmar burned a string of Miami towns on the upper Maumee, in what is now northeastern Indiana, together with large stores of corn. Unhappily, the Indians had in the meantime stolen so many of his horses that he had lost his freedom of movement and he decided to withdraw while he could. Colonel John Hardin, senior militia commander, with a detachment of 340 militia and 60 regulars, was belligerently searching the surrounding woods for Indians to fight when he found more than he wanted. Little Turtle, the Indian commander, had found what he wanted — exactly the opportunity for which he had been waiting. The flexible Indian battle line, admirably adapted to the conditions of forest warfare and under the constant control of platoon leaders who transmitted their orders by piercing whistles, one moment appearing to give way, the next charging viciously, remained most of the time invisible while maintaining an unrelenting blast of rifle fire which seemed to come from all sides at once. These were tactics with which only the most experienced Indian fighters could cope. But there were too few such old hands on this field. The militia, confused by this sudden uproar of whistles, war whoops and gunshots, which seemed less a human assault than a kind of eruption of the smoke-wreathed forest itself, broke and scattered, the most of them, according to reports of Captain Joseph Ashton and Lieutenant John Armstrong, without firing a shot. The few regulars present stood their ground and were cut to pieces. Overtaking the main column Hardin angrily begged for a second chance. He was given one. The result was more disastrous than the first. Again the militia broke and again the outnumbered regulars bore the brunt of the action.

Harmar continued his withdrawal to Fort Washington, convinced that his campaign had been if not a triumph a solid success. It was true that he had lost 183 killed and that more than half of the fallen had been regulars most difficult to replace but he had penetrated into the heart of the Indian country, had burned a number of their towns, had destroyed thousands of bushels of corn, and had killed, he estimated, some hundreds of Indians. St. Clair reported the campaign to Washington as completely successful and a "terrible stroke" which must have had a profound effect upon the Indians.

Actually, the main impression left with the Indians had been the ease with which they had driven the Americans from two fields of battle. The loss of their houses and corn represented to them no more than a nuisance affliction. The one loss considered by Indians to be vital was a loss of human life, upon which they set a supreme value when it was the loss of one of their own. It was the Indian concept that no victory could be glorious if it were gained at the cost of many fallen warriors. As an Indian once succinctly put the case to a white critic: "If you were so brave as to kill a bear while the bear was killing your father and your son would you then dance with delight?" Hardin had been routed twice with an Indian loss of less than twenty. For long the Indians had been dreading the great blow so often threatened by the government of the United States. It had been an apprehension that had shadowed all their councils. Now the blow had

FORT HARMAR IN 1790. The Ohio River is to the right and the Muskingum at the left. The site of Marietta is on the farther bank of the Ohio. Lithograph after a drawing by Joseph Gilman

AN AMERICAN LOG HOUSE IN 1796.
Engraving by Pierre Alexandre (?) Tardieu
from the drawing by Victor Collot

View of Marietta, 1796.
Engraving by Pierre Alexandre (?) Tardieu
from the drawing by Victor Collot

A Typical Flatboat of the Western Waters.
Engraving by Pierre Alexandre (?) Tardieu
after the drawing of Victor Collot

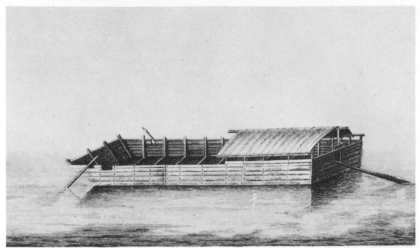

VIEW OF THE RAPIDS
OF THE OHIO AND LOUISVILLE
FROM CLARKSVILLE, 1796.
Engraving by Pierre Alexandre (?)
Tardieu from the drawing by
Victor Collot

A FRENCH HOUSE IN THE ILLINOIS COUNTRY, 1796. Engraving by Pierre Alexandre (?) Tardieu after the drawing by Victor Collot

JOSEPH BRANT. Painting by George Catlin after the portrait by Ezra Ames

PAYTAKOOTHA (FLYING CLOUD), A DISTINGUISHED SHAWNEE WARRIOR.
Lithograph by Lehman and Duval from the painting by Charles Bird King

CATAHECASSA (BLACKHOOF), PRINCIPAL CHIEF OF THE SHAWNEE. Lithograph by Lehman and Duval from the painting by Charles Bird King

TOOANTUH OR DUSTU (SPRING FROG), A CHEROKEE CHIEF. Painted and lithographed by L. T. Bowen Lithographic Establishment

Copyright 1940, by University of Oklahoma Press

THE CHARCOAL DANCE OF THE OSAGES. Reproduced from *Tixier's Travels on the Osage Prairies*, edited by John Francis McDermott

CUT-OFF RIVER, A BRANCH OF THE WABASH. From the painting by Charles Bodmer

been delivered, with the effect of demonstrating how little they had had to fear.

Evidence of their new confidence came swiftly and terribly. On January 2, 1791 they began, for the first time, a series of concerted attacks upon the new settlements in the Northwest which were under the direct protection of the national government and redoubled their efforts against the river traffic on the Ohio. The time had come, they felt, to restore the line of the Ohio and to hold it. Now New England settlers began to experience fully what the other settlements had so long suffered. Now the scalp halloo was ringing in their ears, the smoke of burning homes was drifting across their fields, and children were dying in their dooryards. General Rufus Putnam wrote Washington:

Our situation is truly critical; the Governor and Secretary both being absent, no assistance from Virginia or Pennsylvania can be had. The garrison at Fort Harmar, consisting at this time of little more than twenty men, can afford no protection to our settlements, and the whole number of men, in all our settlements, capable of bearing arms, including all civil and military officers, do not exceed two hundred and eighty-seven, and these, many of them, badly armed. We are in the utmost danger of being swallowed up. . . . We are a people so far detached from all others, in point of situation, that we can hope for no timely relief, in case of emergency, from any of our neighbors; and among the number that compose our present strength, almost one half are young men, hired into the country, intending to settle by and by; these, under present circumstances, will probably leave us soon, unless prospects should brighten; and, as to new settlers, we can expect none in our present situation; so that, instead of increasing in strength, we are likely to diminish daily; and, if we do not fall a prey to the savages, we shall be so reduced and discouraged as to give up the settlement, unless Government shall give us timely protection.

The new Indian assaults gave new food for thought to public opinion in the east. Formerly many easterners had felt that the western settler might better have stayed home, that he was the aggressor and the Indian his victim. This tacit sympathy with the Indian cause began now to fade. To New England, as well as to

Pennsylvania, Virginia and North Carolina, came reports and letters detailing the pitiable murder of friends and relatives. Moreover, the Indian war was no longer a sectional affair. Indian hostility had become an affront to the national honor.

Congress bestirred itself. A second regular regiment of infantry was provided for and to the federal military establishment were added a major general, brigadier general, brigade major, quartermaster and chaplain. The sum of $312,686 was appropriated to cover the expenses of another expedition which was to be adequate beyond question. St. Clair was directed himself to take command and to make certain that this time the Indians were properly chastised.

While St. Clair was laboriously organizing his great effort, impeded by want of supplies and heart-breaking delays in the arrival of the men and equipment to be furnished by the new federal military establishment, Kentucky, with his sanction, impatiently aimed independent blows at the Indian enemy. Expeditions of volunteer Kentuckians, the one under Wilkinson who had suddenly determined to add a military reputation to his other distinctions, the other under General Charles Scott, crossed the Ohio, moved into the edges of the Indian country, burned a number of towns, and withdrew without becoming involved in general engagements. The principal effect was to deepen the impression on the border that the settlers were better able to deal with the Indians without the slow moving help of the regulars. The Indians waited, their attention fixed on St. Clair.

After many delays, St. Clair began his ponderous northward march September 17. Retarded by the late fall rains and by pauses to build forts to guard his line of communications, it was November 3 before he reached the headwaters of the Wabash, still far short of the advance made by Harmar. His effective force had dwindled to 1400, owing to the number of troops left behind to garrison the forts, to sickness, to desertions, and to forces detached to pursue the deserters. The watchful Indian commanders again saw their opportunity. This time Little Turtle and his companion war chiefs, with the instinct of born field marshals, shifted their tactics to achieve a different kind of a surprise. Instead of waiting for the invaders to blunder into some wilderness trap they themselves suddenly took the offensive. Moving across the frozen, snow-covered ground, they assaulted St. Clair's sprawling camp at daybreak, overran his outposts, broke each successive line of resistance that he attempted to set up, captured his artillery and all of his stores, and drove him back southward in utter rout.

St. Clair, attempting, as soldier and commander, to account for the disaster, said, in his report to Secretary of War Knox:

I have nothing, sir, to lay to the charge of the troops, but their want of discipline, which, from the short time they had been in service, it was impossible they should have acquired, and which rendered it very difficult, when they were thrown into confusion, to reduce them again to order, and is one reason why the loss has fallen so heavy on the officers, who did everything in their power to effect it. . . . I have said, sir, in a former part of this letter, that we were overpowered by numbers. Of that, however, I have no other evidence but the weight of the fire, which was always a most deadly one, and generally delivered from the ground — few of the enemy showing themselves afoot, except when they were charged; and that, in a few moments our whole camp, which extended above three hundred and fifty yards in length, was entirely surrounded and attacked on all quarters.

In the greatest former Indian victory over white troops Braddock had lost 714 killed and wounded. St. Clair lost 890. It was without doubt the most complete defeat in battle ever suffered by an American army.

St. Clair, as sick at heart as he had been sick in body throughout the campaign, following in the path of his fleeing army, saw the ground littered with rifles thrown away by his panic-stricken men. The remnant safely reached the refuge of Fort Washington. For the triumphant Indians, as was so often their way, failed to exploit their great victory. They lingered on the battlefield to collect the spoils and to torment the wounded. Among the victims were some 30 women camp followers who were put to death by forcing wooden stakes into their bodies. The Indians then scattered to their towns to celebrate.

Nevertheless, the disastrous culmination of the two years of federal determination to break Indian resistance was to open the whole west to such opportunities as the Indians might choose now to seize. Such a thrill of dismay as had not been known since 1782 swept along the frontier. The new menace was not confined to the Ohio, Kentucky, Tennessee and Georgia frontiers. The borders, also, of Pennsylvania, Virginia and North Carolina, where people had come in recent years to consider themselves relatively secure, again experienced the terrors of anticipation and the shocks of attack.

Pittsburgh, by now commonly considered an interior town, earnestly memorialized Governor Mifflin of Pennsylvania:

At present we have neither garrison, arms, nor ammunition to defend the place. If the enemy should be disposed to pursue the blow they have given, which it is morally certain they will, they would, in our situation, find it easy to destroy us; and, should this place be lost, the whole country is open to them, and must be abandoned.

The people of the southwestern counties of Pennsylvania thus memorialized the governor:

Your Excellency is well aware of the great extent of our frontier; and, when you consider the high degree of spirit which the savages, animated by two successive victories, entertain, you may more easily conceive, than we can describe, the fears which pervade the breasts of those men, women and children, who are more immediately subject to their barbarities and depredations.

The people of Virginia's County of Ohio petitioned their governor:

In the course of last year, upwards of fifty of our people were killed, and a great part of our country plundered, notwithstanding the aid afforded by the Pennsylvanians, who joined the Virginians in our defence. The success of the Indians in their late engagement with General St. Clair will, no doubt, render them more daring and bold in their future incursions and attacks upon our defenceless inhabitants.

Nobody, however, seemed to see any point in petitioning the national government for succor.

The news of the Indian triumph in the north stirred the Southern Indians into a comparable frenzy of jubilation. The successive defeats of Harmar and St. Clair were accepted as convincing evidence that Indians, when they exerted themselves, were masters of the Americans. The doctrine of a concerted North-South attack upon the whites was preached with new fervor. Dragging Canoe rushed to McGillivray with the cry, "Now is the time." McGillivray was willing. The Chickasaw balked, clinging to their unique policy of peace with the Americans and war upon fellow Indians who disagreed with them. But despite this setback the cause of general Indian confederation attracted more earnest support and more nearly approached achievement than ever before.

Hector, Baron de Carondelet, the new Spanish governor, arrived at New Orleans just in time to hear of St. Clair's defeat. He, too, was convinced by this indication of Indian military prowess and, abandoning his predecessor's cautious policy, openly encouraged the Indians to unite and to strike. He hopefully foresaw sepoy-like regiments of Indians, equipped with Spanish arms and fighting for Spanish interests, sweeping the Americans out of the Mississippi Valley. Engaged in such heady discussions as these, the excited Indians rushed from council to council and interrupted their consultations only to redouble, both in number and ferocity, their assaults upon the southern frontier.

The regulars had come to the rescue. But they had failed signally to cement the bonds between the West and the Atlantic states or to enhance, either in the eyes of the settlers or the Indians, the prestige of the national government.

XVII. Frantic Appeasement

THE NEWS of the St. Clair disaster, reaching Philadelphia in mid-December, came as a stunning blow in more than a military sense. It also cut the ground from under the new national government's belated but earnest save the West policy.

Washington, upon taking office, had recognized the urgency of the need to counteract the separatist movement in the west and to reassure the westerners that the East was neither jealous of nor opposed to the West's legitimate aspirations. The administration possessed few resources to attempt much that was immediate and positive but a persistent propaganda effort was made to disarm western discontent, to cater to western prejudices, and to persuade western opinion that future support and protection was the certain reward of continued patience. The stamp of this new effort was upon every early federal act relating to the West.

Jefferson, a recognized western sympathizer, was brought into the cabinet to balance the inclusion of Hamilton and even Hamilton did his bit by announcing his repudiation of the eastern doctrine of acquiescence in Spain's closure of the Mississippi. Congress was induced to appropriate money for the Harmar and St. Clair campaigns. North Carolina having at long last ceded her western lands, thus freeing Cumberland but at the same time leaving the district more than ever exposed, a federal Southwest Territory was organized as assurance that the United States was prepared presently to accept the same responsibility to defend that border as the northern. As further solace to the southern frontier, the hotbed of separatism, federal bribes and threats were brought to bear on the Creek and Cherokee to extract from them new treaties more acceptable to the settlers. Congress kept up the good work by voting, after so many years of beating about the bush, to admit Kentucky as a state.

But in no respect was the national government's new eagerness to mellow the West's temper more extravagantly shown than in its endeavor to recapture the goodwill of the more obstreperous western leaders. Those eminent westerners who were most actively participating in land schemes, separatist movements, and Spanish intrigues were singled out for federal approval and federal preferment. Wilkinson was given a commission as lieutenant colonel commandant in the United States Army (he chose the occasion to dun his Spanish employers for more money on the plea that he was now in a position to prove of greater service to them), together with the promise, soon kept, of unlimited promotion; Blount was made Governor of the Southwest Territory and Superintendent of Indian Affairs for the Southwest; Sebastian was appointed United States attorney-general for the district of Kentucky; Innes was appointed federal judge; and Sevier and Robertson were commissioned brigadier generals in control, under Blount, of military affairs on the southern frontier.

This congenial platform of all is forgiven and from now on everybody is on the same team was abruptly upended by the St. Clair catastrophe. An agonizing reappraisal of the national government's western commitments became imperative. The bad news produced another revulsion of feeling in the east. The new land companies, whose beginnings in the northwest had seemed so auspicious, had fallen into financial difficulties, accompanied, in some instances, by charges of embezzlement and stock manipulation. Two of their officials, Colonel William Duer and Richard Platt, were actually in jail. Wide and sympathetic eastern attention had been attracted to the plight of the colony of French families, lured across the Atlantic by land company misrepresentations and unhappily planted at Gallipolis on the wild shores of the Ohio, where, totally unsuited to frontier conditions, they were cowering under Indian threats and slowly starving to death. The current financial panic engulfing many eastern business houses was associated in the public mind with the recent fever of speculation in western lands. Even Jefferson, the friend of the West, was moved to declare: "The credit and fate of the nation seem to hang on the desperate throws and plunges of gambling scoundrels." The inclination in the east was to lump all their troubles and load them on the West. Oliver Wolcott voiced in Congress the revival of general eastern disapprobation: "These western people are a violent and unjust race in many respects, unrestrained by law and considerations of public policy." All in all, the East was in no mood to pay wartime taxes to continue to bail out western land grabbers and Indian baiters.

Under whatever compulsions of fiscal embarrassment and eastern opinion, the national government promptly shelved its policy of appeasing the West and undertook in its stead even more earnestly to appease the Indians. In the hour of crisis the interests not of the frontiersmen but of their enemies were to be served. The first necessity was some approach to the baffling task of establishing any kind of contact with the Indians in order to assure them that the United States wanted peace with them at almost any price. Resort was had to agents and go-betweens of every description.

Peter Pond and William Stedman, the former an Indian trader whose background might lend color to the assumption that the mission was private and commercial, were employed to make their way into the Indian country, where they were to spy out Indian strength and, more important, were, according to their official instructions, to "insinuate upon all favorable occasions the humane disposition of the United States; and, if you can by any means ripen their judgment, so as to break forth openly, and declare the readiness of the United States to receive, with open arms, the Indians, notwithstanding all that has passed, *do it.*" Reverend Samuel Kirkland, famous missionary to the Iroquois, Reverend John Heckewelder, great Moravian apostle to the Delaware, and Hendrick, the celebrated, semi-Americanized chief of the Stockbridge Indians, were all solicited to spread the gospel of the United States' peaceful intentions.

The official intercession of the Iroquois was sought in the hope that they might use their traditional influence in the Indian world to restrain the belligerency of their Ohio neighbors. During the Revolution the Iroquois ravages along the frontier had been more violent and cruel than those of any other Indians. For years they had burned and massacred and once had carried their depredations to within sight of the city of New York. But in this postwar emergency their favor was anxiously courted. They were begged to send a delegation to the capital in order that by face-to-face contacts with the heads of the American government they might be convinced of the sincerity of the American desire for peace.

Repeated and personal appeals were made to Brant, the great Indian champion of Indian resistance, to accept the role of mediator between the United States and the Ohio confederacy which he himself had founded. He was promised special treatment and a conference with President Washington, if he would consent to come to Philadelphia. There was the intimation that this might be considered a meeting of equals who, it was hoped, might discover a mutual inclination to compose their differences.

Chief reliance, however, was placed upon a direct approach to the Indian enemy. General Rufus Putnam, of the Ohio settlements, Colonel John Hardin of Kentucky, and Major Alexander Trueman of the United States Army were directed to enter the Indian country under flags of truce and to request an Indian hearing for the American peace proposals. The basic message that they were instructed to deliver to the Indians was:

Brothers: The President of the United States entertains the opinion that the war which exists is founded in error and mistake on your parts. That you believe the United States want to deprive you of your lands, and drive you out of the country. Be assured this is not so; on the contrary, that we should be greatly gratified with the opportunity of imparting to you all the blessings of civilized life. . . . The President of the United States requests you . . . to reflect how abundantly more it will be for your interests to be at peace with the United States, and to receive all the benefit thereof, than to continue a war, which, however flattering it may be to you for a moment, must, in the end, prove ruinous. This desire of peace has not arisen in consequence of the late defeat of the troops under Major General St. Clair. . . . Do not suffer the advantages you have gained to mislead your judgment, and to influence you to continue the

war. . . . *Remember that no additional lands will be required
of you, or any other tribe, to those that have been ceded by
former treaties* . . . and the faith of the United States is hereby
pledged to you for the true and liberal performance of everything herein contained and suggested.

Meanwhile St. Clair had come over the mountains to demand
a court of inquiry and Wilkinson had been left the senior officer
in the west. In February he led an expedition into the snow-
bound Indian country to the corpse-strewn site of the great
defeat, noted evidences of the fearful torments that had been
inflicted upon wounded and prisoners, buried the dead, and
safely withdrew. Following this exploit he was promoted to
brigadier general. St. Clair, held personally blameless by a
congressional committee, was forced to resign his military command but was retained as governor.

Despite the array of anxiously pressed peace offers it was
realized that the Indians might doubt the good faith of the
United States, especially the solemn declaration that no more
land would ever be required of them, that all negotiations might
fail, and that minimum preparations for carrying on the war
must be considered. Jefferson proposed the establishment of a
fortified port in the vicinity of the present Erie, Pennsylvania,
and the creation of a fleet to seize command of the waters of
Lake Erie. Hamilton opposed this as certain to lead to war with
England. A more popular plan was the construction of a line of
forts to shield the frontier against Indian attacks. But Washington, the veteran commander, knew the inadequacy of a purely
defensive posture. His decision was to begin to prepare for an
eventual offensive against the Indians, though not against England, but to withhold action during the peace talks. Congress
was persuaded to vote funds for a reorganization of the army.
The new army, Knox's brain child, was to take the shape of a
"legion" of five thousand regulars, backed by an organized reserve of state militia. Except in the west the militia reserve was
never organized and enlistment in the Legion fell far short of the
authorized total. After an anxious canvas of available candidates,
Wayne, a veteran Revolutionary general whose nickname of
"Mad Anthony" reflected not upon his intelligence but upon his

vigor in battle, was appointed to command the new army. It was an appointment bitterly opposed by some and approved by few but Washington knew his man. He needed a commander in the west who, whatever his other faults or virtues, had enough of the old soldier in him to obey orders.

Wayne's sole task for months and years to come was merely to drill and to organize, for the administration clung to the hope that he might never have to take the field. He was made to wait while peace was offered, sought, begged, pursued and implored. The other cheek was turned not once but a hundred times. Seldom until our own time has a nation struggled so pacifistically to get out of getting on with a war. The confused and abortive negotiations dragged on through the summer and the winter, another summer and another winter, while Wayne was strictly enjoined to make no move that might conceivably be construed as an aggressive gesture and, though Indian raids were continuous, the Kentuckians were as strictly forbidden to cross the Ohio and the Tennesseeans to cross their border, in pursuit of their respective Indian tormentors.

The achievements of this headlong pursuit of peace scarcely measured up to the effort exerted. Pond and Stedman were detained by the English at Niagara and failed to get into the Indian country at all. Kirkland, Heckewelder and Hendrick were able to bring their influence to bear only upon those fringes of Indian opinion already disposed to be neutral or pacifist.

The Iroquois delegates, some fifty of them, came to Philadelphia, delighted with the novelty of viewing strange sights, with the pleasure of receiving presents, with the opportunity to show off in conference, and with the satisfaction of eating and drinking their fill. Much eloquence was displayed on both sides and many noble sentiments were reiterated. It was an axiom of Indian diplomacy, as with that of the Communists today, that peace and peace only was forever their dearest aim and that their hearts overflowed with loving kindness for all mankind. The Iroquois left after vague promises to remain neutral and, when the occasion arose, to reason with their recalcitrant Ohio brethren.

Brant also came, after waiting until he had been sufficiently assured that his treatment would be on the order of that accorded a foreign chief of state and until the other Iroquois had come and gone so that he might be the center of attention. His trip was somewhat more eventful. While crossing the New York frontier, where he was remembered as the active partisan leader of some of the most bloody Indian-Tory outrages perpetrated during the Revolution, he was in some danger from the local inhabitants and, in spite of his official escort, in one instance was obliged to hide in a cellar. One vengeful frontiersman followed him to New York City in the hope of finding an opportunity to shoot him down in the street and was deeply puzzled by the city police warning that to shoot an Indian would be considered a crime. However, once past the frontier Brant discovered the Americans more ready to forget the recent past. In New York the press said:

On Monday last arrived in this city, from his settlement on Grand River, on a visit to some of his friends in this quarter, Captain Joseph Brant of the British army, the famous Mohawk chief who so eminently distinguished himself during the late war as the military leader of the Six Nations. We are informed that he intends to visit the city of Philadelphia, and pay his respects to the President of the United States.

In Philadelphia there was the same readiness to receive as a distinguished visitor the man who so recently had been considered a bloodthirsty and inhuman monster. He accepted all attentions with the smiling calm of a cosmopolite who had known the amenities of more than one London season. The English had attempted to prevent his American visit lest he come under American influence but apparently they need not have feared. He later claimed that the Americans had offered him a thousand guineas down, double the pension he received from England, and an ultimate reward of 20,000 pounds if he succeeded in arranging a peace with his fellow Indians. Officially, his meetings with Washington and his advisors were devoted to their attempt to convince him that the United States wanted no more Indian land and to his eventual consent to take this word to the Ohio Indians, which later he failed to do on the excuse of illness.

The attempt at direct negotiations in the west were as ineffectual as this search for go-betweens, and tragic in the bargain. Putnam, though he was shepherded by Heckewelder, prudently remained in the safety of Fort Knox at Vincennes where he worked out with representatives of several lesser tribes a treaty of partial neutrality which was repudiated by the United States Senate because it included a defined relinquishment of certain land claims. Both Hardin and Trueman, though making their separate approaches in the capacity of ambassadors, a role always before deeply respected by Indian protocol, were murdered in the wilderness before they reached the Indian councils which they had hoped to attend.

The results, then, of the first year's diplomatic struggle to escape further fighting approximated zero. The situation had deteriorated rather than improved. The Northern Indians, emboldened by so many signs of American weakness, sent delegations to the Southern Indians, accompanied by English secret agents, to preach the impassioned doctrine that the time had come for the Indian world to strike as one. The Southern Indians, whose operations had been considered a secondary theatre of the Indian war, struck more violent blows against their frontier in 1792 than in any former year.

To the increased Indian tension were added new international tensions. In the north, England, disturbed by the appointment of Wayne whose military capacity she had reason to remember, was strengthening her position on the lakes and more openly exciting the Indians to resist. To take personal charge of Indian and military affairs, Colonel John Graves Simcoe, a distinguished career officer and veteran of the Revolution, was made Lieutenant Governor of the new province of Upper Canada with headquarters at Niagara. As further evidence of English stiffening, Hammond suggested the creation of a neutral Northwest Territory with the integrity of Indian boundaries guaranteed by both England and the United States. The concern felt by Washington's administration that a new collision with the Indians could mean a collision with England was no more than natural in the face of England's curiously anomalous attitude. There can be little doubt that England, foreseeing imminent war with France, was at the moment basically as averse to war in North

America as was the United States. It was studied English policy to maintain her freedom of action by repeatedly warning the Indians that English troops could not be expected to come to their assistance. But the English, too, wanted to have their cake and eat it. They continued to supply the Indians and their western agents continued to undermine every peace effort.

In the south, Carondelet had cast away any remaining hope of enticing western leaders into the Spanish camp by taking in the Indians in their stead. In a treaty negotiated at New Orleans, to which McGillivray, the King of the Creeks, and Panton, the greatest English trader, were the chief other parties, Carondelet promised to supply the Indians with sufficient arms and other support not only to defend themselves but to undertake an organized offensive to regain their lost lands. This abrupt Spanish disavowal of the movement toward uniting the West to Spain merely altered the nature of the national government's apprehensions. For the West, returning happily to its natural antipathy to everything Spanish, began at once making new plans for independent conquest of New Orleans.

Few features of the darkening scene on every frontier missed the anxious eyes in Philadelphia. Washington wrote Jefferson of his strong suspicions "that there is a very clear understanding in all this business between the Courts of London and Madrid; and that it is calculated to check, as far as they can, the rapid increase, extension, and consequence of this country." Faced with the possibility, if not the probability, of war with England or Spain, or both, piled on the Indian war, Washington and his advisers clung doggedly to the policy of continued negotiations in the hope, at the worst, of postponing the issue.

The great Indian congress at the forks of the Auglaize and Maumee Rivers in the fall of 1792 offered a faint gleam not so much of new hope as of a new chance for further postponement. The tremendous conclave was attended not only by the Ohio confederates and the Iroquois but by scores of other nations, from Canada, from the south, and from regions to the northwest, some so distant that their delegations had been many months en route. The Iroquois, who had experienced defeat as well as victory in their innumerable wars with the whites, extended the congress some fatherly advice. They criticized the murder of the peace envoys, pointed to the vastly superior number of the Americans, and suggested that the sheer weight of numbers, even of a people who did not want to fight, should be kept in mind. They were hooted down by the confederates. The war advocates admitted the killing of Hardin and Trueman had been a reflection upon Indian honor but they insisted that these had been the unplanned acts of irresponsible individuals and they bitterly recalled how often in the past, as in the case of Old Tassel, the Americans has assassinated Indian ambassadors. After long discussion the congress repeated the former Indian denunciations of the treaties of Fort McIntosh, Fort Finney and Fort Harmar, proclaimed the Ohio still to be the Indian boundary, and demanded that it be restored by the removal of all white settlements on their side. However, the ultimatum was accompanied by one slight qualification and a term was brought up with which we have become so unhappily familiar today. An armistice was offered, on condition that Wayne's forces be withdrawn across the Ohio. The Indian congress also resolved to reconvene in the spring and offered then to listen to any proposals the American government might wish to make in connection with the restoration of the Indian boundary.

Though the Indian terms were considered unacceptable and the Indian armistice offer was somewhat clouded by a coincidental Indian attack on one of Wayne's supply trains with a loss, keenly felt by Congress, of $15,000 worth of government property, Washington's administration clutched at the excuse to resume negotiations. Wayne was instructed to issue an armistice proclamation directing all Americans, particularly the Kentuckians, to cease hostilities. Benjamin Lincoln, Timothy Pickering, and Beverly Randolph, figures of national reputation, were appointed Peace Commissioners to meet with the Indians and to make a new and more persistent effort to reach an agreement.

The difficulties and delays, evasions and equivocations, subterfuges and tricks, which the commissioners encountered in their quest again have a familiar ring today. They were divided from the representatives of the nations with which they had to deal by so many differences in race, language, and political, moral and ideological points of view as to constitute an abyss across which no bridge of mutual understanding could be thrown, while they were hopelessly handicapped by the activities of aggressive groups on both sides who were determined that there should be no concessions and therefore no peace.

Warned by the fate of Hardin and Trueman, they did not even attempt to contact the Indians directly by way of the wilderness. Instead they proceeded first to Niagara from which point they could make their approach under the official protection of the English authorities. Thereafter what they said to the Indians and what the Indians said to them was largely controlled by what the English wanted either party to hear. Simcoe received them courteously and entertained them hospitably. But the delays commenced at once. The Indian congress had resumed its sessions on the Maumee and the commissioners realized that they must get to it early enough in the season to provide time for Wayne to take the field before the fall rains. The threat of his advance, whether or no he was yet prepared to make one, was the one card the commissioners had to play when they confronted the Indian delegates. Simcoe and his Indian agent and fur trade advisers were equally aware of this. On one pretext or another the commissioners were kept at Niagara the better part of two months.

They had no alternative, for their transportation and their safety were alike dependent upon their English protectors. Certain die-hard elements among the Indians, determined at whatever cost to prevent a peace, were threatening the new envoys with the fate met by Hardin and Trueman. In the circumstances the commissioners were obliged to welcome as well as to accept the personal guardianship of John Butler, Alexander McKee and Matthew Elliott, the three most notorious Tory commanders of frontier-ravaging Indian attacks during the Revolution and, since then, the principal instigators of continuing Indian hostility.

The commissioners once were allowed to start for Detroit but were required to turn back after an encounter with an Indian deputation led by Brant. Brant insisted on the return to Niagara in order that certain grave Indian protests might be lodged in Simcoe's presence. The commissioners had no choice but to

comply. Addressing Simcoe as "Father" and the American plenipotentiaries as "brothers," Brant charged that Wayne's troop
training activities constituted a breach of the armistice and
demanded insultingly to know if the commissioners were "properly authorized to run and establish a new boundary line between
the lands of the United States and the lands of the Indian
nations." They patiently replied that Wayne had been ordered
to make no aggressive move, that they were certain that he had
obeyed, that they realized the definition of a boundary line was the
essence of the treaty that they had come to negotiate, and that
they were fully authorized to define such a line. The Indian
deputation deliberated according to the slow motion technique
of Indian diplomacy and at length, professing to be satisfied, gave
their permission for the commissioners to make another westward
start.

Toward the end of July they reached Detroit. They were forbidden by their English conductors to make a nearer approach
to the Indian congress on the Maumee and were quartered in the
house of Matthew Elliott on the Canadian side of the Detroit
River. They had here no more direct contact with the Indian
congress than they had had at Niagara or, for that matter, in
Philadelphia. It was negotiation by remote control and with the
control in the hands of men like McKee and Elliott whose careers
had been devoted, and were still devoted, to the perpetuation of
hostility between Indians and Americans. Another delay ensued.
The commissioners fumed and sweat, stared out the windows and
wrote in their journals, and waited.

Eventually Elliott appeared with a deputation of twenty
Indian representatives of the principal Indian nations attending
the congress. Their spokesman, a Wyandot chief whose name the
interpreter rendered into English as *Carry-one-about,* announced
the Indian position. By now the commissioners had begun to
expect the worst. They were not disillusioned. The Indian
proposal was a blunt demand that all American settlements be
withdrawn across the Ohio and that the river be established as
the fixed and permanent boundary "between your people and
ours."

At any rate, the commissioners at last could speak their piece.

They dwelt upon the legitimacy of the earlier treaties under which the Indians had ceded a portion of their lands in southeastern Ohio. They undertook to guarantee that never would the United States require more land from them. They explained the prohibitive cost of uprooting the settlements already established on the Indian side of the Ohio. And, coming to their main point, they offered to pay the Indians "such a large sum in money or goods as was never given at one time for any quantity of Indian lands since the white people set their foot on this inland," together with large perpetual annuities.

The deputation listened solemnly and returned to present the American counter proposal to the Indian congress. A week passed. And then another. The commissioners were still forbidden to attend the conference. They dispatched a message addressed to Brant for delivery to the congress, taking a somewhat stronger line, reminding the Indian nations that they had come to make a treaty and that if there was to be no treaty they were prepared to go home.

Then came the final Indian reply. It was a sweeping and defiant rejection of the American terms. To add to its insolence it was read to the commissioners by the infamous renegade, Simon Girty, serving as official interpreter, who appeared before them in Indian costume with a quill thrust through his nose and who interspersed his reading with taunting asides.

Actually, the Indian council had been agitated by days of the most earnest debate. Brant and the Iroquois, with their greater knowledge of the realities of the white world, had worked hard for an acceptance of the American terms. They had enlarged upon the superior strength of the Americans which would become apparent if war were forced upon them and prophesied that never again would the Indians be offered terms so favorable. Afterward Brant said that the tide was turned by the influence of McKee, Elliott, Girty and other Tory agents who resided among the Indians as the representatives of the English government and the English fur trade. Flushed by the memory of their recent great victories and encouraged to believe that England would come to their aid if they ever needed aid, the Indians decided to stand fast.

The Indian ultimatum of the Ohio or war was pronounced unacceptable by the weary American commissioners and the long sustained American search for peace came to an end. Even had they elected further to temporize they might have found the closing words of the Indian declaration somewhat difficult to answer:

Brothers: Money to us is of no value, and to most of us unknown; and as no consideration whatever can induce us to sell our lands, on which we get sustenance for our women and children, we hope we may be allowed to point out a mode by which your settlers may be easily removed, and peace thereby obtained.

Brothers: We know that these settlers are poor, or they never would have ventured to live in a country which has been in continual trouble ever since they crossed the Ohio. Divide, therefore, this large sum of money which you have offered to us among these people; give to each also a proportion of what you say you would give us annually, over and above this large sum of money; and we are persuaded they would most readily accept of it in lieu of the lands you sold to them. If you add, also, the great sums you must expend in raising and paying armies with a view to force us to yield you our country, you will certainly have more than sufficient for the purpose of repaying these settlers for all their labor and improvements.

Brothers: You have talked to us about concessions. It appears strange that you expect any from us, who have only been defending our just rights against your invasions. We want peace. Restore to us our country, and we shall be enemies no longer.

Twenty-four months of frantic appeasement had had the usual consequence. The West had been inspired to regard the national government with new disdain. The enemy had been inspired to expand his demands. The one achievement had been to make clear that war had been inevitable from the first.

XVIII. The Liberty Cap
on a Western Pole

MEMORIES of French aid during the Revolution were still fresh during the 1790's. The public had not yet forgotten how decisive had been that aid or that, for example, Washington's command at Yorktown had numbered 31,000 French soldiers and seamen and but 9,000 Americans.*

This sympathy with everything French was made more poignant by the outbreak of the French revolution. American enthusiasm mounted with each wave of news coming across the Atlantic. Countless bonfires were lighted, orations delivered, thanksgiving proclaimed, and bumpers downed to celebrate the successive tidings that there, too, the rights of man were triumphant, that the king had been deposed, and that France, following in the footsteps of her new world soulmate, had become a sister republic.

In 1793 France, moved to frantic fury by the growing disapproval of her neighbors, added to the array of her enemies by declaring war upon England and Spain. The whole world was taking sides in a conflict that was to endure for twenty-two years. This compulsion to take sides spread to the United States which was obliged immediately to consider the new threat to her long and already troubled English and Spanish borders. Every first impulse of natural gratitude and political sympathy suggested an alliance with France. But this general early enthusiasm began to sag under the weight of the progressive intemperance of

* A sidelight on these French sentiments is cast by early western place names. The first settlements adopted English suffixes: Pittsburgh, Harrodstown, Boonesborough, Lexington. Then came the sudden change to: Louisville, Knoxville, Nashville, and, as a climax, Marietta, an affectionate and familiar diminutive intended as a tribute to Marie Antoinette.

the French Revolution. Affection for republican France, hatred of monarchic England, and aversion to papist Spain were not sufficient in themselves completely to offset the spectacle of French iniquity. Most Americans held the sanctity of religion and the sanctity of property in high regard. French atheism and French communism were striking at both.

The division in American opinion rapidly widened and deepened, the cleavage following the timeless pattern set by temperament, economic standing, religious conviction, and political philosophy. The man of property, the earnest church goer, and the advocate of a stronger central government tended to recoil from French excess and the less well to do, the political theorist, and the opponent of a stronger central government to hail French reform.

In the west, however, there was no division. Nobody was rich enough to fear for his property or religious enough to fear for his church and everybody despised the central government. Neither were the westerners appalled by the violence of the French outburst. They were in a mood to become violent themselves. The conviction was growing that by no other method could they win their own natural rights. Stirred by the French example, they set up committees of correspondence, democratic societies, and outright Jacobin clubs in every hamlet. People began to call one another "citizen" and to wear tri-colored cockades.

At first these organizations were preoccupied with the interchange of declarations and memorials expressing their republican sympathies for republican France and their republican attachment to the rights of man. This was the identical paraphernalia of protest employed so successfully by prerevolutionary seaboard patriots to organize resentment against England and here, too, the circulation of correspondence became the forum for attacks upon a distant and obnoxious government. The blast of propaganda found a public prepared to listen. More than ten years had passed without providing redress for the West's principal grievances. The one great change had been the increase in population which had merely served to make the West more independent and less patient. More and more westerners were regarding the national government's policy as instigated by the malignant jealousy of the East and part of a deliberate design to keep the Spaniards on the Mississippi, the English in the lake posts, and the Indians at their doors. The sudden furor of pro-French sentiment, presently, therefore, developed into a movement more against the United States than for France or against Spain and England.

In Philadelphia Washington's administration was rocked by crisis. The division of opinion in the country extended also to his cabinet. Jefferson proposed to relieve the West by an alliance with France and an opening of the Mississippi by force. Hamilton admitted the necessity of doing something about the Mississippi but favored enlisting English aid, by the cession to England of a part of the northwest if necessary. The split in the country had assumed geographical as well as class proportions. New England, having discovered her trade flowed as inevitably to England as before the Revolution, was as anti-French as the West was pro-French, and Virginia, where most planters had long owed English merchants, was strongly opposed to any rapprochement with England that might lead to debt collection. Washington's calm resolution continued to represent the cement that bound the nation together. He rejected Hamilton's cession proposal as a cure worse than the disease but he saw clearly the great danger in a simultaneous war with England and Spain in which control of the seas must be lost at once and possession of the west certainly soon thereafter. He decided upon a policy of neutrality.

Clark, the one great westerner, also saw clearly. For years he had been shunted aside by his nation, by his state, and even by the more influential among his fellow Kentuckians, his magnificent energy unharnessed, his talents unused. He had attempted, without much success, to accept his eclipse philosophically. In a letter to a friend he wrote, "As for the Politicks of this country [the West] first suppose a swarm of Hungary persons gaping for bread you may conclude that their ideas are not Genly Virtuous but as I dont meddle in their affairs I know but little about them." He was devoting some of his time to writing his memoirs, which was like writing the history of his times. His restless intelligence seized upon other interests. Irritated by the various attempts to account for the thousands of Indian mounds

spread across the Mississippi Valley, which had mystified observers since the arrival of the first white man, ascribing their
origins to the Welsh, the ancient Britons, the Carthaginians, the
Goths and Vandals, the Mexicans or the lost tribes of Israel, he
wrote the *American Museum,* "I dont suppose there is a person
living that knows the Geography and Natural History of the back
country better if so well as I do myself, it hath been my study
for years." His theory to account for the mounds, that they were
raised by the ancestors of the present Indians, is now generally
accepted by anthropologists. About this time he was applying
for a patent on a mechanical boat which he argued was a con-
trivance certain to revolutionize commerce on the western rivers.
But these interests paled for him as the tremendous events of the
early 1790's began to unfold. Here was a threat to his homeland
as portentous as the one he had countered in 1779. He had
reason to hope that Wayne's appointment would come to him
for he alone among American commanders had known triumph
in western wilderness warfare. He was disappointed in this and
again disappointed when Virginia once more refused to reim-
burse him for the funds he had advanced the common cause during his Revolutionary campaigns. "I have given the United
States half the property they possess," he had declared in support
of his petition, "and for them to suffer me to remain in poverty,
in consequence of it, will not redound much to their honor hereafter."

He was not yet forty. His confidence in himself was unshaken.
The fate of the West was in the balance. Too much was at stake
for such a spirit to remain inactive. His vision encompassed the
international scene as well as the range of realities in the west.
He understood the eagerness of the French inhabitants on the
Mississippi to revolt and the weakness of their Spanish governors and he was willing to gamble with the threat of England's interference. A revival of his Yazoo project was certainly indicated.
The opportunity to save the West by opening the Mississippi
forthwith was too promising to be lost through the official inaction of the United States. Toward the close of 1792 he wrote
the French government offering to raise a force of Kentuckians
to take New Orleans in the name of France.

The French needed no reminder. They, too, knew the west. The Mississippi Valley had been the intense concern of their colonial office for the past hundred and fifty years. French interests there had been placed not in the keeping but in the temporary custody of Spain. Revolutionary France, already stirring with that explosion of national energy which was to overwhelm Europe and to embark upon adventures in Egypt and India, determined now to repossess her own in North America.

Citizen Genet, the regime's first minister to the United States, disembarked in Charleston with the air of a Roman proconsul come to bring order to a confused province. He took for granted his enthusiastic reception by the local pro-French political faction and proceeded to act as though the United States were as much a New World projection of French power as it had been during the American Revolution. He commissioned American privateers to prey on English commerce and organized expeditions of American frontiersmen to attack Spanish possessions. Samuel Hammond and William Tate in South Carolina and Elijah Clarke in Georgia were asked to command these invasions of a country with which the United States was not at war and accepted with alacrity since the projects coincided so appropriately with their own land company enterprises.

Genet's northward progress to Philadelphia was triumphal. At every stop he accepted addresses of welcome and preached the gospel of American participation in France's holy war. It was plain that the majority of the people, at any rate of the common people, regarded him as the heroic representative of a revolution which was but the continuation of their own. Some not so common were of the same mind. Jefferson was writing Monroe of "the old spirit of 1776, rekindling. The old Tories joined by our merchants, who trade on British capital, and the idle rich, are with the kings. All other descriptions with the French." Madison was writing Jefferson, "It is mortifying that the President should have anything to apprehend from the success of liberty in another country, since he owes his preeminence to the success of it in his own." It is not remarkable that Genet was so little subdued by the news awaiting him in Philadelphia of Washington's neutrality proclamation. Or that he was elated by the letter, also awaiting him there, written him by Clark in Kentucky, February 2nd. Clark wrote:

I can raise abundance of men in this western country — men as well Americans as French who have repeatedly fought, obtained laurels, and never yet met with a repuls under my command, men through whose courage, fidelity to their country and confidence in my arrangements, which never yet failed them of success, took the Illinois and Pos St. Vincennes from the Britons, saved St. Louis and the rest of Louisiana for the Spaniards, from that nation, humbled the whole Northern and Southern tribes of Indians (those in particular who are now so hostile and triumphant) to the very dust, preserved Kentucky, Cumberland, and the whole territory northwest of the Ohio to the United States, and protected the western frontiers of Virginia and Pennsylvania from British and Indian depredations. . . . Out of Kentucky, Cumberland, the settlement on Holston, the Wabash and the Illinois I can (by my name alone) raise 1500 brave men — and the French at St. Louis and throughout the rest of Louisiana, together with the American Spanish subjects at the Natchez would, I am sure of it (for they all know me) flock to my Standard. . . . With the first 1500 alone I can take the whole of Louisiana for France. If France will be hearty and secret in this business — my success borders on certainty.

Genet was hearty enough but there was nothing secret about his reaction. It was the essence of his method publicly to capture American aid in defiance of Washington's proclamation. He enlisted the services of André Michaux, the eminent French naturalist, who was familiar with the west as a result of his botanizing travels. Michaux was not an experienced political agent but he was discreet, distinguished and of irreproachable reputation. He hurried down the Ohio, accompanied by two French artillery officers and carrying in his pocket a commission appointing Clark "Major-General in the Armies of France and Commander-in-Chief of the French Revolutionary Legion on the Mississippi River" and a letter of introduction to Governor Shelby of Kentucky. He was further empowered to negotiate treaties of alliance with Indian nations in American territory and to foment revolt among French communities in Spanish territory.

Clark felt his great moment had come and with gusto he began preparations to rise to it. The total design was ambitious and flamboyant enough to tax the imagination even of a Genet. The expeditions from the southern frontier, already promoted at Charleston, were to invade Florida and either to win the support of or to contain the Southern Indians. The main stroke was to be delivered by Clark's army of Kentuckians advancing down the Mississippi upon New Orleans, liberating en route the French river communities whose men were to join him. A French fleet would appear in the Gulf to threaten the city from the sea and another would blockade the St. Lawrence to hamper English interference.

There was no more secrecy about Clark's preparations than there was about Genet's other activities. Clark advertised his commission, his purpose, and his call for volunteers in the press. Footloose Kentuckians who were moved to enlist in the enterprise were promised up to three thousand acres of Spanish land together with their share in the plunder of New Orleans. The sole Kentucky newspaper, the *Gazette,* was an enthusiastic supporter of his program. The democratic societies hailed it as a crusade. Attracted by the glittering prospects of loot and land, thousands of impoverished and landless Kentuckians were eager to volunteer. Many more substantial men subscribed funds along with their services. The problem was not to find men but to supply a tenth of those who wanted to serve. The major financial support was to come from Genet but that had been promised and was believed on its way. No important segment of western opinion actively opposed the undertaking. The possibility that the Spanish Old Man of the Sea might at last be thrown off was welcomed by all. Frantic appeals from Philadelphia found Governor Shelby evasive. He professed to know of no organized preparations in his state to attack Spain. His official position was that there was no law on the books to prohibit any American taking his rifle off the wall, picking up a sack of corn, and moving anywhere within the United States and that there was equally no law to cover whatever he did once he had crossed the country's border.

Carondelet was terrified by the sudden loom of this new menace. He had been hoping to bring off a general Indian assault upon the southern frontier but his scheme was over-shadowed by this counter threat of a Kentucky descent upon New Orleans. He did what he could to strengthen his garrisons, be-seeched Madrid for more troops, established a new Spanish post, Fort Confederation, in the Southern Indian country, hysterically advised the Northern Indians that they could count on Spanish support against Wayne, and sent off an earnest appeal to Simcoe in Canada for cooperation.

St. Clair, Governor of the Northwest Territory, was raising his own cries of alarm. He could see what an explosive effect Clark's New Orleans preparations were having upon the already pre-carious balance of power in the west. England and Spain had been enemies for centuries but at the moment they were allies in the sense that they were both at war with France. He thought it unlikely that England would remain indifferent while an ex-pedition sponsored by France attacked Spain on the Mississippi. The collapse of the Detroit peace negotiations with the Indians had left a decisive resumption of the Indian war inevitable in the spring. There was the greatest doubt that the forces Wayne was painfully gathering on the Ohio would prove able to cope with the Indians alone. If the Indian strength were augmented by active English assistance then certain disaster was obviously in prospect.

In Philadelphia the grim realities in the west became apparent even to Jefferson, for all his enthusiasm for a military alliance with France. He acquiesced in Washington's decision to re-quest Genet's recall and, realizing how far out of step he was with Washington's basic policies, resigned as Secretary of State on the last day of this threatening year of 1793.

Again the tensions in the west were relieved by the impact of unrelated and distant events. Revolutionary France, in the throes of the Reign of Terror and military reverses in Europe, was compelled to jettison such peripheral projects as Genet's in North America. Fauchet, arriving to replace Genet in the early spring of 1794, repudiated the entire Genet program. He with-held the funds promised Clark, rescinded his commission, and disavowed French sponsorship of the expedition. Washington was encouraged to issue a proclamation specifically denouncing the project and Congress passed a law imposing fines and imprisonment upon American citizens who assembled for the purpose of making an attack upon a friendly country.

The relaxation of tension was scarcely visible at the time. The Jacobin convention meeting at Lexington preached the crusade as ardently as before. Clark was slowed but not brought to a stop. Far from giving up he continued to build boats and to gather supplies. As many men as he could use were ready. What he and his Kentucky supporters had had in mind all along was not so much taking New Orleans for France as opening the Mississsippi for Kentucky.

And from north of the Ohio had come the most ominous rolls of thunder yet. Dorchester had astonished and enraptured the Indians with his sudden official pronouncement that they might expect England soon to join them in their war with the Americans. Simcoe had advanced from Detroit to the Maumee and at the center of that collection of villages which amounted to the capital of the Indian confederacy had built and garrisoned an English fort. For the retention of the lake posts England had had originally the excuse of American failure to fulfill some of the treaty terms. But no sophistry could cover this aggressive move. It was an invasion of American territory. It was, in effect, an act of war.

If so, it produced no loyal closing of ranks among the Americans in the west. Their dissatisfaction with their own national government was stronger than their aversion to the Indians or their fear of the English. Largely relieved, since 1792, of Indian attacks upon the northern frontier, first by the armistice and then by Wayne's advanced position at Fort Greenville, they had been free to dwell upon this dissatisfaction. In the spring of 1794 western discontent had reached the breaking point.

The break came in southwestern Pennsylvania. This was the one section of the frontier that had not been subjected to the vicissitudes of working out its own government. The people here lived in counties which were corporate parts of the substantial, prosperous and politically well organized state of Pennsylvania. But they were also a people who lived west of the mountains and they were far more akin to Kentuckians and

Tennesseeans than they were to the good burghers of Philadelphia.

Their mushrooming democratic societies lent themselves to
the same rigamarole of liberty caps on poles and tri-colored
cockades on hats, of declarations of solidarity with France, of
declamations upon liberty, fraternity and equality, and of fren-
zied denunciations of federal tyranny. Nowhere in the west were
the societies more active and violent and nowhere were the cries
of up with France intended more clearly to mean down with the
United States. The southwestern Pennsylvanians sympathized
with Kentucky's determination to break the Spanish Mississippi
barrier but their own paramount grievance was federal taxation.
Among Hamilton's fiscal measures to bolster the national credit
was a tax on spirits. The impost amounted to seven cents a
gallon, which in the east represented about an eighth of the
value but in the west more than a quarter. The toll imposed a
very nearly prohibitive burden upon traffic in the one important
product the West could export over the mountains to the eastern
market. A horse could pack but four bushels of rye while after
the grain was converted into whisky he could transport the
equivalent of twenty-four bushels. In view of their geographic
and economic isolation the westerners had some grounds for
feeling the excise to be a clear case of taxation without representation and they opposed its collection with as much indignation and conviction as ever had their fathers the tax on tea and
the stamp tax.

From the outset resistance took violent and physical forms.
Collectors, marshals and process servers were humiliated and
terrorized and if they turned up a second time were tarred,
feathered and whipped. Inhabitants who gave them food or
shelter were burned out. "Tom Tinker's men" roamed the
region at night "mending" with axe and torch the stills of
farmers who had consented to pay the tax. The intimidation of
individuals spread to include all types of federal office holders
and then to anyone who voiced any attachment whatever to the
federal government.

This spirit of violence was enormously stimulated by the
sudden upsurge of pro-French excitement. In the spring of

1794 a meeting of local militiamen on Mingo Creek formed an "association" for the purpose of organizing resistance to the tax. The more they talked the more exercised they became and before they were through they had determined to resist by force every manifestation of federal authority. Demagogic leaders sprang up to carry the movement on from riotous disobedience to actual armed rebellion.

Outrages committed upon the persons of federal officers multiplied. Occasions were manufactured to show contempt for federal authority. General John Neville, a wealthy, public-spirited and until then universally respected pioneer and Revolutionary hero, was opposed to the whisky tax but had accepted the post of chief collector in the hope of easing the strain between his community and his country. In the course of attempting to serve a warrant Neville and a United States marshal were fired upon and driven from the scene. The feeling against Neville mounted. The popular cry was that he had been "bought" by the national government. A party of militiamen assembled about his house to demand possession of his official records and papers. The general had escaped and a detachment of eleven regulars from the tiny Pittsburgh garrison had arrived to protect his property. The "committee of safety" in charge of the demonstration nevertheless directed an assault in which one rebel was killed and a number on both sides were wounded. The soldiers were forced to surrender and Neville's home, reputed to be the finest in the west, was burned.

After this deliberate attack upon the uniform and flag of the United States the rebel leaders pressed feverishly on toward the point of no return. The United States mails were seized, partly to cut off any chance of reconciliation with the national government and partly to learn the names of inhabitants who might still entertain government sympathies. A list of names was served upon Pittsburgh, where a certain spirit of moderation continued to exist, demanding the expulsion of those who had been so indiscreet as to trust their loyal sentiments to the mails. Pittsburgh complied with anxious haste and the loyalists fled down the Ohio to take refuge in Kentucky or the wilderness.

Some thousands of the militia of all five western counties

assembled at Braddock's Field at the call of the rebel leaders. There was still much dissatisfaction with Pittsburgh where enthusiasm for the revolt remained lukewarm. A proposal to burn the backward city found much favor. Hundreds of women from the back country joined the march to enjoy the spectacle and, possibly, to participate in the looting. The city fathers cannily countered the threat with irresistible good will. The marchers were greeted with open barrels of whisky and tables laden with food. More amiable second thought prevailed and Pittsburgh escaped destruction. Nevertheless, thousands of restless men were under arms. The movement had become a rebellion in fact as well as name. The writ of the United States no longer ran west of the mountains.

The news from southwestern Pennsylvania and Kentucky strained Washington's so painfully marshaled patience and moved him to express his exasperation with all westerners in one of the outstanding understatements of all time: "There must exist a predisposition among them to be dissatisfied." But he had need to remain patient. In Kentucky Clark was still building boats and enrolling men for his reckless New Orleans adventure. North of the Ohio Wayne was making his slow and fateful approach to the English-guarded Indian citadel. France and England were beginning to seize American shipping en route to their rival's ports. The clouds of world war hung on every horizon. This was no moment to visit his just indignation upon the frontier rebellion.

The Supreme Court certified the western counties of Pennsylvania to be in a state of insurrection. Washington issued another of his proclamations, reminding the dissidents of federal authority and denouncing continued resistance to it. But instead of making any prompt move to reestablish respect for that authority he appointed five commissioners, three representing the United States and two the State of Pennsylvania, to go over the mountains and endeavor to reason with the rebels. The commissioners found that many of the more substantial inhabitants had become disposed, upon reflection, to make their peace with the national government. But the great mass of the populace remained rebellious and gathered in unruly numbers about every conference for the express purpose of intimidating the moderates. After a month of confused negotiations the commissioners returned, as had the peace commissioners from Detroit, to report the failure of another effort to appease.

Meanwhile the irrespressible Carondelet had taken another full turn. Instead of preparing to fight the Americans in cooperation with his Indian allies he sought once more the greater advantage of joining them. Perceiving that the sense of outrage kindled in Kentucky by the national government's opposition to Clark's project had revived the secessionist agitation, he impetuously threw new Spanish support to the movement. An insurrection in Kentucky, capping the one in Southwestern Pennsylvania, could split the United States into rival eastern and western republics much easier for Spain to deal with. He proposed to open the Mississippi to such an independent western republic and, to hasten the happy moment, dispatched northward heavier cargoes of silver than ever before had found their way into American pockets. For this new Spanish intrigue he saw certain success; this time, he reported to his government, the maneuver was "infallible."

Simcoe, likewise, was struck by the dark mood of the westerners. Their dissatisfaction with their own country had reached such a pitch, he was convinced, that in their passion to turn away from it they might even turn back to England. "It is generally understood that above half the inhabitants of Kentucky and the western waters," he reported to his government, "are already inclined to a connection with Great Britain."

And meanwhile Wayne pressed with deliberate resolution deeper into the wilderness. All depended now on him.

XIX. The Darkest Hour

MAJOR GENERAL Anthony Wayne, upon whose shoulders so great a burden had been laid, was still only forty-seven. But he had been aged by many other and more personal problems. After retiring with a military reputation second only to Greene's among Washington's lieutenants he had encountered a series of commercial failures and financial reverses and, in an excursion into politics, a field for which he was scarcely fitted, had suffered a humiliation which narrowly approached becoming a reflection upon his integrity. Meanwhile his formidable constitution had been undermined by the after effects of wounds received in the Revolution. As a consequence of one of them a disease resembling gout had developed in his left leg which periodically swelled to twice its normal size and caused him constant pain. But the body that was growing weak and fat and flabby housed a spirit that still burned with undiminished vigor. And he possessed the born commander's confidence in his own judgment which made him capable of forming a plan and then of waiting, however long, with resolution unshaken by delay, for the moment to execute it.

Responsibility had descended upon him unaccompanied by the moral support of feeling that the country had turned to him or even that he had been singled out by the President as the man most fitted for the task. His appointment had been not only a second choice but an almost accidental one which had been widely criticized. Washington had wanted Light Horse Harry Lee but Lee had been outranked by too many members of the jealous corps of Continental ex-officers. St. Clair was handicapped by the stigma of his great defeat. Either Wilkinson or

Clark would have been more acceptable to the West than any easterner but neither, Washington felt, could have been trusted either to restrain his personal ambitions or to conform to the directives of a government committed to caution first. While Washington was casting about for the least undesirable alternative to Lee, Congress unwittingly solved his dilemma by voting that Wayne was not entitled to the seat to which ostensibly he had been elected by the voters of Georgia. Wayne, a failure at politics, commerce, and planting, was ready to return to the profession he understood. Still Washington hesitated. He appreciated Wayne's proven military capacities but an aggressive fighting general was not necessarily the man for this kind of an emergency. The administration was bent not upon making war but upon making peace. Weeks passed without finding a man considered more eligible. At last Washington sent Wayne's name to the Senate, which protested long and loudly. It required the President's personal persuasion to gain a confirmation of the appointment.

That June of 1792 Wayne painfully crawled from his saddle and stood in the dusty street of Pittsburgh, face to face with his problem. The situation with which he was confronted must have seemed staggering. The army which he had been named to command did not yet exist. Ahead of him down the Ohio the discouraged survivors of St. Clair's defeat huddled in half a dozen forest-girt army posts, half starved, half armed, and seldom paid. Desertion had become so common that civilian scouts, experienced in following tracks through the wilderness, had been offered a standing reward of $40 for the head of a deserter. Behind him scanty columns of recruits for the new Legion of the United States, grudgingly authorized by a most doubting Congress, were marching reluctantly over the mountains. The regular army was unable to offer either the pay or the prestige to attract men capable of self respect in any other field. Desperate recruiting officers had been driven to impress the off scourings of poorhouse, jail, hospital and gutter.

The frontier inhabitants, disillusioned by repeated disaster, managed soon to complete the disillusionment of the newcomers. Surveying these sad reinforcements, the settlers made no effort to conceal either their contempt or their pity. The frontier needed defenders and had been supplied instead with new victims. The wearied recruits, equally unfamiliar with war, with the wilderness, and with Indians, were quick to sense this atmosphere of universal foreboding. More than half had deserted before the footsore companies even reached Pittsburgh.

The people about the Forks of the Ohio had a right to their opinion. Nowhere else on the continent was there a stage on which had been enacted so often the macabre drama of Indian war. For more than half a century successive waves of Indian attack had swept across the river and, in earlier days, on over the mountains and all the way to the Delaware. The hushed talk now was mostly of more recent disasters, of Crawford, and Harmar, and St. Clair, but older men had not forgotten the bodies of Lochry's men bobbing down the Ohio, the murder of Logan's kin, the fierce shock of battle at Point Pleasant, the Highlanders falling in rows at Bushy Run, Pontiac's siege of Pittsburgh, the bears devouring Braddock's dead, or the young Washington surrendering at Fort Necessity. A half century of war and still no family could rest easily at night, still the smoke of burning cabins rose in the morning air. Across the Ohio loomed an Indian power more ominous than any before, better armed, better led, elated by repeated triumph. To cope with a peril so monumental there had come this fat, sickly, and crippled general with his handful of scarecrow soldiers, sent by a panic-stricken government whose one active policy was to plead with the Indians for peace.

Wayne kept his counsel and took his forlorn recruits in hand. They were a less promising batch than any he had ever seen during the worst days of the Revolution but somehow they had to be taught how to fight. Sooner or later he would have to take this collection of misfits into the wilderness to meet an enemy who had so often proved they already knew. The news of Hardin's and Trueman's fate indicated how unfounded was the government's hope for a negotiated peace. A report that Pittsburgh was about to be attacked turned out to be a false alarm but the confusion of that night demonstrated how much the "legionnaires" had to learn. Few of the officers were much help. Most spent their time gambling, drinking, raising scandals among the sergeants' wives, and fighting duels with each other.

Wayne's grip tightened, upon officers and men alike, and, as winter approached, he moved the whole command twenty miles down river where he set the men to building the fortified camp that became Legionville. And here, removed from the distractions of Pittsburgh, he drilled them, day after day, throughout the winter. In addition to the drudgery of close order he pounded into them instruction and practice in how to take cover as skirmishers, how to reload on the run, and, above all else, how to fix bayonets. Slowly their bodies hardened and then their minds. Slowly the clumsy recruits were beginning to look faintly like soldiers. Before Wayne was through with them they were to become soldiers. The training was to go on until it had become second nature to them to wait for orders and to obey orders, in every situation and under whatever circumstances, and not until then was he to subject them to the ultimate shock of battle.

For Wayne had worked out his formula for beating Indians. The first principle was never to permit surprise. The one possible guard against surprise was discipline. Only thoroughly disciplined troops never became confused, never bolted, never yielded to panic. The second principle was to bring the battle immediately to close quarters — to charge and keep on charging to counteract the favorite Indian tactic of enveloping the field in converging fire from a fluid line of hidden riflemen. Again absolute discipline was required. Only the most thoroughly trained troops would take their losses and keep on going forward until the enemy line was met and broken. With patient determination Wayne drilled and drilled and kept on drilling. Gradually he warmed to his men and they to him.

In the spring he received some hundreds of additional recruits, though his strength remained little more than half of the authorized five thousand. In May he loaded his little army on flatboats and drifted down to Fort Washington. The river was so high, flooding the entire lower valley, that it was with difficulty he forced his boats through the half-submerged treetops to find a place to land. At this campsite of Hobson's choice he built another fortified camp and resumed drilling.

Wayne and his Legion had not appeared on the Kentucky

frontier as a champion flying to the rescue. Of necessity his first act was to proclaim the armistice and to forbid the Kentuckians to continue their personal war with the Indians. His arrival was accompanied by an aura of appeasement and defeatism. The government's attention was concentrated on the peace negotiations. All emphasis was on schemes to avoid his ever having to take the field. The settlements regarded his necessary immobility with scorn. The West was in a treasonable ferment of impatient dealings with Spain, France and England but to the average westerner any move to deal with the Indians was the one great treason. The Indian was his implacable enemy, his perpetual and personal antagonist, the incessant destroyer of his property and his people. Either he or the Indian must give way. Coexistence was inconceivable. And yet, after fifty years of outrage, after twenty years of uninterrupted war along the Ohio, three years after Harmar's humiliation, two years after St. Clair's debacle, and a year after the murder of the ambassadors, here was a new federal army, such as it was, idling away another year, huddled supinely behind stockades, while the representatives of the United States crept to the English at Niagara and then all the way to the Indians at Detroit, begging for peace.

Wayne was soldier enough to sense the threat to such morale as he had been able to instil into his Legionnaires. They were in addition afflicted by epidemics of influenza and small pox. He worked shrewdly at creating in them soldierly pride in themselves and in their corps. He sought to make them feel superior not only to the Indian enemy but to the scoffing frontiersmen they had come to defend. The simplest first step in making a soldier feel pride in being a soldier was to put him in uniform but no uniforms were available. Wayne directed them to attach distinctive plumes to their home-made bearskin caps, white for the 1st sub-legion, red for the 2nd, yellow for the 3rd, and green for the 4th. And he sent off to the east for decorations, battalion colors and, most important of all, a legionary standard. It was traditional that a legion possess its own official standard. This was to be one behind which the Legion of the United States would march, around which it would camp, and which, Wayne assured Knox, was most definitely never to be lost.

On September 11, after so many dreary months of inaction,

the word came. The foredoomed peace negotiations at Detroit had failed. The armistice was over. The long contemplated time had come for Wayne to lead his regulars into the wilderness as, before him, had St. Clair, Harmar, Sullivan, Bouquet, Forbes, Braddock. In every campaign there was a large element of risk. But, as he was so well aware the experiences of his forerunners had demonstrated, in no campaign were the risks so varied and unforeseeable as in an advance by regular troops upon Indians waiting in the recesses of their own country. Some of his younger officers were jubilant over the prospect of action but these optimistic expectations were shared by few. To most observers either in Philadelphia or on the frontier Wayne was embarking upon an undertaking in which failure meant catastrophe and success, at best, but limited advantage. His orders from Secretary of War Knox emphasized this view: "Let it therefore be again, and for the last time, impressed deeply upon your mind, that as little as possible is to be hazarded . . . and that a defeat at the present time, and under the present circumstances, would be pernicious in the highest degree to the interests of our country."

Wayne had no intention of suffering defeat. His men, though few in numbers, had been, he hoped, imbued with some of his own sober resolution. He had taken relentless precautions never to afford the Indians the fatal opportunity of surprise. He proposed to launch his own attack upon them only at a moment of his own choosing. "I pray you not to permit present appearance," he wrote Knox, "to cause too much anxiety either in the mind of the President, or yourself, on account of this army."

His chief concern was not with what lay ahead but, as well it might be, with what lay behind. Hundreds of his men, incapacitated by illness, had had to be left at Fort Washington. Another epidemic had cut his line of supply. Communications between Pittsburgh and the east had been interrupted by a yellow fever outbreak in Philadelphia. The frontier, his immediate base, was offering him indifferent support. Kentucky was now a state and a full-fledged member of the Union but admission had come too reluctantly and too late to assuage public opinion. Dissatisfaction with the national government and all its works was more bitter than ever before. Wayne's plan of operations had included dependence upon a corps of mounted Kentucky riflemen but there had been a general unwillingness to volunteer to serve with another army of regulars as apparently predestined to disaster as its predecessors. Protected, for the moment, from Indian inroads by the interposition of that army, most Kentuckians were preoccupied with Genet's manifestoes and Clark's preparations and the prospect of sweeping the Spaniards from the Mississippi.

Wayne's greatest cause for concern, however, was at his elbow, in the person of his second in command, Brigadier General Wilkinson. He had distrusted his glib subordinate from the beginning but on account of Wilkinson's popularity in Kentucky had hesitated to insist upon his removal. For his part, Wilkinson bitterly resented Wayne, whose arrival had reduced his own former importance as senior officer in the west and whose presence hampered the conduct of his various intrigues. Wayne's disapproval of Wilkinson must have been fed by the arrest of Reuben Reynolds in Pittsburgh. Both men vigorously denied everything but it was apparent that Reynolds had been acting as a species of personal agent for Wilkinson when, in the role of deserter, he had visited Detroit, Mackinac, Montreal and the Vermont-Canadian border before returning by way of Philadelphia. How much greater must have been Wayne's concern had he known that Wilkinson had been establishing calculated contacts with English authorities, that he was now drawing an annual Spanish pension of $2000, a tidy addition to his $94 a month pay as brigadier general, and that he was deluging Carondelet with cipher messages dilating upon the deepening dissension within the United States, the incompetence of the Secretary of War, the ignorance of his commanding general, and the readiness of the West to secede.

Wayne moved northward by deliberate marches, each night building a fortified camp, as had the original legion of Roman times. Four hundred sentinels were kept on guard, day and night. Indian scouts, peering from the forest, sent thoughtful reports to their commanders. This expedition had from the start a different look than the sprawling and straggling advances of a St. Clair, a Harmar, or a Braddock.

But Wayne was far from satisfied. Training had given his men the outward air of soldiers, not the inner assurance. They marched on steadily and obeyed orders promptly but he did not miss the furtive sidewise glances, the whispers, the nervous laughs. Before them stretched the freshly cut road on either side of which rose the dark and ghostly walls of forest. Their spirits were subdued by the reflection that they were not the first to follow such a path. Time and again before them just such well formed columns as theirs had pressed on along such a lane to find disaster at the shadowed end of it. In ordinary warfare troops knew when battle was imminent and had time to brace themselves for the shock. In the wilderness the tension and the suspense were constant. No man could know that the next moment there might not pounce upon him out of that silent forest the roar of gunfire and the screech of warwhoops.

Already, Indians were lurking ahead, flitting along the flanks, and dogging the rear. At every alarm, most of them false, that one had been sighted, men paled and muttered. Wayne ordered the vanguard to simulate an attack. The sudden clatter of musketry struck the main body like the shove of an invisible hand, though later all sheepishly insisted that they had known all along that it was only a sham battle. An actual attack by no more than fifty Indians upon a wagon train on the road to Fort Washington was even more disturbing. At the first howling onslaught most of the ninety man escort broke and scattered. Lieutenant Lowry, Ensign Boyd, and thirteen men who stood fast were butchered. The exultant Indians made off with 64 horses and as much corn and bacon and as many pieces of wagons as they could pack on them. Wayne held a court martial but abandoned any idea of punishment. The fact of the matter was that, for all his rigorous training, the Legion was not yet ready to fight so resourceful and difficult an enemy.

Seventy miles north of Cincinnati he built a permanent fort and named it Fort Greenville, in honor of his old comrade in arms, General Nathanael Greene. Here he went into winter quarters. Here, also, he extracted such advantage as he could from his situation by calling upon Governor Shelby for the promised support of Kentucky volunteers and militia. A thousand came, grudgingly, and more out of curiosity than in any expectation of active service this late in the season. Wayne soon dismissed them, his purpose achieved. They had had an opportunity to observe the soldierly care with which the camp was fortified and picketed and the plumed precision with which the Legionnaires performed their every duty. Outwardly all was prepossessingly most military. The militia would return to Kentucky to spread the report that here was a new sort of regular army. Next year when he did need the Kentuckians they would come more willingly.

The decision to go into winter quarters automatically prolonged the war for at best another year. It was an agonizing prolongation for all involved of the expense, the suspense, and the tension. Many elements entered into his determination which had been largely formed before he left Fort Washington. His troops needed more training under wilderness conditions. The season was late to risk a decisive campaign. The position already reached was sufficiently advanced to keep the Indians in a defensive posture and to restrain them from weakening their central force by the dispatch of detachments to attack the frontier. The delay was welcomed by Knox, who was brooding with increasing anxiety over the "unlimited evils" certain to follow a defeat, and by the administration, which was engaged in a new series of frantic negotiations with the Iroquois, who were threatening actively to join the hostile coalition. But the basic factor in Wayne's thinking was the effect of the delay upon Indian morale. They had keyed themselves up to sustain the shock of his attack. Now the issue was postponed to another season. Yet, while waiting, they were required to take into account the possibility of a sudden winter march such as Clark had made upon Vincennes. They could not scatter, as had been their immemorial winter custom, to hunt for food to support their families. Wayne was calculatingly initiating a war of nerves. The Indian's excitable and volatile nature was none too fitted to endure the pressures of long continued delay and suspense.

In December Wayne stepped up the pressure. To make certain that the Indians did not take his winter immobility too much for granted, he emerged from his fortified camp with a force of eight companies and darted northward twenty-five miles to St. Clair's battlefield. On Christmas Eve the Legionnaires pitched their tents among the frost-encrusted heaps of skulls and bones which had been dragged to the surface again by wild animals after Wilkinson's hasty interment. On this grisly and ill-omened site Fort Recovery was built, an outpost small enough to be garrisoned by a modest force and yet strong enough to hold against any Indian attack unsupported by artillery. Major Henry Burbeck, left in command of this lonely outpost of the Legion, set his men to gathering and burying the acres of skeletons. One of his working parties uncovered four brass cannon, hidden in a trench beneath some fallen trees by the Indians after the pieces' capture from St. Clair. They had thought one day to return to repossess them but now the guns were gratefully added to the defences of Fort Recovery. The incident moved Wayne to an order of the day:

The commander-in-chief returns his most grateful thanks to Major Henry Burbeck, and to every officer, non-commissioned officer and private belonging to the detachment under his command, for their soldierly and exemplary good conduct . . . the cheerfulness with which they surmounted every difficulty at this inclement season, in repossessing General Saint Clair's field of battle . . . as also for piously and carefully collecting and interring the bones, and paying the last respects and military honors to the remains of the heroes who fell on the 9th of November, 1791, by three times three discharges from the same artillery that was lost on that fatal day, but now recovered by this detachment of the Legion.

The spring of 1794 came. The wilderness flood waters slowly subsided, making land travel possible and bringing nearer the moment of decision. Wayne looked northward with a calm and steady eye. He was confident that his little army now was ready. His campaign plan involved making as great demands upon it in the way of patience, endurance and headlong audacity as could ever be required of soldiers. But he knew his men and they knew him. Each felt the other equal to the coming test. However, in every other respect the scene had darkened immeasurably. From end to end of the frontier, in the east, and on the seas, old threats grew graver, while new ones, far more dangerous, multiplied.

On the Georgia border, Elijah Clarke, support of his Genet-inspired Florida invasion withdrawn by the French, had, as an alternative, moved with his followers into the Creek country where he had set up an independent republic in defiance of the Creek nation, of Spain, of the State of Georgia, and of the United States. Governor Mathews of Georgia was reluctant to excite local public opinion, here, as everywhere else in the west, flagrantly sympathetic toward any secessionist adventure, by making any overt move against the insurrectionists. Hamilton, appealing to the governor to use South Carolina troops, if necessary, was writing that it was:

impossible to conceive a settlement more unjustifiable in its pretexts, or more dangerous in its principle. . . . It is not only a high handed usurpation of the rights of the General and State Governments, and a most unwarrantable encroachment upon those of the Indians; but, proceeding upon the idea of a separate and independent government, to be erected upon a *military basis,* it is essentially hostile to our republican systems of government, and is pregnant with incalculable mischiefs. It deeply concerns the great interests of the country that such an establishment should be checked by adequate punishment.

North of Georgia the Holston-Cumberland frontier was suffering under a veritable drumbeat of attacks. During the early months of 1794 there were forty such important losses in property and lives as to be considered of enough moment to be listed in the sparse written records of the time. A number of the most notable incidents of border history occurred during this culminating year of the Indian war, such as the abduction of the women and slaves of the Scott party at Muscle Shoals, in the course of achieving which Chief Bowl's band of Cherokee assaulted a large, multi-family flatboat, killed the thirteen white men, and then, in order to assure themselves permanent possession of their booty of Negroes and white women, migrated with their captives beyond the reach of any future prisoner exchange to the farther wilderness across the Mississippi. Blockhouses and stations were assailed almost within sight of Knoxville and Nashville. Other parties of raiders penetrated far beyond the outer fringe of settlements to carry their depredations into Virginia's Washington County. The Wilderness Road became less safe than in Daniel Boone's time. In this twelfth long year since the Revolution the Indian menace had again increased, not lessened.

The endeavor of the settlers to defend themselves was handicapped by the federal government's insistent objection to pursuit or retaliation by the local militia. The United States was once more making desperate efforts to negotiate a peace with the Southern Indians, whose passivity was sought while Wayne was so critically involved in the north. Knox was writing Governor Blount, in response to the settlers' violent protestations, "the whole matter was before Congress at its last session, and they did not think proper to authorize or direct offensive measures, notwithstanding the ideas to the contrary which prevail on your frontier."

An illustration of the success of the federal pacification program was provided by the 1794 calendar of adventures of Doublehead, one of the more enterprising of the Cherokee war chiefs. On April 1 Doublehead ambushed a party of travelers on the Wilderness Road, killing, among others, Thomas Sharpe Spencer, a veteran Indian fighter and one of the earliest and most noted of frontiersmen, who had been affectionately known as "Big Foot" ever since the day, more than twenty years before, when the mere sight of his moccasined footprints had caused a French trader to jump into the Cumberland in the apprehension that a monster bear was upon him. The following week Doublehead accepted an invitation to head a delegation of fellow Cherokee chiefs on a peace pilgrimage to Philadelphia. There he was entertained, cajoled, granted a personal interview with Washington, handed an annuity of $5000, and dispatched back to Savannah in state on a warship. The week after his return home, much refreshed by his summer junket, he led an attack upon the station of Colonel Valentine Sevier, brother of the great John, in which among the many scalped and mutilated victims were three of Valentine's children.

The Indian effort against the southern frontier might have been far more destructive had it not been for the deterrent influence of three developments for which neither the settlers nor the federal government were responsible. The Creek and Cherokee, traditionally suspicious of one another, became embroiled in another of their violent quarrels, this one precipitated by the Cherokee delivery of a Creek to the Americans who hanged him. Panton, Leslie and Company, their shipping disorganized by the activities of French privateers, was forced to advise its Indian customers to go to the Spaniards for the gunpowder they needed to keep up a large scale war. Carondelet, however, bemused by the sudden prospect of reviving his Kentucky intrigue, returned to the earlier Spanish policy of limiting the scope of the Indian war by limiting Indian supplies.

The Kentuckians, in Wayne's immediate rear, saved for the moment from Indian inroads by the advanced position of his army, were preoccupied not with his fortunes but with their chaotic popular debate upon the Mississippi question. One faction, led by the pro-French democratic societies, was still in full cry in support of Clark's projected descent upon New Orleans. Another group, fewer in number, but insidiously influential and better furnished with money, was as earnestly advocating, alternately, secessionist deals with Spain or England as a surer method of opening the Mississippi which possessed the added advantage of an escape from the clutch of the federal government. Kentucky's civil disorder was not Wayne's principal responsibility but it shrouded his base in clouds of uncertainty, caused the diversion to Clark of supplies he needed, and required the detachment from his small army of troops to garrison Fort Massac on the lower Ohio to block Clark's descent of the river.

In southwestern Pennsylvania the open rebellion against federal authority had entirely cut his main line of communications. He could no longer expect, whatever his need, reinforcements of Pennsylvania militia and, no matter what difficulties he fell into, there was no longer the possibility that federal aid of any character could get through to him.

At the upper tip of the frontier the Iroquois situation had taken a most ominous turn. All winter English and American authorities had competed for Iroquois favor, deluging the constantly conferring sachems with presents, money, clothing and food. By spring Iroquois-American relations were becoming progressively less friendly. The hope of a last minute peace conference at Venango was fading. At this most ill-chosen moment the State of Pennsylvania occupied Presqu'Isle on Lake Erie in territory claimed by the Iroquois. This venture brought an instant blast of indignation from the Six Nations. Washington demanded a Pennsylvania withdrawal. Governor Mifflin reluctantly complied. But the damage had been done. The Iroquois, who, as mediators, the previous year had so earnestly begged the Ohio confederacy to accept the Muskingham line, now came out flat-footedly in support of the Ohio line and announced their decision in a message as warlike as an ultimatum:

General Washington, attend. What gives us room for the making of so many speeches, is, because you relate all the former deceptions that have been used. . . .
Brother: We are determined now, as we were before, that the line shall remain. . . .
Brother: If you do not comply with our request, we shall determine on something else. . . .
Brother: We are determined to be a free people. You know, General Washington, that we, the Six Nations, have always been able to defend ourselves, and we are still determined to maintain our freedom.

Wayne was thus faced with the prospect that even if the Iroquois as a nation did not enter the war many hundreds of their warriors under Brant would stream westward to reinforce the confederates.

All these unpropitious circumstances, from Elijah Clarke's absurd little republic in the far south to Brant's marshaling of Indian power in the north, must have been on Wayne's mind as he sat in Fort Greenville that early summer of 1794, weighing each separate risk inherent in his plan of campaign. But all of these were as nothing compared to the stunning development within the defenses of the Indian stronghold upon which he was about to advance. Until now the English had supplied and encouraged the Indians but had taken the greatest care to hold their support within the limitations of their threadbare short of war formula. Again and again they had discreetly reminded the Indians that they could not expect actual armed assistance. The official English attitude had been succinctly defined in a letter from Hammond, English minister to the United States, to Lieutenant Governor Simcoe, July 11, 1792, in which he said, "I think everything short of hostilities should be employed to give weight to our interference." Now, as though in answer to Wayne's preparations, there had been officially announced a complete reversal of this policy of restraint. Lord Dorchester, Governor General of Canada, returning from a sojourn in England during which he obviously had been in full consultation with his government, addressing a deputation of Northern Indians, assured them:

Children: I was in expectation of hearing from the people of the United States what was required by them: I hoped that I should have been able to bring you together, and make you friends.

Children: I have waited long and listened with great attention, but I have not heard one word from them.

Children: I flattered myself with the hope that the line proposed in the year eighty-three, to separate us from the United States, which was immediately broken by themselves as soon as peace was signed, would have been mended, or a new one drawn, in an amicable manner. Here, also, I have been disappointed.

Children: Since my return, I find no appearance of a line remains; and from the manner in which the people of the United States rush on, and act, and talk, on this side; and from what I learn of their conduct toward the sea, *I shall not be surprised if we are at war with them in the course of the present year;* and if so, a line must be drawn by the warriors.

Children: . . . I have told you that there is no line between them and us. I shall acknowledge no line to be their's which have been encroached on by them since the year 1783. . . . Therefore all their approaches toward us since that time, and all the purchases made by them, I consider as an infringement on the King's rights. And when a line is drawn between us, be it in peace or war, they must lose all their improvements and houses on our side of it. *Those people must all be gone who do not obtain leave to become the King's subjects.* What belongs to the Indians will, of course, be secured and confirmed to them.

Children: What farther can I say to you? You are witnesses that on our parts we have acted in the most peaceable manner, and borne the language and conduct of the people of the United States with patience. But I believe our patience is almost exhausted.

He might well ask his audience what more he could say. He had said everything. He had denounced the peace treaty ending the Revolution. He had offered the Indians armed support if they needed it to regain the Ohio line and he had warned the American settlers that if they remained north of the Ohio they must become British subjects. In so far as the highest ranking English official in North America could speak for England he had placed England squarely in the forefront of the American-Indian war.

A week later Dorchester had implemented his belligerent words with belligerent action, having ordered Simcoe to march deeper into American territory and to build an advanced post for the protection of England's Indian allies. The fort rose on the Maumee in the heart of the Indian capital, manned by English soldiers and defended by English guns. Copies of the address and notices of the establishment of Fort Miami were distributed to all Indian nations for their information and assurance. Not only the overjoyed Indians but all Canada accepted Dorchester's moves, following so immediately upon his return from London, as certain evidence that England had decided upon war with the United States. The most conservative construction that could have been placed upon these events at the time, or now, for that matter, was that England, impressed by Genet's intrigues, American pro-French sympathies, and American resentment of the ship seizures, foresaw the inevitability of war, sooner or later, and had determined to maintain the Indian barrier in the face of Wayne's projected assault upon it.

These thunderheads of a new war were not rising only in the west. The east, too, was in a tumult. To pro-French excitement had been added a sudden outburst of anti-English fury. England, under the "Rule of 1756" which denied the right of neutrals to take over a belligerent's carrying trade, had suddenly and without warning seized and confiscated every American ship in West Indian waters that her cruisers could overhaul. News of Dorchester's inflammatory address to the Indians added to the storm of indignation sweeping the United States. The administration clapped on an embargo to reduce the shipping loss. But this negative approach satisfied few. The House passed a non-intercourse act aimed directly at England. Bills were introduced in Congress for the establishment of arsenals, the accumulation of naval supplies, the enlargement of the army.

Cooler heads in the government were aghast at this sudden courting of a new war with England for which the struggling young republic was so ill prepared. Washington persuaded Chief Justice Jay to step into the breach. Hastily, lest the mounting war fever prevent his departure, Jay was sent off to London to endeavor to reason with the English government. But whatever the success of his mission trans-Atlantic communications were too slow for his peace efforts to have any bearing on Wayne's bearding of English power in the western wilderness. Nevertheless, Washington did not countermand his marching orders. The American interests Wayne was committed to guarding were too critical to permit their surrender under any pressure.

These were some of the anxieties superimposed upon Wayne's primary concern — the task of advancing into the Indian country and destroying the Indian army which had so often and so recently, under comparable circumstances, so convincingly proved its military superiority. Few commanders in history, since Cortez stepped on the shore of Mexico, have surveyed a scene across there played fewer rays of hope. But now, as always before, our story cannot go forward unaccompanied by the tom toms of melodrama. For there was fixed upon Wayne a final incredible encumbrance, clinging as closely as his shadow, which must completely have demoralized any resolution less calm and single-purposed. Wilkinson, the necessary sharer of his secrets and companion of his councils, his second in command, was devoting his cunning, his ingenuity and his vast capacity for mischief to endless attempts to obstruct, confound, betray and destroy his chief.

Wilkinson's second Spanish intrigue was in full flower that spring. He was receiving more Spanish money than ever before. He was reporting on Clark's New Orleans project and taking personal credit for Clark's delays. He was urging upon Carondelet a more drastic closing of the Mississippi as a means of precipitating Kentucky's secession. He was forecasting Wayne's certain defeat but warning Carondelet that this was certain to tip the West toward union with England and requesting $200,000 as the sum necessary to ward off this development. He was maintaining his English contacts, established through Reuben Reynolds and others, and regularly sending information to Detroit of Wayne's military intentions and movements.

One passage in this counterpoint of melodrama was a 1794 financial transaction that led to a comedy of errors so ludicrously lurid that it was a shame Wayne could not have learned of it, since it might have produced a smile at a time one would have been a relief to him. Three barrels of silver were en route up the Mississippi in the custody of one of Wilkinson's agents, Henry Owen. After the Spanish military escort was necessarily dropped at the mouth of the Ohio, the barge crew mutinied, murdered Owen, and made off with the money. Greater disaster impended. Three of the pirates were arrested in Kentucky. Judge Innes, horrified lest judicial proceedings disclose the origin and destination of the treasure, hastily sent the prisoners to Fort Washington for Wilkinson himself to deal with. Wilkinson, as desperately afraid of any investigation and particularly of one which might attract Wayne's attention, hastily packed them off to the Spanish commandant at New Madrid. Still the agony was prolonged. The party was stopped by the vigilant American commander at Fort Massac and the prisoners, after some sceptical scrutiny, were sent back again to the civil authorities in Kentucky. This time Judge Innes kept his wits about him and managed to see that the charges were dismissed for lack of evidence. Wilkinson breathed again. The money was gone. But his contemporary reputation, once more, was spared.

Intent as he was upon his Spanish and English intrigues Wilkinson found ample time to attempt directly and officially to destroy his chief. In June and July, on the very eve of the momentous campaign, he wrote Secretary of War Knox, laying five general charges against Wayne and urging that the campaign be ordered suspended for the purpose of holding an inquiry to determine Wayne's fitness to command. Wilkinson's Spanish and English schemes, though in competition with one another, had one feature in common: neither could survive an American victory.

Knox, characteristically, took no action with regard to this astounding attitude on the part of a second in command. He permitted the commander and his ranking lieutenant, the accused and his accuser, to serve together to the end of the supremely critical operation. At the end of the campaign he furnished Wayne with copies of Wilkinson's letters. Wayne pronounced the charges "as unexpected as they are groundless, and as false as they are base and insidious."

Unfortunately, Wilkinson's letters to Knox have somewhere along the line been lost to sight and we may judge their content only by the tone of Knox's replies to him and Wayne's to Knox. More than likely the charges were of a piece Wilkinson was broadcasting at the time in letters to many influential westerners, asserting that "such feeble & improvident arrangements, and such guardless & disorderly conduct was never before witnessed in any military corps," declaring "the whole operation presents us a tissue of improvidence, disarray, precipitancy, Error & Ignorance, of thoughtless temerity, unseasonable cautions, and shameful omissions," and characterizing Wayne as "a liar, a drunkard, a Fool . . . a Coward" and "a Hypocrite."

Wayne, beginning to guess Wilkinson's malevolence but not yet beginning actively to suspect the extent of his treason, closed his mind to this and all other distractions, whether near or far, however significant or threatening, and kept his attention fixed upon the enemy in the field. Until midsummer he remained immobile in Fort Greenville, preferring to wait for drier ground and for Indian excitability to mount. His patience bore fruit. In the war of nerves the Indians, tormented by the suspense, made a premature move. But they made it with alarming ferocity and great dexterity. Eluding Wayne's screen of scouts, an Indian column descended upon Fort Recovery, June 30, just as a supply train, under Major William MacMahon, was pulling out along the road to Fort Greenville. Achieving surprise, as so often they had before, the attackers sprang at one bound from the forest into the midst of the convoy. MacMahon was among the first to fall. The escort was broken and driven back upon the fort. The Indians followed with a rush, hoping to overwhelm the place during the initial confusion. But the Legionnaires of the garrison, by now wilderness veterans, remained steady, though the hail of rifle fire was so intense that many defenders were struck down by bullets entering the loopholes through which they were endeavoring to return the fire. The Indians persisted in the assault with a disregard for their own losses that they had occasionally displayed in the field but had never before accepted in an attack upon a fortified place. A part of their advance planning had been the expectation of digging up the by now historic four brass cannon to use in breaching the walls but they were confronted instead with the guns mounted on the ramparts. The storm continued until half the defenders had fallen but those still on their feet did not weaken. Finally the Indians drew off, reappeared to attempt a surprise night attack, and then broke off the battle.

The most significant feature of the engagement was not the disciplined vigor of the Indian attack or the narrow margin by which it had eventually been repulsed. It was the appearance among the assailants of so many white men. The Tory Rangers were back in harness, reviving the bitter days when they had accompanied and animated savage invasions of the frontier from New York to Georgia. While in the background, clearly visible from the fort, had stood three red-coated English officers, observing and advising, if not directing, the operation. Twelve years after the Revolution here again were Englishmen marching shoulder to shoulder with their Indian allies. Wayne could have had no further doubt that in marching into the Indian country he was marching also into the mouth of the lion's den.

Nevertheless, the time had come to put all his painstaking plans and preparations to the test. On July 26 the Kentucky auxiliaries, 1600 mounted riflemen under General Scott, arrived in response to his summons. This time, as Wayne had foreseen, they came ungrudgingly. There now at last existed a regular army with which they could be glad to serve. Two days later Wayne set out on his northward march. His regulars numbered but 2634. It was a small army but perhaps never has there been an American force more fitted, man for man, for its mission, or one whose defeat could have proved more disastrous to the nation.

Wayne moved forward with the deliberation that remained

essential to his plan, taking time to cut an adequate road, to organize a sufficient supply, to maintain a wide screen of scouts and pickets, and each night to fortify his camp. Little Turtle, the previously invincible Indian commander, had been observing Wayne for two years. Everything he saw had impressed him the more disagreeably. "The Americans are now led by a chief who never sleeps," he is reported to have said in council. "He is like a blacksnake, the night and the day are alike to him."

Some of Wayne's followers were not so impressed. Not only Wilkinson but many of his loyal officers became increasingly vocal. Scouts brought reports of an Indian town off to the flank which appeared to invite a surprise attack. Wayne was not interested. He was in no mood for side shows. The murmurs of criticism swelled. Young William Clark, whose association with Meriwether Lewis while with Wayne's command was to lead to a longer and equally historic march, confided disgustedly to his journal that apparently it was not Wayne's wish "to Embrace so probable a means for ending the War by compelling them to peace."

The Indians, finding no favorable opportunity to attack, continued to withdraw. Wayne reached the junction of the Auglaize and Maumee rivers, where so recently the Indian world had held its great congress from which had issued its memorable defiance of the United States. Here he paused and devoted eight leisurely days to the construction of another fortress which he named Fort Defiance.

Downstream, along the Maumee's fifty mile course to Lake Erie, the rolling forested hills rose on either side of a narrow lane of bottom land which had been converted into one almost uninterrupted corn field. Ranged through the corn were the towns of such noted Indian war chiefs as Blue Jacket, Blackhoof, Red Pole, Captain Pipe, Black Wolf, Cat's Eyes, Tarhe the Crane, and many others whose names were as familiar to the settlers as the names of big league ball players to today's sports fans. The Miami, Shawnee, Wyandot and Delaware towns had until recently been scattered over a far wider area but for mutual protection had now been concentrated in this single valley. Here was the Indian inner citadel, the fountainhead of Indian power. At its center, by the foot of the rapids, grimly squatted the new English fort. Above it flew the Union Jack, a flaunted symbol of that covering mantle of official patronage in which for twenty years the Indians had been wrapped, of that sanctuary of English protection from which they had issued to attack and to which they had returned for comfort.

Wayne, gazing down that valley, studying its military features, must have had his gaze fixed as well upon the incalculable consequences of his every next move. Before him loomed the risk of a far greater catastrophe than had befallen St. Clair — war with England, loss of the West, irretrievable disaster to his country. In his pocket was Washington's final admonition. He was at all costs but one to avoid attacking the English post. That one was defeat. If in the last resort victory depended upon it he was to attack. In no event was he to return without victory.

While building Fort Defiance Wayne turned again to his war of nerves. He dispatched to the Indians one last appeal for peace:

I, Anthony Wayne, Major General and Commander in Chief of the federal army now at Grand Glaize, and commissioner plenipotentiary of the United States of America . . . urged by pity for the errors into which bad and designing men have led you, from the head of my army, now in possession of your abandoned villages and settlements, do hereby once more extend the friendly hand of peace toward you . . . . Be no longer deceived or led astray by the false promises and language of the bad white men at the foot of the rapids; *they have neither power nor inclination to protect you.*

Wayne had not expected submission. But he saw no harm, at so critical a moment, in giving the Indians a topic for discussion which might excite their cowed peace faction, distract their councils, and breed suspicion of English sincerity. He succeeded better than he could have hoped. A sudden sense of impending isolation seized upon the more perceptive Indian leaders. The American army was almost in sight, the hour of decision was at hand, and yet the much advertised English support had not stirred beyond the former limits of ammunition, rations, and admonitions to be brave. Neither had Brant and

the heralded Iroquois reinforcements arrived. Even the redoubt-
able Little Turtle was depressed. He proposed an attempt to
gain at least the delay of prolonging negotiations with Wayne.
But any such open admission of weakening confidence was fiercely
rejected by the council majority. Indian public opinion demanded another of the great victories to which it had become
accustomed. Accused of cowardice by several of his fellow coun-
cillors Little Turtle observed calmly that this was a matter that
they could judge for themselves by remaining in his company
when battle was joined.

Since the confederacy's determination was to fight, he chose
his position with care. A stronger could scarcely have been
imagined. Near the head of the rapids a recent tornado had
felled a wide belt of forest. The bristling barrier of uprooted
and interlaced trees, two miles from front to back, formed an
abattis more formidable than the most diligent corps of military
engineers could have contrived. This barrier, ideally adapted
to Indian skill in making use of cover, extended from the river
to the wooded hills, straight across the one feasible route of
advance available to Wayne. He must make a frontal attack upon it or attempt exceedingly awkward flank movements through
the forest where the Indians would possess the tactical advantage
invariably theirs in such terrain. If he did make the frontal
attack his cavalry could not get into action against the main
Indian position and his so carefully drilled infantry battalions,
necessarily losing their formations before they had penetrated
ten yards into the belt of fallen timbers, must become easy prey
as individuals to the hidden Indian sharpshooters. Though
Major William Campbell, commander of the English fort, for
all his intense interest in proceedings, still showed no sign of
permitting his garrison to step outside the walls, Little Turtle
had little reason to feel dismay. To defend his seemingly in-
vulnerable position he had at his disposal an estimated 2,000
Indian warriors and some hundreds of white volunteers, Detroit
militia, traders, trappers, squaw men and battle-hardened ex-
Tory Rangers.

To gain more time for Brant and other possible reinforcements to arrive, the Indian reply to Wayne's peace overture

was their usual one. They would give him a reply in ten days. Wayne's response was to move to the head of the rapids. Here he built a fortified camp, Fort Deposit, in which to place his baggage and supply train. His troops stripped for action. Thereupon he tightened the screws of his war of nerves to the last excruciating pitch. Though in the very presence of the enemy he remained motionless for the next three days. It was the custom for the Indian warrior on the eve of battle, or any exceptional trial, to purify and strengthen himself by fasting and prayer. The Indian defenders, crouched among their fallen timbers, anticipating attack any hour, day after day, muttered and sweat and starved, their excitable spirits alternately fired by false alarms and chilled by new delays.

Reports from scouts and spies fully informed Wayne of the strength of the Indian position. He remained imperturbable. He was content to fight them on grounds of their own choosing. He intended to beat them. He wanted it to be decisive victory, with no residue of excuses or explanations to account for their defeat. Until now he had been plagued by many anxieties. But now that he had arrived upon the battlefield he was calm. He was sure of his men, sure of what they could do, sure that they could win. At dawn on August 20 he ordered the attack.

His game leg, which was to cause his death two years later, was troubling him more than usual that morning. He had it bound with flannel from hip to ankle. Tears of pain started from his eyes when he was hoisted into the saddle. But his vision was clear enough when he had picked up the reins. He rode off, well to the fore. When an aide protested that if he were killed there would be no one to give the army orders, he replied testily that the orders would remain the same — "charge the damn rascals with the bayonet."

All went exactly as he had foreseen and planned. The army advanced along the strip of bottom land on the left bank of the river, through fields of corn and occasional patches of woods, with a battalion of mounted Kentuckians in the van as skirmishers, the main body of Kentuckians on the left, the Legion cavalry in reserve, and the Legion infantry in position to storm the belt of fallen timbers. The advancing mounted militia came under sudden heavy fire. They broke and fell back upon the infantry. But there was no confusion. These were indeed a new kind of regular troops. They opened ranks to let the fleeing horsemen through, closed again, wheeled into attack formation as though on the drill ground, and went on, their multicolored plumes gleaming in the summer sun. As they approached the smoke-wreathed barrier of fallen trees they took the murderous fire without flinching or replying and kept on, their own pieces at the trail. At the last moment they lifted the glittering blades mounted on the still cold muzzles of their muskets and plunged into the labyrinth, reaching that ritualistic climax of a soldier's career, the charge driven home with the bayonet.

The battle was won in that first moment. The impact proved Wayne's theory of the key to victory, proved the fatal flaw in the Indian military character. The Indian's traditional way of making war prepared him to display the most extraordinary bursts of courage when himself choosing the moment of attack but did not endow him with the disciplined and phlegmatic stamina to endure such an onset. Little Turtle's line broke and the charge swept on with an impetus that gave the Indians no time to reload or reform. The Legionnaires kept going, without once losing that impetus, through the whole two miles of the barrier of fallen trees, until they broke out into the open beyond in pursuit of the demoralized enemy. The Legion cavalry, discovering a narrow space of open ground between the river and the barrier, wheeled into it, burst like a whirlwind upon the entrenched defenders, and circled that flank in time to add swifter terror to the general rout.

The Indian power had been broken but the graver crisis still remained. Ahead stood the English post and the greater power of England. English soldiers on the ramparts were watching, matches alight, this overthrow of England's allies. The crucial moment came. Fleeing Indians swarmed about the gate of the fort, pleading for refuge. If they were admitted Wayne must go in after them. But they were not admitted. Red-coated soldiers prodded them away with bayonets and they fled on, howling imprecations upon English ingratitude and English perfidy.

Wayne relaxed slightly, for the first time in two years. The great English bluff had at last been called. He realized Campbell's orders, like his own, envisaged risks but risks short of war. For all the recent display of apparent belligerent intentions England had no more wanted war than had the United States. The Indians had been made the victims of a calculated, prolonged and officially nourished illusion.

The essence of Wayne's victory was the proof at last forced upon them that this was so, that the Revolution had meant for them an actual change of masters, that they were confronted not with the sovereignty of England but with the sovereignty of the United States. He drove the point home. He wanted to leave no vestige of doubt in the Indian mind. Devastation of the towns and cornfields of their central fastness was carried for miles up and down the Maumee Valley and to the very muzzles of the English guns. With special relish he burned the trading post of Alexander McKee just below the English fort. McKee, more than any other one man, personified the illegitimate union of English policy and Indian hostility. Since he had escaped from American arrest in Pittsburgh in 1778, he had, as Tory partisan, as professional trader, as English agent, and as uncrowned king of the Ohio Indians, devoted his remarkable influence, talent and energy to persuading the Indians that their future depended upon their continuing attachment to England and an unrelenting war with the Americans. At times leading them in person, he had had for sixteen years a hand in every attack against the settlements. The spectacle of his headquarters in flames in full view of the English garrison could not have left much doubt in the simplest Indian mind.

The three days Wayne remained before the English fort were nevertheless days in which each moment presented new hazards. Two nations could not well come closer to war. A single shot from either side would have been enough. Either of the two commanders, as they exchanged insulting notes, each virtually daring the other to knock the chip off his shoulder, each cut off by weeks of wilderness travel from consultation with his government, had it in his power to start one by a single slip of judgment. It was a war that was to be proved inevitable but it did not come for another eighteen years. In 1812 additional hundreds of thousands of hardy and by then completely loyal settlers had taken root in the west, Tennessee and Ohio had joined Kentucky upon the roll of states, the nation had developed under the constitution a coherent voice and a cohesive structure and yet the war was accompanied by innumerable humiliations and disasters. In 1794 the evil would have been, as Knox so soberly said: "unlimited." Happily, both commanders were soldiers and the shot was not fired. Wayne, having accomplished his purpose, moved westward to build and garrison another stronghold, Fort Wayne, on Miami land, to complete his grasp upon the Indian country.

Americans have fought few battles more decisive than the Battle of Fallen Timbers. Wayne, at the time, was dissatisfied because the Indians had fled before he had killed as many as he could have wished. But the consequences that flew from the victory were like the upending of a cluster of tenpins. The whole national scene was completely changed.

The Northern Indians, ignoring final desperate English clutches at their confidence, after a winter of earnest consultation among themselves came to Wayne at Fort Greenville to sign, this time without equivocation or reservation, a peace of his dictation. The Southern Indians, likewise convinced of the inevitable, called a halt to their organized depredations upon that frontier. The country was never again to be confronted by an Indian war of strategic significance. From Fallen Timbers to the Pacific every future Indian campaign was to be in the nature of a police or punitive action.

Jay's lost cause mission to England took on unforeseen life with the news of the victory. The English policy of maintaining the Indian barrier without paying the price to maintain it had fallen in ruins. Jay was able to win English agreement, this time speedily fulfilled, to turn over the lake posts. Indian power had lost political significance and the West's northern border had become what it is today.

United States Minister Pinckney in Madrid was at the same time gaining Spanish agreement to open the Mississippi. The issue which had provoked the West to more oratory, ill feeling, intrigue, and outright treason than all others combined had become a thing of the past. Upon Wilkinson, of all people, fell command of the American forces taking over Natchez upon its evacuation by the Spaniards. The collapse of Spanish hopes, foreshadowing the purchase of Louisiana, left wide open the door to empire.

Equally enduring results as swiftly became evident in the west. The survival of Wayne's army as a military force in being revitalized federal authority. Clark's New Orleans venture faded away. Two days after news of Wayne's victory reached Philadelphia Washington called out troops to suppress the rebellion in southwestern Pennsylvania, which was already collapsing. But the most notable effect of the battle was upon the West's state of mind. Gusts of dissastisfaction with the national government persisted, as they have to this day, but emphasis shifted to efforts to gain a redress of grievances within the union rather than by threats of withdrawal from it. Sporadic secessionist intrigues continued but no longer enjoyed popular support and that species of impulsive resort to treason died out in the final comic flicker of Aaron Burr's conspiracy.

So do we come finally to the genesis of the fateful decision. The First American had made it before he was fully aware that he had made it. There was in him the instinct to survive as the kind of man that he had already become. His choice had been made by a practical process of first considering and then rejecting all possible alternatives. He had been like a suitor casting about for the most eligible of available brides. Union with Spain had offered various immediate rewards but in the long run the sterile and rigid controls of a distant state and church. Union with England had offered a blessed relief from the Indian war, an open Mississippi, a share in the fur trade, but the handicapped future of a province. Union with republican France could have been romantically perfect, accompanied by a freedom amounting to license, but the calculating suitor had presently recognized this to be an unattainable ideal. Continued bachelorhood, by way of secession and independence, had offered countless attractions but as well the burdens of coping unaided on the battlefield and at the council table with a host of enemies. The least of evils had been to wait and see, to concede, for the moment at least and until other opportunities chanced to develop, a tacit attachment to the distant government on the Atlantic which while too weak to offer more than nominal support possessed at the same time the inestimable advantage of being too weak to interfere.

This was at no time a conscious decision. There came no day or hour when it was voiced. Several of the Kentucky conventions which had voted, in effect, to wait and see may be said to have approached voicing one. But no one at the time was aware that a significant decision had been reached. The persisting wait and see attitude had been purely an instinct — an instinct felt in common by men of a special kind who sensed a need to guard the qualities that made them special. Neither had been Kentucky's acceptance of the much belated invitation to become a state a final decision. This was generally regarded then as an expedient which might be rescinded at will. More suitable arrangements, such as the French alliance, appeared already in the offing. The enormous significance of the great doctrine of an ever expanding union of new, free and equal states had not been at once recognized. To the self-seeking and hard-headed westerner the principle of federal union had not yet proved its clear and present value.

Some time during the months after Fallen Timbers the light began to dawn. And it was a dazzling light. Other powers striving for the great valley, England, France, Spain, the United States, had sought to have their cake and eat it, to gain advantage without paying advantage's price. It was now left to the West itself to perform this exceptional feat. The national government had at last been proved capable of providing measurable support and yet the West under the doctrine of free and equal states was not to be required to pay the price of submission to dictation. Under the shield of his nation's name and his nation's flag the westerner retained full freedom of action to grapple with his every opportunity and to make his freebooting way on westward. He was free to grab land, to trade as and where he chose, to exploit a continent's resources, to dispossess the Indian, to seize Spanish provinces, to seek his fortune wherever and however it might be found, to exhaust his every potentiality. At last he had chosen his nation. He had become that nation in the sense that he represented the irresistible growth factor which was to galvanize its perspectives and to prescribe its dimensions.

Never has instinct been more fully justified. It had become pragmatically clear to him that his interests and his country's interests were identical and that the principle of federal union gave him the strength of ten together with perpetual freedom of action. He understood bargains and his side of the bargain was a surge of deep and compulsive loyalty. The time was to come when the South might attempt to secede but never again was the West's allegiance to waver.

It may be argued that other influences than the Battle of Fallen Timbers played upon these great consequences. However, to estimate the full decisiveness of a battle it is necessary first of all to consider the contrary consequences had it been lost. Had Wayne lost none of these most agreeable rewards would have been forthcoming. Every English and Spanish design must have been pressed with new energy. The Indian war, exploding into new offensive intensity, must have thrust upon the embittered West the alternatives of seeking English or Spanish protection. Western contempt for a national government too timid to support Clark and too weak to support Wayne must have passed all bounds. So fierce a strain upon the West's faltering allegiance must almost certainly have split the Mississippi Valley into a confused welter of independent republics, buffer states, Indian sanctuaries, and foreign provinces. But, as always before in our story, at the most critical moment rescue was at hand. Wayne did win and his winning brought a fortunate end to an era, one of the most critical, if not the most critical, in our history.

The First Americans had survived — as Americans.

Appe

During those three August days of 1794 Majo
Campbell of the English army and Major General
Wayne of the American army had not only the pow
strong an incentive as a soldier can feel to commit
spective nations to a war which must have vastly ch[
history of North America. Their official sentiments as
under the stress of the moment may therefore prove o[
terest. Campbell initiated the correspondence, though
until the day after the battle before venturing to [
dignity:

August 2

Sir: An Army of the United States of America, said to be u
command, having taken post on the banks of the Maumee, fo[
of the last twenty-four hours, almost within reach of the gu[
fort, being a post belonging to his Majesty, the King of Grea
occupied by His Majesty's troops, and which I have the hono
mand, it becomes my duty to inform myself, as speedily as p[
what light I am to view your making such near approache
garrison. I have no hesitation, on my part, to say, that I kn[
war existing between Great Britain and America.

I have the honor to be, sir, with great respect, your most
and humble servant,

William Campbell, Major 24t[

To this Wayne replied:

August 21,

Sir: I have received your letter of this date, requiring from
motives which have moved the army under my command to t[
tion they at present occupy, far within the acknowledged jurs

Great Britain and America." I, on my part, declare the same, and that the only cause I have to entertain a contrary idea at present, is the hostile act you are now in commission of, i.e. by recently taking post far within the well known and acknowledged limits of the United States, and erecting a fortification in the heart of the settlements of the Indian tribes now at war with the United States. This, sir, appears to be an act of the highest aggression, and destructive to the peace and interest of the Union. Hence it becomes my duty to desire, and I do hereby desire and demand, in the name of the President of the United States, that you immediately desist from any further act of hostility or aggression, by forbearing to fortify, and by withdrawing the troops, artillery, and stores, under your orders and direction, forthwith, and removing to the nearest post occupied by his Britannic Majesty's troops at the peace of 1783, and which you will be permitted to do unmolested, by the troops under my command.

I am, with very great respect, sir, your most obedient and very humble servant,

ANTHONY WAYNE.

But Campbell, the loser, had the last word:

22nd August, 1794.

Sir: I have this moment to acknowledge the receipt of your letter of this date; in answer to which I have only to say, that, being placed here in command of a British post, and acting in a military capacity only, I cannot enter into any discussion either on the right or impropriety of my occupying my present position. Those are matters that I conceive will be best left to the ambassadors of our different nations.

Having said this much, permit me to inform you that I certainly will not abandon this post, at the summons of any power whatever, until I receive orders for that purpose from those I have the honor to serve under, or the fortune of war should oblige me. I must still adhere, sir, to the purport of my letter this morning, to desire that your army, or individuals belonging to it, will not approach within reach of my cannon, without expecting the consequences attending it.

Although I have said, in the former part of my letter, that my situation here is totally military, yet, let me add, sir, that I am much deceived, if His Majesty, the King of Great Britain, had not a post on this river, at and prior to the period you mention.

I have the honor to be, sir, with the greatest respect, your most obedient and very humble servant,

WILLIAM CAMPBELL, Major 24th Regiment.

Appendix B

A FRAME of reference in time for the 1782-1794 period in the evolution of the West might include the dates:

1535 Cartier visits site of Montreal.
1539 De Soto crosses Mississippi River.
1540 Coronado on Kansas plains.
1542 Cabrillo sights California coast.
1560 Spanish develop mines in northern Georgia.
1565 Spanish found St. Augustine.
1579 Drake lands near Golden Gate.
1598 Spanish occupy New Mexico.
1607 Jamestown founded.
1609 Hudson ascends Hudson River.
      Champlain antagonizes Iroquois.
1610 Hudson discovers Hudson Bay.
1615 Dutch establish trading post at Albany.
      Champlain sights Lake Huron.
1620 Pilgrims land.
1626 Dutch purchase Manhattan.
1633 Maryland founded.
1640–
1696 Era of Iroquois conquest.
1641 French reach Lake Superior.
1660 North Carolina founded.
1664 English capture New York.
1668 English establish trading post on Hudson Bay.
1670 Charleston, S. C., founded.
1671 French proclaim possession Great Lakes basin.
1673 Marquette and Joliet on Mississippi.
1678 Duluth builds post on west end Lake Superior.
1681 First settlement in Pennsylvania.
1682 La Salle reaches mouth Mississippi.
1699 French found Biloxi.

1700   French found Kaskaskia.
1701   French found Detroit.
1703   English traders begin gaining Southern Indian market.
1714   French found Natchez.
1718   French found New Orleans.
        Spanish found San Antonio.
1721   Pennsylvania authorities burn cabins to prevent English settle-
        ment west of Susquehanna.
1724   French build Fort Orleans on Missouri.
1727   French found Vincennes.
1733   Savannah founded.
1740   Pennsylvania traders begin gaining Ohio market.
1741   Russians visit Alaska coast.
1742   Verendrye sights Rocky Mountains.
1748   Ohio Company founded.
1750   Pennsylvania traders dominate Ohio Indian market.
        Dr. Walker explores parts of Kentucky and Tennessee.
1751   Gist explores parts of Ohio and Kentucky.
1753   Washington sent to demand French withdrawal from upper
        Ohio.
1754   French build Fort Duquesne.
        Washington surrenders at Fort Necessity.
1755   Braddock's defeat.
1755–
1761   French and Indian War.
1759   Quebec captured.
1760   Detroit occupied.
1763   Pontiac's rebellion.
        France cedes North American territories to England and Spain.
        Royal proclamation reserving region west of mountains to
        Indians.
1766   Great expansion English-Indian trade.
1768   First Treaty of Fort Stanwix opens southwestern Pennsylvania
        and northwestern Virginia to land companies.
1769   Settlers rush into new purchases.
        First settlements on Watauga and Monongahela.
        Spanish occupy California.
1773   First house in Kentucky at Harrodsburg.
1774   Dunmore's War between Virginians and Shawnee.
1775   Boonesborough, first permanent settlement in Kentucky, founded.
        Lexington, Concord, Bunker Hill and Siege of Quebec.
1776   Indian war spreads from southern to northern frontiers.
1777   Known in Kentucky as "The Bloody Year."
        Burgoyne's surrender and Valley Forge.
1778   France enters war.

Clark's conquest of Illinois.
Boone's capture, escape and court martial.
Wyoming and Cherry Valley massacres.
Siege of Boonesborough.
1779 Spain enters war.
Clark's capture of Vincennes and Hamilton.
Sullivan devastates Iroquois country.
Spanish take Natchez.
1780 Cumberland settlement established.
Spanish take Mobile.
English take Charleston.
Battle of King's Mountain.
Failure of English invasion of West.
France proposes Proclamation line of 1763 as U. S. western
boundary after independence.
1781 Spanish capture Pensacola and St. Joseph's.
Near collapse of frontier defense.
Congress votes acceptance Appalachian boundary.
Cornwallis surrenders at Yorktown.

1782

Feb.–Apr.		Unprecedented Indian raids.
Mar.	2	Parliament votes for peace with colonies.
Mar.	3	Moravian massacre.
Mar.	22	Estill's defeat.
Apr.	12	English fleet defeats French in West Indies.
Apr.	15	Bald Eagle blockhouse destroyed.
May		Chickasaw and Tory refugees raid Spanish river traffic.
June		Indian congress at Wapatomica.
June	5	Crawford's defeat.
July	11	English evacuate Savannah.
July	13	Hannastown destroyed.
Aug.		Indian council at Chilicothe.
Aug.	12	Holder's defeat.
Aug.	15	Attack on Bryant's Station.
Aug.	19	Battle of Blue Licks.
Aug.	27	English order defensive in west.
Aug.	27	Kentucky petitions Congress for statehood.
Sept.		Sevier destroys Chickamauga towns.
Sept.		Salt River station captured.
Sept.		Tories begin embarkation from New York.
Sept.		Statehood agitation in southwestern Pennsylvania.
Sept.	1	Destruction Kincheloe's Station.
Sept.	4	English peace commissioners agree deal directly with U.S.

Sept.	6	French and Spanish propose England to have territory north of Ohio and Spain all south of Tennessee.
Sept.	11	Siege of Wheeling.
Sept.	13	French and Spanish attack Gibraltar.
Sept.	14	Rice's fort attacked.
Oct.	6	U.S. and England reach agreement on Mississippi and Canadian boundary independently of France and Spain.
Oct.	29	New York cedes western lands to U.S.
Nov.		Clark burns Shawnee towns.
Nov.	30	Provisional peace treaty between U.S. and England.
Dec.	3	Pennsylvania assembly makes statehood agitation treason.
Dec.	14	Charleston evacuated.

1783

Mar.	3	Name Kentucky becomes official with creation Judicial District of Kentucky.
Apr.		Chickasaw and Tory refugees attack Spanish posts on Arkansas.
Apr.	19	Washington proclaims peace to Continental Army.
May		News of peace reaches Pittsburgh.
May		North Carolina claims western lands to Mississippi River and expropriates and opens to entry all Indian lands.
May		McGillivray made chief of Creek nation.
June		Miro calls conference of Southern Indians.
June		U.S. treaty of Nashville with Chickasaw, Creek, and Cherokee.
July		English at Detroit and Niagara advise Indians recognize peace.
July	2	Virginia discharges Clark from service.
July	13	Washington sends von Steuben to arrange transfer lake posts.
Aug.	1	Haldimand forbids entry Americans into English-Indian territory.
Aug.	11	Haldimand informs von Steuben England to retain lake posts.
Sept.	3	Simultaneous signatures English peace treaties with Spain, France and U.S. leaving southwest border undefined.
Sept.	22	Congress forbids settlers occupy Indian lands.
Oct.	15	Virginia votes Clark's veterans 150,000 acres north of Ohio.

Oct.	18	Congress directs disbanding of Continental Army.
Nov.	1	Treaty of Augusta with Creek.
Nov.	6	Treaty of French Lick with Chickasaw.
Nov.	25	English evacuate New York.

1784

Jan.	14	Congress ratifies peace with England.
Feb.	29	Blount wins first Muscle Shoals land grant from Georgia.
Mar.	1	Virginia completes cession territory north of Ohio.
Mar.	4	Clark appointed to federal Indian commission.
Apr.–Sept.		40 deaths listed along southern frontier.
Apr.	9	George III ratifies peace treaty.
Apr.	23	First Northwest Ordinance.
May	12	England refuses new request for lake posts.
June–July		Spain negotiates treaties with Southern Indians at Pensacola and Mobile.
June	26	Spain proclaims closure Mississippi River to American trade.
Summer		100 listed killed on Wilderness Road.
July		Kenton establishes station at Limestone on Ohio.
Aug.	23	Franklin declared independent state.
Sept.		Washington visits his western lands.
Oct.	22	Second Treaty of Fort Stanwix relinquishes Iroquois claims in west.
Nov.	7	Kentucky militia officers determine call state convention.
Dec.	5	First company of Harmar force reaches Pittsburgh.
Dec.	14	Sevier elected governor of Franklin.
Dec.	27	First Kentucky Convention.

1785

Jan.–May		Settlers west of Ohio evicted by federal troops.
Jan.	2	Treaty of Fort McIntosh.
Feb.		Georgia attempts seizure of Natchez.
Apr.	19	Massachusetts cedes western land claims to U.S.
May–Nov.		Renewed violence in Georgia-Creek war.
May	17	Virginia creates companies to develop routes west.
May	20	Congress directs and regulates surveys west of Ohio.
May	23	Second Kentucky Convention.
June	15	Congress renews prohibition settlement west of Ohio.
Summer		1,000 immigrant boats counted on Ohio.
July	6	Congress establishes dollar as unit of U.S. currency.

July	20	Gardoqui arrives to negotiate Spanish claims to Southwest.
Aug.		Fort Harmar started.
Aug.		Ouiatanon Indian congress plans resistance.
Aug.	8	Third Kentucky Convention.
Aug.	25	Pennsylvania-Virginia line run to Ohio.
Fall		Virginia legislature makes statehood agitation treason.
Oct.		Southern Indians extend raids to Kentucky frontier.
Nov.	10	Fort Finney established.
Nov.	12	Treaty of Galphinton with Creek.
Nov.	28	Treaty of Hopewell with Cherokee.

1786

Jan.		Brant pressing Indian case in London.
Jan.	3	Treaty of Hopewell with Choctaw.
Jan.	10	Virginia agrees conditionally to Kentucky independence.
Jan.	16	Treaty of Hopewell with Chickasaw.
Jan.	31	Treaty of Fort Finney.
Mar.	6	New Ohio Company formed in Boston.
Spring		Increased Indian hostilities along all frontiers.
Spring		Sevier destroys Cherokee valley towns.
Spring		Limestone, Licking and Beargrass areas devastated.
Apr.		Creek attacks on Georgia and Cumberland frontiers.
Apr.		Donelson and Christian killed by Indians.
Summer		Cherokee press attacks on southern frontier.
July		Hardin's expedition to relieve Vincennes Americans.
July	25	Indian congress at Niagara.
July	29	*Pittsburgh Gazette* begins publication.
Aug.		Franklin forces new land cession from Cherokee.
Aug.		Jay offers Gardoqui 25-year closure of Mississippi.
Aug.	7	Congress establishes Northern and Southern Indian Districts.
Aug.	8	Congress sets value silver dollar.
Aug.	29	First outbreaks violence Shay's Rebellion in Massachusetts.
Sept.		Clark's abortive Wabash campaign.
Sept.		Fourth Kentucky Convention delayed by Indian hostilities.
Sept.	14	Connecticut conditionally cedes western lands.
Oct.–Dec.		Rising western indignation over Spanish blockade.
Oct.	3	26 killed or captured in single Wilderness Road attack.
Oct.	6	Logan burns Shawnee towns.
Oct.	8	Clark seizes Spanish property at Vincennes.

Nov.	3	Shoulderbone Treaty with Creek.
Dec.	18	Northern Indian congress challenges U.S.
Dec.	19	Wilkinson committee condemns Clark Vincennes seizure.
Dec.	20	Wilkinson warns Spanish of Clark project.

1787

Jan.		Fourth Kentucky Convention.
Jan.	25	Virginia proclaims opening bounty lands between Scioto and Little Miami.
Feb.	3	Congress approves calling constitutional convention.
Feb.	27	Virginia condemns Clark Vincennes seizure.
Feb.	27	Last engagement Shay's Rebellion.
Apr.	24	Congress directs federal troops dispossess Clark.
May	14	Constitutional Convention convenes.
May–June		Northern and Southern Indians plan confederation at Little Tallasie.
June		Robertson destroys Cherokee town at Coldwater.
July		Brant writes Congress demanding Ohio surveys cease.
July	2	Wilkinson arrives at New Orleans.
July	13	Northwest Ordinance.
Aug.		Creek join Cherokee in Cumberland raids.
Aug.	1	Virginia opens surveyor's office for Ohio lands.
Aug.	18	*Kentucke Gazette* founded.
Aug.	22	Wilkinson takes oath of allegiance to King of Spain.
Sept.	5	Wilkinson memorial proposing Spanish support revolt in west.
Sept.	17	Constitution signed.
Sept.	17	Fifth Kentucky Convention.
Sept.	28	Congress refers Constitution to states.
Oct.	5	St. Clair appointed Governor Northwest Territory.
Dec.	7	Delaware ratifies Constitution.
Dec.	12	Pennsylvania and New Jersey ratify Constitution.

1788

Jan.	2	Georgia ratifies Constitution.
Jan.	9	Connecticut ratifies Constitution.
Feb.		Wilkinson returns to Kentucky.
Feb.	7	Massachusetts ratifies Constitution.
Feb.	14	Wilkinson proposes found colony on Yazoo.
Feb.	28	Battle between Sevier and Tipton forces in Franklin.
Spring		Tecumseh joins Cherokee with Shawnee war party.
Mar.	15	Clark proposes become Spanish subject in return for colonization rights.

Mar.	21	Great New Orleans fire.
Apr.	7	Marietta founded.
Apr.	28	Maryland ratifies Constitution.
May–Sept.		Federal detachments repeatedly attacked between Louisville and Vincennes.
May		Kirk and Brown massacres.
May	1	White leaves on tour of west to co-ordinate Spanish relations of western leaders.
May	23	South Carolina ratifies Constitution.
Summer		"Great Immigration" to west.
Summer		Harmon's Station repeatedly attacked.
June		Sevier attacks Cherokee in defiance of North Carolina.
June		Murder Old Tassel.
June		First Wilkinson trading fleet reaches New Orleans.
June		Bowles arrives from Bahamas with extra supplies for Creek.
June	21	New Hampshire, ninth state, ratifies and Constitution adopted.
June	25	Virginia ratifies.
July		Spanish fortify Natchez and New Madrid.
July	3	Congress refuses admit Kentucky.
July	15	St. Clair proclaims federal government at Marietta.
July	18	Sevier's first letter to Gardoqui.
July	20	Attack on Bledsoe's Station.
July	26	New York ratifies.
July	28	Sixth Kentucky Convention.
Aug.		Fain's defeat at Settico.
Aug.		Siege Houston's Station.
Aug.	20	McGillivray resigns from Spanish service.
Aug.	23	Martin's defeat at Lookout Mountain.
Fall		Harmon's Station abandoned.
Sept.		Sevier raids Cherokee country.
Sept.	13	New York becomes first capital U.S.
Sept.	21	Sevier's relief of Sherrill's Station.
Oct.		Creek and Cherokee take field in force.
Oct.	3	Morgan accepts New Madrid colony proposal.
Oct.	10	Sevier arrested.
Oct.	17	Destruction Gillespie's Station.
Oct.	25	Dr. Connolly arrives Louisville with English proposals.
Nov.		Cumberland renamed Mero.
Nov.	4	Seventh Kentucky Convention.
Nov.	18	Columbia founded.
Dec.	1	Spanish royal order directing more cautious relations with American West.

1789

Jan.		Columbia destroyed by flood.
Jan.	3	Morgan embarks for his New Madrid colony.
Jan.	7	Cincinnati founded under name Losantiville.
Jan.	9	Fort Harmar Treaty.
Jan.	10	Sevier defeats Cherokee at Flint's Creek.
Feb.	12	Wilkinson writes Miro details of English project.
Feb.	17	Sevier takes North Carolina oath of allegiance.
Spring		Wilkinson's great trading fleet leaves for New Orleans.
Mar.		Miro receives royal order limiting American conspiracy.
Mar.	4	Constitution takes effect.
Apr.		White arrives New Orleans for conference with Miro.
Apr.	6	Washington declared President.
Apr.	11	Dorchester reports on progress English intrigue in west.
Apr.	30	Washington inaugurated.
June		Fort Washington begun.
June		Wilkinson's second New Orleans visit.
July	20	Eighth Kentucky Convention.
Sept.	17	Wilkinson's second memorial.
Sept.	29	Congress establishes regular army.
Oct.	18	Washington authorizes St. Clair call out western militia.
Nov.	21	North Carolina ratifies Constitution.
Dec.		Defeat of Doughty on Tennessee.
Dec.	21	Georgia legislature grants 25,400,000 acres to land companies.
Dec.	25	Wilkinson returns to Kentucky with two mule loads silver.
Dec.	29	Harmar advances to Fort Washington with 300 troops.

1790

Jan.		Cincinnati named.
Jan.		Yazoo project launched.
Jan.–Feb.		St. Clair tours Northwest Territory establishing local government.
Feb.	25	North Carolina cedes western lands to U.S.
Apr.		Gamelin fails conciliate Miami.
May		Six boat federal convoy on Ohio destroyed with 5 killed and 8 captured.
May		Dorchester instructed offer Kentucky help in driving Spanish from Mississippi.
May	5	Imminence war with Spain announced in parliament.

May	9	Capital changed to Philadelphia.
May	20	Congress establishes Southwest Territory.
May	29	Rhode Island ratifies Constitution.
June		McGillivray visits Washington in New York.
July		Clark offered command Yazoo expedition.
July	15	St. Clair calls out western militia.
July	26	Ninth Kentucky Convention.
Aug.		Wilkinson withdraws from Yazoo company.
Aug.	7	Treaty of New York with Creek.
Aug.	7	Blount becomes governor S.W. Territory.
Aug.	26	Washington proclamation denounces Yazoo project.
Sept.	30	Harmar marches from Fort Washington.
Oct.		Gallipolis settled.
Oct.	19	Hardin's first defeat.
Oct.	22	Hardin's second defeat.
Oct.	28	England and Spain sign Nootka convention.
Dec.		Iroquois delegation visits Washington at Philadelphia.

1791

Jan.	2	First attacks on Muskingum settlements.
Jan.	2	Big Bottom settlement destroyed.
Jan.	8	Siege Dunlop's Station.
Feb.	4	Congress agrees admit Kentucky.
Mar.	4	Vermont admitted.
Mar.	19	Boatload traders and discharged soldiers massacred on Ohio.
Mar.	26	Greathouse boat massacre on Ohio.
Apr.	10	Kenton ambushes Indian raiders recrossing Ohio.
Apr.	30	St. Clair organizing new army in Pittsburgh.
May	5	Proctor, U.S. peace envoy, halted by English at Niagara.
May	15	St. Clair preparing expeditionary force at Fort Washington.
June	1	Scott burns Wabash towns.
July	1	McKee addresses North-South council at Maumee Rapids.
July	2	Blount forces Treaty of Holston on Cherokee.
Aug.		Doublehead and Bench raid Cumberland and southwest Virginia.
Aug.		Indians demand more support from Dorchester.
Aug.	7	Wilkinson's Wabash expedition.
Aug.	23	Southwestern Pennsylvania meeting denounces federal taxation.
Sept.		St. Clair builds Fort Harrison.

Sept.	17	St. Clair's army marches from Fort Washington.
Oct.	12	St. Clair builds Fort Jefferson.
Oct.	22	Wilkinson commissioned lt. commandant in U.S. Army.
Oct.	24	St. Clair marches into wilderness.
Nov.	4	St. Clair's disaster.
Nov.	5	*Knoxville Gazette* started.
Nov.	8	St. Clair survivors reach Fort Washington.
Dec.	15	Bill of Rights becomes effective.
Dec.	30	Carondelet succeeds Miro as Spanish governor.

1792

Jan.	2	U.S. asks intercession of Iroquois.
Jan.	9	Pond and Stedman dispatched as unofficial peace envoys.
Feb.		Cherokee press raids along Kentucky and Tennessee roads.
Feb.	1	Wilkinson column visits St. Clair battlefield.
Feb.	1	Wilkinson granted permanent Spanish pension.
Feb.	25	Brant invited to Philadelphia.
Mar.	1	Wilkinson commissioned Brigadier-General in U.S. Army.
Mar.	5	Congress authorizes new army.
Mar.	5	St. Clair resigns commission.
Mar.	13	Iroquois delegation arrives Philadelphia.
Apr.		Bench raids Holston.
Apr.		U.S. forbids Tennessee militia pursue Indians across treaty line.
Apr.	3	Trueman and Hardin instructed on peace missions.
Apr.	3	Wayne appointed commander in chief in west.
May		Wilkinson sends Reuben Reynolds to Canada.
May	8	Hendrick sent to intercede with hostile Indians.
May	11	Captain Gray discovers mouth Columbia River.
May	14	Spanish treaty of confederation with Southern Indians.
May	22	Trueman killed en route to Miami villages.
May	22	Hardin killed en route to Sandusky villages.
June		Carondelet offers Southern Indians unlimited supplies.
June		Wayne reaches Pittsburgh.
June	1	Kentucky becomes state with Isaac Shelby first governor.
June	20	Brant reaches Philadelphia.
June	26	Ziegler's Station burned.
June	28	Innes appointed Chief Justice of Kentucky and Sebastian to Court of Appeals.

Appendix C

A LIST of books available at most public libraries, for the reader moved to pursue the subject, might include the following:

ABERNETHY, Thomas Perkins. *Western Lands and the American Revolution.* New York, 1937. Thorough and scholarly study of the frontier land problem.

ABERNETHY, Thomas Perkins. *From Frontier to Plantation in Tennessee.* Chapel Hill, 1932. Brief but considered history of early Tennessee.

ADAIR, James. *History of the American Indians.* London, 1775. Reprint (Samuel Cole Williams, ed.). Johnson City, Tenn. 1930. The personal adventures and observations of an early English trader with the Southern Indians.

ALBACH, James R. (James H. Perkins and J. M. Peck, eds.). *Annals of the West.* St. Louis, 1850. A sketchy but useful compilation of much contemporary source material.

ALVORD, Clarence Walworth and BIDGOOD, Lee. *First Explorations of Trans-Allegheny Region by the Virginians.* Cleveland, 1912. Documented study of the first Englishmen to find streams flowing west.

BAILEY, Kenneth P. *The Ohio Company of Virginia.* Glendale, Calif., 1939. A full account of the great land company that employed George Washington and George Rogers Clark.

BAKELESS, John. *Daniel Boone.* New York, 1939. Most complete life of Boone.

BARTRAM, William. *Travels.* Philadelphia, 1791. Reprint (Mark Van Doren, ed.). New York, 1940. Contemporary local color on the land and the Indians provided by a great naturalist who was also a great writer.

BILLINGTON, Ray Allen. *Westward Expansion.* New York, 1949. Amazingly comprehensive, detailed, and evaluated one volume history of the frontier from 1492 to 1896.

BILLON, Frederick L. *Annals of St. Louis.* 2 Vol. St. Louis, 1886–88. Much contemporary and regional detail on the French and Spanish background to the American frontier.

BOND, Beverley W. *The Foundations of Ohio.* Columbus, 1941. A brief history of the settlement, development and Indian relations of pioneer Ohio.

BOYD, Thomas A. *Mad Anthony Wayne.* New York, 1928. Colorful and adequate life of the general.

BREBNER, John Bartlet. *Explorers of North America.* New York, 1933. Brief history of exploration to 1806.

BROWN, John P. *Old Frontiers.* Kingsport, Tenn., 1938. A vivid yet well-documented account of the wars of the Cherokee.

BUCK, Solon J. and Elizabeth H. *The Planting of Civilization in Western Pennsylvania.* Pittsburgh, 1939. Splendid and fully informative study of the economic, political and social development of a frontier.

BURT, A. L. *The United States, Great Britain, and British North America, 1783–1815.* New Haven, 1940. A penetrating examination of the official English attitude toward the advancing American frontier.

BUTLER, Mann. *A History of the Commonwealth of Kentucky.* Louisville, 1834. Written by a man who had been able to interview most of the participants.

BUTTERFIELD, Consul Willshire. *History of the Girtys.* Cincinnati, 1890. Painstaking account of the famous renegades by a somewhat opinionated scholar.

BUTTERFIELD, Consul Willshire. *Washington-Irvine Correspondence.* Madison, Wisc., 1882. Light on the facts of life that faced contemporary authority.

BUTTERFIELD, Consul Willshire. *Journal of Jonathan Heart* and *Dickinson-Harmer Correspondence* (in 1 vol) Albany, 1885. More light on the contemporary facts of life.

BUTTERFIELD, Consul Willshire. *Crawford's Expedition Against Sandusky.* Cincinnati, 1873. Contemporary detail on the tragedy.

COLLINS, Richard H. *History of Kentucky.* 2 vols. Covington, Ky., 1877. A useful assembly of fact and detail drawn from Kentucky sources.

CONNELLEY, William Elsey. *The Founding of Harman's Station.* New York, 1910. An account of the typical vicissitudes of a frontier settlement.

COOK, Frederick (ed.). *Journals of the Sullivan Expedition.* Auburn, N.Y., 1887. A collection of original documents relating to the Iroquois campaign of 1779.

COTTERILL, Robert S. *History of Pioneer Kentucky.* Cincinnati, 1917. Standard history of early Kentucky.

COTTERILL, R. S. *The Southern Indians.* Norman, Okla., 1954. Authoritative study of the long struggle of the civilized tribes against their white enemies.

CRUIKSHANK, E. *Butler's Rangers*. Welland, Ont., 1893. Brief account of the exploits of the Tory rangers written from a loyalist point of view.

DILLON, John G. *The Kentucky Rifle*. Washington, D.C., 1924. Expert discussion of the frontiersman's primary tool.

DODDRIDGE, Joseph. *Notes on the Settlement and Indian Wars of Virginia and Pennsylvania*. Wellsburg 1824. Reprint (Alfred Williams, ed.) Albany, 1876. Somewhat colloquial historically but possessing the inestimable advantage of having been written by an educated and perceptive man who had himself experienced most of what he was writing about.

DOWNES, Randolph C. *Council Fires on the Upper Ohio*. Pittsburgh, 1940. A detailed and documented study of Indian diplomacy in the region from 1720 to 1795.

DRAKE, Daniel. *Pioneer Life in Kentucky*. New York, 1948. Revealing letters to his children about his boyhood on the frontier.

DUNBAR, Seymour. *History of Travel in America*. 4 vols. Indianapolis, 1915. Much detail on frontier travel conditions.

FILSON, John. *The Discovery, Settlement and Present State of Kentucky*, Wilmington, 1784. Reprint (Willard Rouse Hillson, ed.). Louisville, 1929. The first history of Kentucky.

Frontier Forts of Pennsylvania. Report of the Commission to Locate Sites. 2 vols. Harrisburg, 1896. A mine of source material on Indian campaigns from the Delaware to the Ohio.

HANNA, Charles A. *The Wilderness Trail*. 2 vols. New York, 1911. Unorganized but completely documented and enormously detailed account of the migrations of the Indian tribes in the Pennsylvania-Ohio area, the changing locations of their towns, and their relations with the traders.

HART, Freeman H. *The Valley of Virginia in the American Revolution*. Chapel Hill, 1942. Much striking and pertinent detail on the frontier way of life.

HAYWOOD, John. *Civil and Political History of Tennessee*. Nashville, 1823. Reprint Nashville, 1891. Includes a collection and recapitulation of contemporary reports upon more than 400 Indian attacks along southern frontier.

HECKEWELDER, John. *History, Manners and Customs of the Indian Nations*. Philadelphia, 1819. Reprint. (William C. Reichel, ed.). Philadelphia, 1876. The great Moravian missionary describes the Indians as he knew them.

HECKEWELDER, John. *Narrative of the Mission of the United Brethren*. Philadelphia, 1820. Reprint (William Elsey Connelley, ed.). Cleveland, 1907. An eyewitness account of Indian war by a man who suffered with both sides.

HODGE, Frederick Webb. *Handbook of the American Indians*. 2 vols.

Washington, D.C., 1907–10. Invaluable cross reference detail on everything pertaining to Indians.

HORNADAY, William T. *Extermination of the American Bison.* Washinton, D.C., 1889. Includes a study of the original distribution of a food supply that was so important to the Indian and the frontiersman; the extermination began in eastern Pennsylvania, Virginia, the Carolinas and Georgia.

HOUCK, Louis. *History of Missouri.* 3 vols. Chicago, 1908. Much contemporary detail on the French and Spanish background.

HULBERT, Archer Butler. *Historic Highways of America.* 16 vols. Cleveland, 1902–05. Detail on the early paths used by Indian and pioneer.

HUNT, George T. *The Wars of the Iroquois.* Madison, Wisc., 1940. Provocative study of the conquests of the Iroquois.

HUTCHINS, Thomas. *Topographical Description.* London, 1778. Reprint (Frederick Charles Hicks, ed.). Cleveland, 1904. Famous contemporary account of the early west by a professional geographer.

IMLAY, Gilbert. *A Topographical Description of the Western Territory of North America.* 4th ed. London, 1797. The famous and enthusiastic account of a temporary resident.

JACOBS, James R. *Tarnished Warrior.* New York, 1938. Detailed study of the intricate life and works of James Wilkinson.

JAMES, James Alton. *Life of George Rogers Clark.* Chicago, 1928. Not only the best life of Clark but the best short history of his times.

JAMES, James Alton (ed.). *George Rogers Clark Papers 1771–1784.* 2 vols. Springfield, Ill., 1912 and 1926. Comprehensive and invaluable collection of contemporary documents.

JILLSON, Willard Rouse. *Pioneer Kentucky.* Frankfort, Ky., 1934. Useful manual for the identification and location of early stations and geographical features.

KENTON, Edna. *Simon Kenton.* New York, 1930. The life of a great frontiersman by a scholarly descendant, together with as much of the original flavor of pioneer Kentucky as may be found in any single book.

KENTON, Edna (ed.). *The Indians of North America.* 2 vols. New York, 1927. Selected extracts from the *Jesuit Relations* presenting both comprehensive and intimately detailed pictures of the Indian's original way of life.

KINCAID, Robert L. *The Wilderness Road.* Indianapolis, 1947. Excellent account of the experiences of the people who followed Daniel Boone's track over the mountains.

KOONTZ, Louis Knott. *Robert Dinwiddie.* Glendale, Calif., 1941. Documented treatment of the governor who sent the young Washington to open the American road west.

LEWIS, George E. *The Indiana Company.* Glendale, Calif., 1941. Detailed documented study of one of the great land companies.

McKnight, Charles. *Our Western Border.* Philadelphia, 1875. The most comprehensive collection, of the type common three quarters of a century ago, of contemporary anecdotes, community narratives and personal adventures, of little historical value but helpful for the light thrown on the way people of the time lived.

Marshall, H. *History of Kentucky.* 2 vols. Frankfort, Ky., 1824. The partisan account of a participant, largely devoted to passionate attacks upon the separatist leaders.

Mooney, James. *Myths of the Cherokee.* Washington, D.C., 1900. Includes a history of the Cherokee nation.

Morgan, Lewis H. (Herbert M. Lloyd, ed.) *League of the Iroquois.* 2 vols. in 1. New York, 1904. Standard work on the social, economic, and political organization of the greatest of Indian nations.

Morgan, Lewis H. *The American Beaver.* Philadelphia, 1868. Fascinating account of the ways and works of the ingenious animal that had more to do than any explorer or general with shaping the history of the West.

Parkman, Francis. *Works.* Any edition. One of the great histories of all time and essential to an understanding of the French and Indian background of the American frontier.

Pittman, Philip. *European Settlements on the Mississippi.* London, 1770. Reprint (Frank Heywood Hodder, ed.). Cleveland, 1906. Description by an English army officer of the Mississippi Valley before the coming of the first American settler.

Ramsey, J.G.M. *Annals of Tennessee.* Charleston, S.C., 1853. Reprint Kingsport, Tenn., 1926. History of pioneer Tennessee, drawn largely from Haywood, but with addition of many contemporary letters, reports and documents.

Riegel, Robert E. *America Moves West.* New York, 1930. Brief history of westward expansion from the Appalachians to the Pacific.

Robertson, James Alexander. *Louisiana Under Spain, France and the United States.* 2 vols. Cleveland, 1911. Important collection of contemporary documents dealing with the period 1785–1807.

Roosevelt, Theodore. *The Winning of the West.* 6 vols. New York, 1889–96. The only complete history of the early frontier but more notable for the vigor of the author's style and personal opinions.

Royce, Charles C. *Indian Land Cessions.* Washington, D.C., 1900. A detailed compilation, illustrated by maps, of the terms of the 720 Indian cessions of land to the United States between 1784 and 1894.

Stevens, Wayne E. *The Northwest Fur Trade 1763–1800.* Urbana, Ill., 1926. An examination of the influence of English fur traders on English policy.

Stone, William L. *Life of Joseph Brant.* 2 vols. New York, 1838. Includes the texts of many of Brant's letters and papers.

Thwaites, Reuben Gold (ed.). *Early Western Travels.* 32 vols. Cleveland, 1904–07. Though only the first three volumes are devoted to pre-1800 journals the monumental index is essential to any study of the frontier.

TURNER, Frederick Jackson. *The Frontier in American History.* New York, 1920. Read this first of all.

TURNER, Frederick Jackson. *The Significance of Sections in American History.* New York, 1932. And this next.

VOLWILER, Albert T. *George Croghan and the Westward Movement.* Cleveland, 1926. A study of the traders who were the forerunners of the settlers.

WALTON, Joseph S. *Conrad Weiser.* Philadelphia, 1900. The picturesque life of a man who played a leading part in the Indian affairs of colonial Pennsylvania.

WHITAKER, Arthur Preston. *The Spanish-American Frontier.* Boston and New York, 1927. The standard authority on the Spanish conspiracy.

WILDES, Harry E. *Anthony Wayne.* New York, 1941. A life of the general with some detail on his Fallen Timbers campaign.

WILLIAMS, Samuel Cole. *Tennessee During the Revolutionary War.* Nashville, 1944. Documented treatment of events on the Cumberland-Holston frontier from 1776 to 1784.

WILLIAMS, Samuel Cole (ed.). *Early Travels in the Tennessee Country.* Johnson City, Tenn., 1928. A collection of captivating extracts from the journals of observers who saw the valley of the Tennessee while it was still a wilderness.

WINSOR, Justin. *Narrative and Critical History of America.* 8 vols. Boston and New York, 1889. An important storehouse of illustrative and bibliographical detail.

WINSOR, Justin. *The Westward Movement.* Boston and New York, 1897. Balanced and comprehensive one volume account of the 1763–1798 frontier.

WITHERS, Alexander Scott. *Chronicles of Border Warfare.* Clarksburg, W. Virginia, 1831. Reprint (Reuben Gold Thwaites, ed.). Cincinnati, 1895. Written by a man who had been able to talk with hundreds of the participants in the events he describes, and annotated by an outstanding modern authority.

Index

GENERAL ANTHONY WAYNE. Painting by Edward Savage

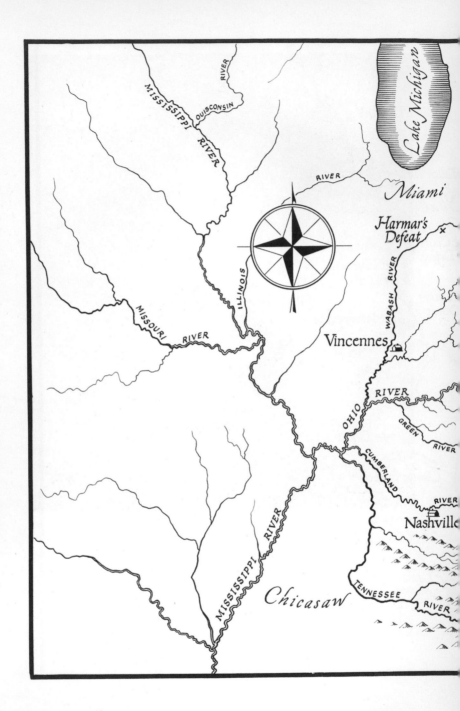

Lake Michigan

MISSISSIPPI RIVER

OUISCONSIN RIVER

RIVER

Miami

Harmar's Defeat ×

WABASH RIVER

ILLINOIS

MISSOURI RIVER

Vincennes

OHIO RIVER

GREEN RIVER

CUMBERLAND RIVER

RIVER

Nashville

MISSISSIPPI RIVER

Chicasaw

TENNESSEE RIVER

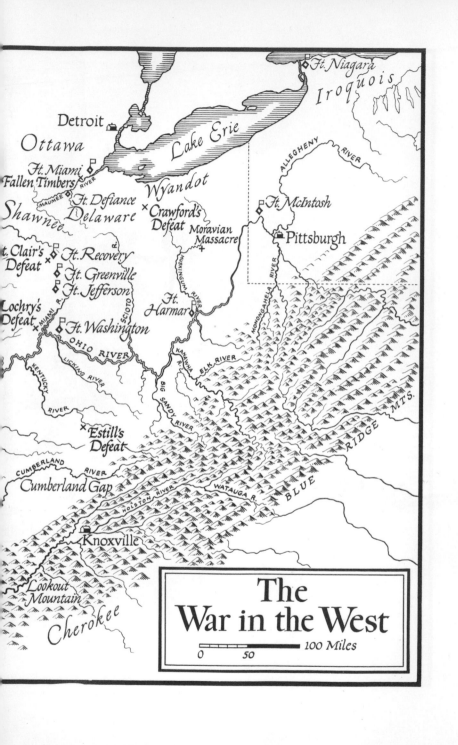

Detroit

Ottawa

Ft. Miami
Fallen Timbers

Shawnee

Ft. Defiance
Delaware

Wyandot

t. Clair's
Defeat

Ft. Recovery

Ft. Greenville

Ft. Jefferson

Lochry's
Defeat

Ft. Washington

Crawford's
Defeat

Moravian
Massacre

Lake Erie

Ft. Niagara

Iroquois

ALLEGHENY RIVER

Ft. McIntosh

Pittsburgh

MAUMEE RIVER

MIAMI R.

SCIOTO

MUSKINGUM RIVER

OHIO RIVER

LICKING RIVER

KENTUCKY RIVER

Ft. Harmar

KANAWHA R.

ELK RIVER

MONONGAHELA RIVER

Estill's
Defeat

BIG SANDY RIVER

CUMBERLAND RIVER

Cumberland Gap

HOLSTON RIVER

WATAUGA R.

BLUE RIDGE MTS.

Knoxville

Lookout
Mountain

Cherokee

The
War in the West

0   50   100 Miles

THE SIGNING OF THE TREATY OF GREENVILLE, 1795. A contemporary, anonymous painting, reputedly by a member of Wayne's staff